Shirley Hardy-Rix & Brian Rix

Now enjoying retirement, Brian was a policeman in Victoria for 36 years. During that time he headed up the Homicide Squad, investigated drug trafficking, kidnappings, armed robberies and worked undercover. He spent the final five years of his career as President of the powerful police union, The Police Association.

Shirley met Brian when she was working as a crime reporter on Melbourne TV and radio. She is now a freelance journalist working as a magazine editor and publicist for film, TV and publishing.

As well as *Two for the Road,* in 2013 Shirley and Brian published *Circle to Circle: a journey through the Americas and beyond* — an account of their 16-month 83,000-kilometres, 32-country motorcycle adventure.

First published in Australia in 2005 by Pan Macmillan Australia

This expanded edition first published in 2014 by Aussies Overland
www.aussiesoverland.com.au
aussiesoverland@hardyrix.com.au

National Library of Australia
Cataloguing-in-Publication entry

Hardy-Rix, Shirley & Rix, Brian.

Two for the Road: 56,671 km, 27 countries, one dream

2nd edition.
ISBN: 9780646918518 (paperback)

Subjects: Hardy-Rix, Shirley--Travel. Rix, Brian--Travel.
Motorcyclists--Australia--Biography. Motorcycling. Voyages around the world.

796.6092

Re-design and additional graphics
High Horse Books
www.highhorse.com.au

SHIRLEY HARDY-RIX
and BRIAN RIX

We dedicate our journey and this book to Fran, Shirley's sister, whose courageous battle with cancer and extraordinary will to continue living was an inspiration to all who knew her.

And to Paul Carr, a friend who lost his life on a Tibetan mountain trying to achieve his dream only days before our journey began.

Their spirits journey with us.

CONTENTS

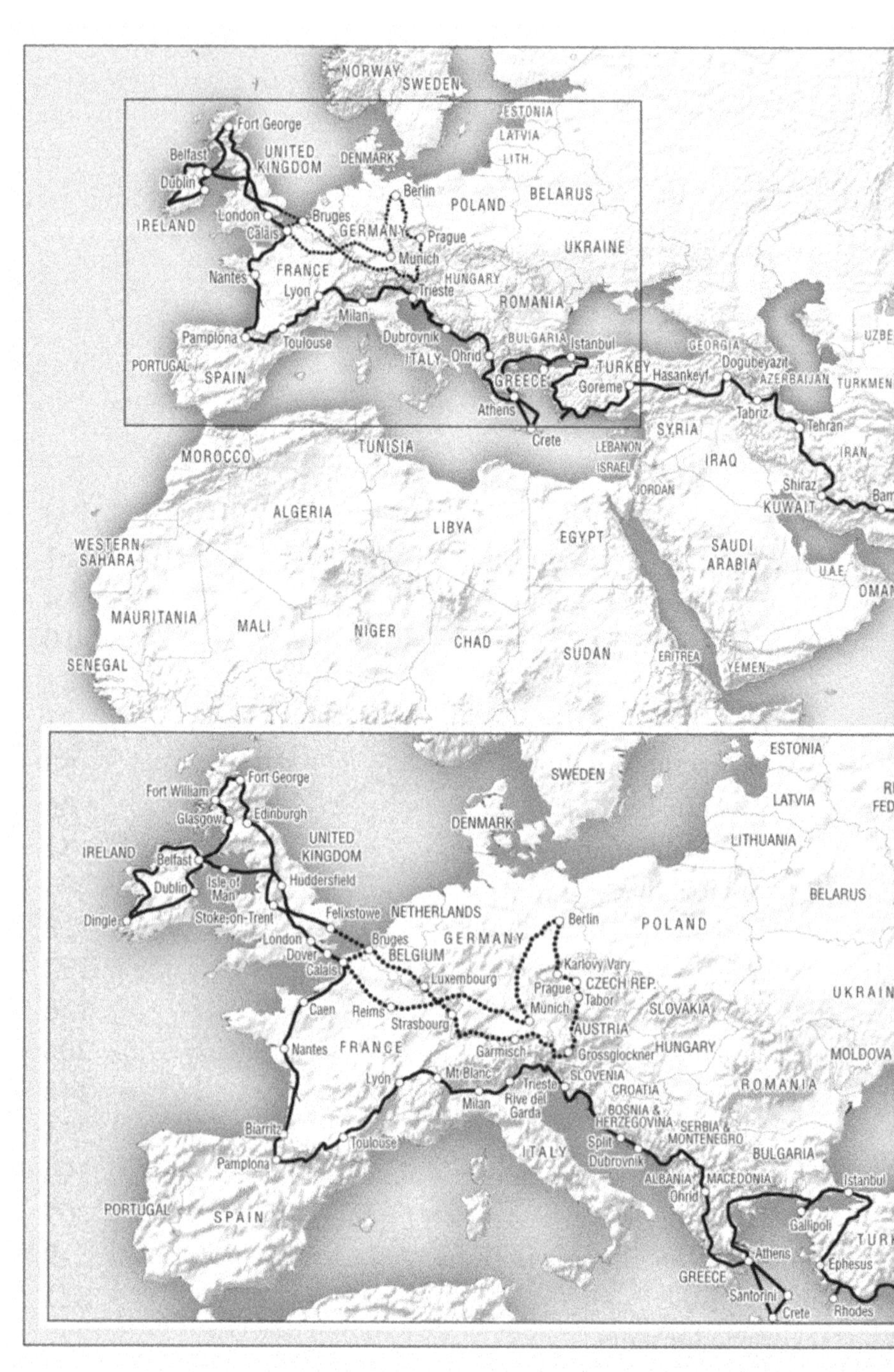

NORWAY
SWEDEN
ESTONIA
LATVIA
LITH.
Fort George
Belfast
UNITED KINGDOM
DENMARK
Dublin
Berlin
BELARUS
POLAND
London
Bruges
IRELAND
Calais
GERMANY
Prague
UKRAINE
Munich
Nantes
FRANCE
HUNGARY
Lyon
Trieste
ROMANIA
Milan
Pamplona
Toulouse
Dubrovnik
BULGARIA
Istanbul
GEORGIA
UZBEK
PORTUGAL
ITALY
Ohrid
TURKEY
Hasankeyf
Dogubeyazit
SPAIN
GREECE
Goreme
AZERBAIJAN
TURKMENI
Tabriz
Athens
SYRIA
Tehran
Crete
LEBANON
IRAQ
IRAN
TUNISIA
ISRAEL
MOROCCO
JORDAN
Shiraz
Bam
KUWAIT
ALGERIA
LIBYA
EGYPT
WESTERN SAHARA
SAUDI ARABIA
U.A.E.
OMAN
MAURITANIA
MALI
NIGER
CHAD
SUDAN
ERITREA
YEMEN
SENEGAL
ESTONIA
SWEDEN
LATVIA
Fort George
Fort William
Edinburgh
Glasgow
DENMARK
UNITED KINGDOM
LITHUANIA
IRELAND
Belfast
Isle of Man
Huddersfield
Dublin
BELARUS
Felixstowe
NETHERLANDS
Dingle
Stoke-on-Trent
Berlin
POLAND
London
Bruges
GERMANY
Dover
BELGIUM
Calais
Karlovy Vary
Luxembourg
Prague
CZECH REP.
Caen
Reims
Munich
Tabor
SLOVAKIA
Strasbourg
AUSTRIA
Garmisch
Nantes
FRANCE
Grossglockner
HUNGARY
MOLDOVA
Lyon
Mt Blanc
Trieste
SLOVENIA
CROATIA
ROMANIA
Milan
Rive del Garda
BOSNIA & HERZEGOVINA
Biarritz
SERBIA & MONTENEGRO
Toulouse
Split
BULGARIA
Pamplona
ITALY
Dubrovnik
ALBANIA
MACEDONIA
Istanbul
Ohrid
PORTUGAL
SPAIN
Gallipoli
Athens
Ephesus
GREECE
Santorini
Crete
Rhodes

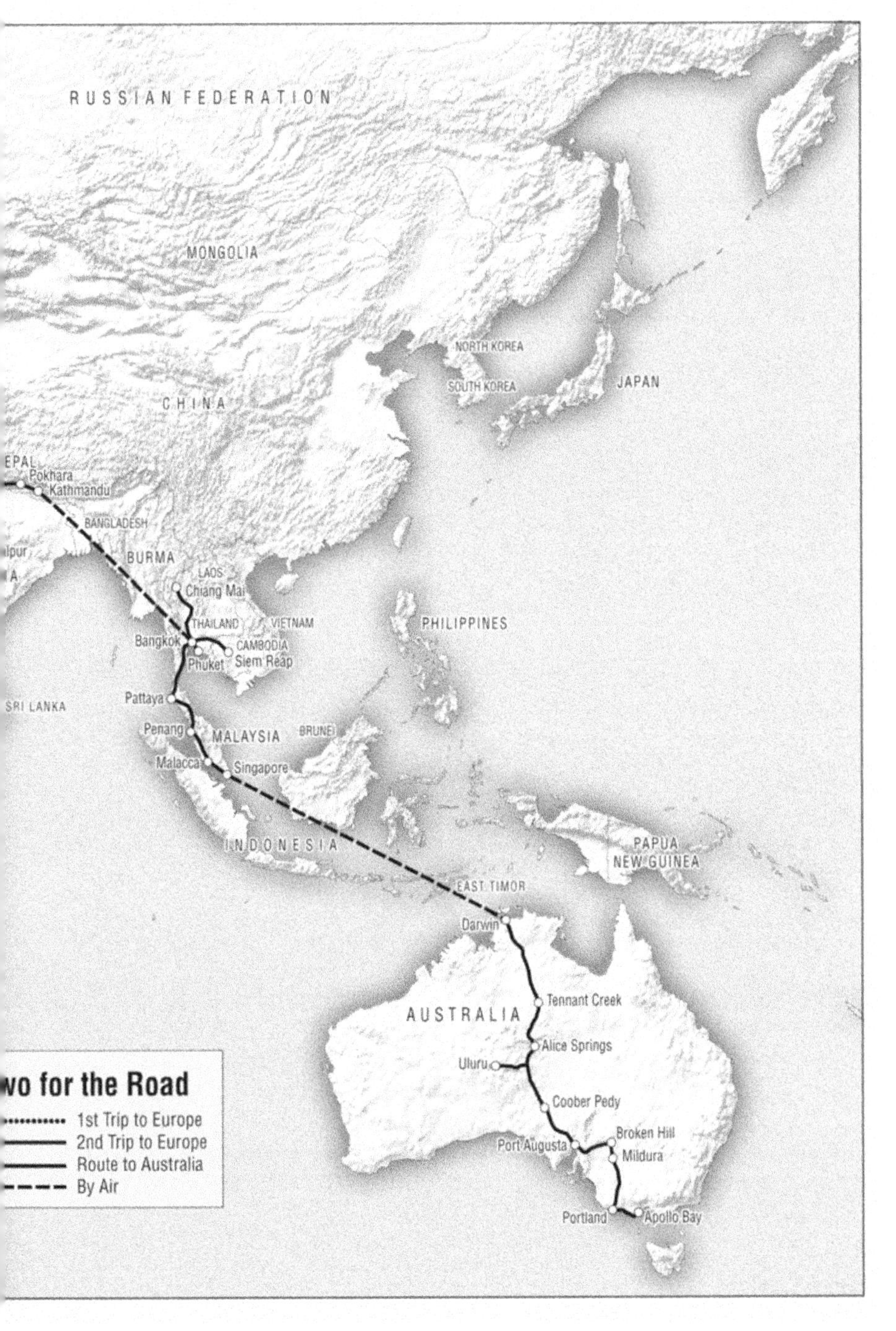

RUSSIAN FEDERATION
MONGOLIA
NORTH KOREA
SOUTH KOREA
JAPAN
CHINA
EPAL
Pokhara
Kathmandu
BANGLADESH
BURMA
LAOS
Chiang Mai
THAILAND
VIETNAM
PHILIPPINES
Bangkok
CAMBODIA
Phuket
Siem Reap
Pattaya
SRI LANKA
Penang
MALAYSIA
BRUNEI
Malacca
Singapore
INDONESIA
PAPUA NEW GUINEA
EAST TIMOR
Darwin
Tennant Creek
AUSTRALIA
Alice Springs
Uluru
Coober Pedy
Broken Hill
Port Augusta
Mildura
Portland
Apollo Bay
wo for the Road
1st Trip to Europe
2nd Trip to Europe
Route to Australia
By Air

INTRODUCTION

10 November 2003

Pakistan, and there is absolutely nothing out here. Dirt, a few rocks and dust as far as the eye can see. I crane my neck to look over Brian's shoulder and what lies ahead is no different. The road is taking us through desert; flat, rocky terrain. The only living things we see are a few camels. A dried-up carcass shows that even these beasts find life hard out here. The shifting sands drift over the road, making our progress slow. In some places it is virtually impossible to gauge the depth of the sand, which makes for some slippery riding.

We've been warned about this road from Iran into the heart of Pakistan. It hugs the border with Afghanistan, at times taking us less than 20 km from Afghanistan. We are in the heart of Taliban country, an area where, we've been told, foreigners are not welcome – particularly foreigners from the West, countries that are part of the Coalition of the Willing put together by the US to topple Saddam Hussein.

We don't see people out here. Scattered along the

roadway are military outposts, where soldiers living in mud huts record the name and passport number of everyone travelling through. They aren't here to be a nuisance. And they aren't here to protect us – not really. They are here so, if we disappear, they will be able to find out when and where we were last seen alive. Hardly a comforting thought. The isolation is palpable when we stop to eat on the side of the road. There is no-one in sight. No cars pass by. From roadside to horizon there is nothing but more of the same rocky landscape.

When we stop at the checkpoints, Brian gets off the bike, takes our passports out of the tank bag and wanders into the hut with a grin. The soldiers are friendly, keen to have their photo taken with the digital camera. They nod and smile, practising their English as Brian fills in our details in the old ledgers propped on ancient wooden tables. On our BMW R1150 GS, we are a novelty. They don't get too many motorbikes out here, or visitors. And when four bikes and a Land Rover pull up, the soldiers seem overwhelmed. It is comforting to be travelling in a group with our German and South African companions, whom we met in Iran a few days ago. We all feel a safety in numbers.

Most of the soldiers are a little perplexed by our arrival but are usually happy to wave us on – apart from one remote outpost. Here the guards are agitated by the thought of us moving through on our own. They want us to take a guard. There is a problem, though. They don't have a vehicle (imagine being out here without transport!) and there is no room for him on the bikes or in the Land Rover. Eventually, after much head-scratching, they let us move on.

Then we get to Nushki, the closest town to the Afghan border, and we are berated for not taking a guard. There is no room for argument. On the next leg of our journey we are led by an armed officer, ensuring we make it to our destination.

Barren hills now line the roadway and we can see the sun glinting off rifles. Gunmen are hidden in the rocks, watching the roadway below. But they are not there to harm us – they are there to protect us . . . just in case. I can't help but think, 'What the hell are we doing here?'

ONE

THE JOURNEY BEGINS

20 May 2003

Shirley: What possesses two normal, middle-class professional people to give up the comforts of home for 12 months, jump on a motorcycle and ride from one side of the world to the other?

Brian and I have always loved motorcycling and it was our dream to combine our love of travel and the joy of two-wheel touring. We met in the 1980s and made an unusual couple – he was a policeman and I was a journalist reporting on crime in our home city of Melbourne. Many people disapproved of our relationship, but we were made for each other.

Brian had a motorbike and couldn't believe his luck when he discovered that not only did I love the role of pillion passenger – having spent my teenage years with boys who rode motorbikes in Sydney – but also enjoyed a day at the motorbike races. As a teenager all my friends had bikes and I spent many hours riding on the back of a 250cc bike hurtling around the Sydney suburbs. I even dated a bloke who raced his bike. We would ride to Amaroo Park and he would take all the glass off the bike, race it, put the glass back on and ride home with me on the back! Brian honed his motorcycle riding skills on the banks of the Murray River near his home town in Victoria. There were 90 miles of public land to explore and Brian cut his riding teeth on dirt riding. He'd always had bikes.

We both loved the idea of exploring the world and soon our holidays were spent travelling on Brian's bike. We joined the FrontLine Tourers, the Emergency Services Motorcycle Touring Club, a group of police, ambulance officers and fire fighters who ride motorcycles. Through the club we've met many great people and enjoyed some of the best roads on offer around Australia.

In 1992 I gave up a senior position with a major magazine publisher to set up my own media business. This gave us the flexibility to enjoy Brian's nine weeks annual leave and, like so many couples with no children, our lives were our own. Brian's sons, Stephen and Gavan, are leading their own successful lives. While we share an incredible closeness and strong emotional bonds, they don't rely on us on a day-to-day basis.

When the boys were growing up we talked more and more about making an overland journey to the UK on a bike. This was to be our retirement plan, before tragedy hit the family. My older sister, Fran, became ill with cancer. She was a fighter and wouldn't just lie down and die. She battled this insidious disease for years, but it soon became obvious her time was running out. At Christmas 1995 Fran was virtually bedridden. We spent a great Christmas together, the entire family, with Fran holding court from her big blue chair in the living area, the smile never leaving her face beneath a bald head. My favourite photo is one showing all of us gathered around Fran, taken on Christmas Day.

Early in 1996 I spent some time with Fran, to help look after her. The cancer was attacking her spine and she could no longer walk; she needed people around her to perform the most menial tasks. One morning I was helping her dress. I'm not a nurse and Fran hadn't been used to dependence on others. I made a real meal of getting Fran into her clothes for the day. We just couldn't coordinate this seemingly simple task and fell onto her bed laughing. It was a great moment of closeness between us.

There were many things left unsaid that day, but they were said days later, when Fran and I were sitting together in the living room. I was filing her nails and she said, 'I'm not ready to die.' I was so moved by her honesty.

'I'm not ready for you to die, either,' I said.

That was enough. Fran knew I loved her and I knew she loved me. And she loved Brian. She once told her girlfriends that Brian was her ideal husband!

When Fran finally lost her battle with cancer, Brian and I talked at length about her wish to live. We vowed then that we would have as few 'if onlys' in our lives as possible. Our plans for the future began to take form. Brian had always dreamed of travelling around the world on his motorcycle and this would be our future – Aussie overlanders! But it would have to wait until Brian retired. Under the current police superannuation scheme, that would be when he was between 52 and 55. It wasn't that far away. My life as a freelance journalist could be put on hold.

As Brian's interest in round-the-world motorcycle travel took hold, we met Chris and Erin Ratay, two New Yorkers travelling the world and visiting Melbourne. We helped them with accommodation, found a mechanic to work on their BMW bikes and provided some good old Aussie hospitality. Little did we realise that meeting them would change our lives. Chris's advice to us was two-fold and simple: 'Once you've made up your mind, tell people. That way you can't back out.' And 'Don't leave it until you retire. So much can happen. You might never do it.' That was enough for us – we decided to head off sooner rather than later. Brian would take long-service leave and I would arrange for people to look after my business.

It took a couple of years to get things organised. Brian started researching the world of motorcycles to make sure we took the right bike for our journey. He settled on a BMW GS pretty early on. It was big enough for two-up touring and versatile enough to take some of the rough roads that lay ahead.

After planning a rough route, we checked out the visa and health requirements of the countries we would travel through. We found a good travel medicine doctor – whom we quickly nicknamed the 'witch doctor' – who administered vaccinations to protect us from most of the ills that can befall overland travellers. Being an experienced overlander, he also had plenty of advice on eating and drinking and staying healthy.

We read books written by other motorcycle travellers to see if there were any pitfalls we could avoid. I devoured guidebooks checking out the scenic routes and not-to-be-missed sites along the way. I started to think I'd missed my vocation – I should have been a travel agent.

We knew keeping in touch with home on such a journey could end up being a nightmare. Murphy's Law was sure to mean we would forget to send postcards to the most important people in our lives. The easiest way of letting anyone interested know where we were and what we were up to seemed to be to have a web page. With some help from talented friends, we set up www.aussiesoverland.com.

ABC Radio Melbourne's breakfast program, hosted by Red Symons, heard about our journey and asked if I would be able to talk to them along the way. Why not?

By May 2003 we were ready to go – or as ready as we would ever be.

The Isle of Man TT is a motorcycle-racing mecca. Riders who have no thought for their own safety take to the streets of this wonderful island in the middle of the Irish Sea and race. And there is nothing demure or safe about the racing. It is right on the edge. Each year people die, racers and visitors alike.

It is totally exhilarating. Spectators sit on fences, behind hedges and in the front yards of houses and churches to watch racers go by. They are so close, the spectators – who are as crazy as the racers – can touch them. We'd watched it on television and dreamed of being there, but always commented on how stupid the spectators were for watching the races from such dangerous spots.

Our initial plan was to ride to London, go to the Isle of Man TT and ship the bike home. A look at the world weather over the next couple of months, however, made us realise that to be in the UK for the Isle of Man TT in May and June, we would have to ride through the wet season in Asia and arrive in Europe in the dead of winter! So we turned the whole thing around – we would ship our bike to the UK, attend the Isle of Man TT and then head home through Europe in summer and Asia in the dry season, arriving back in Australia while it was still warm in the north and the cold in the south wouldn't kill you.

When, on 20 May 2003, it's time to begin our journey, Brian is keen to sneak out of the country, but it is not to be. Our friends and families insist on parties and more parties. In the end, we opt for one big farewell, which provides plenty of memories to comfort us during the times when homesickness hits.

Brian: At last we are on our way. Shirley sleeps fitfully on the plane. I don't at all, but luckily I have a window seat and after lights out, I look at clusters of lights from towns some 10,000 m below.

I think about my friend, Paul 'Possum' Carr, who has just perished on Cho Oyu in Tibet, the world's sixth-highest peak. It was Possum's ambition to climb Everest and Cho Oyu was a training run with three other climbers. Paul and I worked together on many criminal investigations over our time together with the Victoria Police and we were both members of The Police Association (the police union) Executive Committee. We often spoke about our adventurous ambitions and he died living out his, the week before we depart to live out ours.

What should be a happy time is tinged with sadness as we fly a mere 200 m higher than Everest's 8850 m. Paul died at 7400 m and, for the first time ever on Cho Oyu, a recovery operation will take his body down. I know this is unusual because Paul told me that if you die on the mountain, you stay on the mountain, and I can't help thinking that he may prefer to stay there.

It made me reflect on why Shirl and I are doing this. There is certainly the desire to have adventure and experience other cultures, but there is also a deep-seated fear of the 'if onlys' – the regrets you have to contend with when your life is nearing its end and you haven't achieved all you wanted to. There may be no tomorrow, so you have to live life to its fullest.

TWO

THE ISLE OF MAN TT

31 May – 6 June 2003

Shirley: There is an interminable wait for the bike in the UK. The shipping agent said 40 days, so we allow 50 and it takes 60! Thank goodness for family. My brother's niece, Bettina, and her English husband, Tim, live in Surrey. Their friendship and spare bed are lifesavers. When we finally get to the bike in Felixstowe, our stress levels are peaking. We have a single day to get from one side of the UK to the other to catch the ferry to the Isle of Man.

We arrive at customs early and the officials are more than helpful. They check out the bike registration from Australia, our green-card insurance, ask a couple of questions about what else is in the crate and that is it. They don't even want to see the carnet.

'You know you have to take the crate with you?' is all the bloke at the freight-terminal office has to say as he points us to the back of the shed. Brian walks towards a freight officer only to be sharply told to move back to the car. 'You can't walk around here, because you don't have green vests on. And you know you have to take the crate away with you?' Of course we do!

No-one seems even to think that we might not be able to take the crate away. Brian and I will be on the bike and Bettina and Tim, who kindly drove us to collect the bike, are in a hatchback. When the crate appears we are pleased to see there are no telltale tyre marks to indicate it had been run over, or bits of tape holding it together to show it had been dropped off the forklift. Everything seems to be as it should. Tim and Brian take to the crate with hammers and crowbars. Inside, the bike is in perfect condition. The metres of bubble wrap, tape and tie-downs have worked their magic.

We're pleased to hear it fire up straightaway after 60 days in the crate, but there is a hint of panic in Tim's voice when he points out there seems to be fuel pouring out from the bottom of the bike. It takes just a bit of fiddling with the fuel lines to fix that problem and we are away – without the crate. Tim has hidden bits of it under a nearby skip, behind it and alongside it, making sure the address labels are removed.

As we get to the gate, the man comes out of the office and walks to the car. From the bike I can see into the office and the CCTV screens. Guilt and anxiety come to the surface as I realise they have been able to see us on their monitors the entire time we've been working on the bike. I am waiting for the 'What about the crate?' question when the man says he is after the copy of the paperwork the forklift driver gave us.

I can't help but let forth a scream of joy as we ride out of the yard.

Brian: There is no fast way to get from one side of England to the other, which we of course need to do in a day to get the Saturday ferry from Heysham to the Isle of Man. The traffic is unbearable and every time we come to a roundabout it banks back for more than a kilometre. I've been a long time out of the saddle and take my time to get the feel of the bike again, but one thing I notice is how good the English drivers are compared with those in Australia. They are polite and move over to let you cut the traffic when the going gets slow.

Along the way we see rolling green pastures, sheep and small villages on either side of the roads. Every now and then a church steeple pops up among coppices; we are starting to feel like we are in England. We turn off the main roads at Harrogate and are in typical English countryside: narrow, hedge-lined roads with fields of sheep hemmed in by walls of stone.

Roadworks see us taking a detour through the Yorkshire Dales and ending up on the wrong road without us knowing it. We find a great guesthouse and, after a home-cooked meal, take a walk in the twilight. We wander through fields, over the rivers, past the sheep, climb over stiles and end up in town. It is just about perfect. The only problem is we really don't know where we are or how we will get on the road to Heysham in the morning.

Shirley: Our hostess, Joan, gives us directions for a short cut to the main road. It is picture-book stuff – a narrow lane cuts through lush pastures with grazing sheep. We pass through the tiny village of Giggleswick near Settle. Once we are on the main road it is clear sailing through to the port of Heysham, home to a nuclear power station, a sea port and a caravan park for tourists to take in the wondrous sights.

We make it in good time and are on board the ferry by 11 a.m., which gives us 2 hours and 45 minutes to wait. Obviously, very few cars or vans are making the journey to the Isle of Man, but there are hundreds of bikes. The deck hands load the bikes alongside parallel barriers. The bikes are then roped onto these barriers, a bit like cattle. To protect the bikes from the ropes, they use old rags. It doesn't seem very technical, but we hope they know what they are doing.

After an uneventful sail, thanks to a calm Irish Sea, we are finally at the Isle of Man. Getting off the ferry is nowhere near as easy as getting on. There is almost a free-for-all after an hour's delay. We are wedged into a crowd of bikers on the tight stairway heading to the vehicle deck. The people behind us are pushing while the people in front are standing firm – they have nowhere to go. It turns out a couple of Harley riders had blocked the exits as they stuffed around.

Everyone on the island gets involved in the Isle of Man TT and bikers are welcomed with open arms. The police even turn a blind eye to some 'safe speeding' – and don't mind a bit of larrikin behaviour as long as it doesn't get out of hand. The authorities recognise the huge financial benefit this event brings to the island and have a sensible attitude to allowing people to let off steam. They let everyone know what is and is not allowed and, in the main, people comply.

But when we arrive on the island there is an undercurrent of sadness and foreboding. Some of the racers seem subdued. We soon learn that last year's champ, Dave Jefferies, crashed into a stone wall during practice a couple of days earlier. There is no room for error here. Skidding across the narrow country road, Dave and his bike snapped off a telegraph pole before coming to a sudden halt at the wall. He died instantly. As they say here, everyone knows the risks and you take your chances. A journalist once said the racers have 'balls the size of watermelons'. This isn't an exaggeration.

Take Jim Moodie, who was following Dave Jefferies that day. The telegraph lines were strung across the road and Jim, riding a Triumph Daytona 600, hit the wires hanging over the track. He travelled 140 m further with the wires snaked around his chest and neck. He was nearly garrotted, yet he raced the next day. However, it does put a damper on the event to ride past the accident scene and see the flowers propped along the wall.

Riders here think nothing of completing one race of more than 160 km then competing in the next race on different bikes. Some would race up to 560 km in one day. It's amazing – the laps are 60 km and the races are three or four laps. Most races take more than an hour to complete and up to 15 minutes to start, with 10 seconds between each starter.

It's 'Mad Sunday', when the track is closed to two-way traffic and it's open for all to play. There are no speed restrictions on the open roads but dangerous driving will bring the full weight of the law down on your wallet. We are warned not to disobey speed-restriction signs in towns. The police have a system where they pull you up, book you and you must go directly to the station to pay the very steep fine.

As Brian fuels up the bike, a mature gent takes an interest in our Phillip Island Motorcycle GP sticker. Kiwi Mac Trilford is here with his mate John Hudson, an expat Pom speedway rider based in New Zealand. John will ride in the 'parade lap' on a four-cylinder 250cc Honda owned by famous trials rider Sammy Miller. At 67 years of age Miller broke three ribs and his collarbone in a competition in France, so couldn't ride in this year's parade lap. John has taken the hire car out for a few laps of the 60 km-plus track. He was out at 5 a.m. and admits he frightened the living daylights out of himself on his way around. This doesn't augur well for me. I am more than a little anxious about our high-speed lap of the island.

Brian: On Mad Sunday, any motorcycle can take to the track at any speed. Shirley and I work out which way everyone is going around the track and join in the fun. We ride into

Crosby and see the flowers and bikes pulled up, people paying their respects to Dave Jefferies. They think he hit an oil spill from another bike, losing control. Jefferies won nine IOM races, including last year's open. Just three minutes before his accident, he set the fastest lap ever, averaging more than 200 km/h on a track that has riders down almost to walking pace at some hairpin turns.

We carry on in a snaking conga line up the mountain, taking it in turns to overtake cars. As we get to an unrestricted area, the sports bikes wind out and so do I, pushing the big Beemer up to around 160 km/h – and still we are being overtaken as though we're standing still. We are overtaken at 200 km/h-plus on sweeping corners over the top of the mountain. I remain conservative and keep my speed down to around 160–70 km/h. Some of these guys can really ride, particularly the ones with the 'legs of Man' symbol on their number plates. This is their home track and they know every bump.

It feels surreal to whip past parked police cars, three and four abreast on the wrong side of the road, and knowing it's all legal as long as they deem you are riding safely. I'm travelling at about half the pace of the racing bikes, but my concentration levels still have to be high. I wonder how the racers can maintain such levels for six laps, or over 364 km. My respect for their abilities as riders grows.

We pull up at Snaefell, the top of the track in the clouds. It's bitterly cold and the crowd enjoys the antics of the boys dropping wheel stands and roaring past the 'Bobbies', who look decidedly uninterested.

Back on the bike, it's a fast run, and I mean *fast*, down the hill to the start–finish line. This is an awesome experience for any motorcyclist. I know the dangers and accept the consequences, but the exhilaration is intoxicating. Just ask anyone who rides.

Shirley: The first thing I notice are the crowds, all hanging around the dangerous parts of the track. Like the ones in the Roman Forum, they are out for blood, waiting for crashes. It's hardly comforting. Other bikes hurtle past us – so close the draft nearly sucks off my right boot. I can feel Brian's enjoyment. He's having a ball, so I just hang on and go with the flow, moving with the bike and feeling the line through his body. It is exhilarating and terrifying at the same time. I have the utmost confidence in Brian's riding, but the others on the road are an unknown quantity.

When we ride through Crosby, the floral tributes are a sobering reminder of the dangers of this track. When we get to the start–finish line, I draw a deep breath but I am suffering from mixed emotions. Despite myself, I loved the ride, the speed and the terror, but once is enough. 'I'm happy for you to go around again, but I think I'd rather have a look around town,' I tell Brian. I am secretly pleased when he says that once is enough!

Brian: Everyone brings out their bikes during race time – the fast and modern like the ones we met on the track, and the vintage and classic. The courtyard outside Castletown's Castle Rushen is the meeting point for the classic bikes. It is nirvana. An old man in a tweed jacket and porkpie hat puffs as he passes us, push-starting a racing Velocette motorcycle circa 1950. As it roars into life, the noise is deafening. He revs it until evil-looking blue smoke comes out the 'megaphone'. As he lets the engine die to a stop, it's as if others have to fill the void.

We bump into our Kiwi friends John and Mac. They have the little 250 Honda, which John obligingly fires up. The four small megaphones are even louder than the Velo and drown out an old busker plying his trade on a squeezebox. The busker gives up and moves on. John revs the little bike up to 10,000 rpm, still well shy of its 17,000 red line. I sit on the bike and pretend just for a minute or two.

I look over and see an exotic MV Agusta racer and an old gent in full racing leathers as he fires it up. The 750cc racer is at least twice as loud as the Honda and people close by put their fingers in their ears to block out the noise. I look at the old guy and think he looks familiar. He should be – it's Phil Read, a highly successful GP racer of the 1960s. As the noise dies down, two women old enough to collect the pension but dressed in bike leathers rush to his side for a photo opportunity. There is a display of trophies, helmets and a worn-through bike boot once belonging to the late Mike 'The Bike' Hailwood, a legendary English racer. Mike Hailwood's son, David, is here to take part in the so-called 'parade lap'. We ogle plenty of other exotic machinery before heading to the pub.

Shirley: Race day presents a couple of drawbacks. One is the need to settle into your viewing spot before the first race and stay put until after the last. The roads are closed to all but the racers. There are roads around the outskirts of the island, but they have 'Shirley will get lost' written all over them.

Once on the track, Brian and I climb the mountain and pass through the clouds. It is bloody cold and doesn't seem like perfect racing weather. This is the second drawback – the delays caused by bad weather. While it might be sunny on one part of the track it can be foggy and icy on the top of the mountain, where visibility is only a few metres. These guys might be crazy, but they won't race when it is really dangerous.

We ride around the track (within the speed limit today) to find the best vantage point. We end up at Sulby Bridge, behind a low stone wall. We have become two of those people we think are crazy for hiding behind a wall to watch the races! It is sunny but the top of the mountain is shrouded in fog. This delays the race by three hours. They finally get under way at 1.45, but it is well worth the wait.

Sulby Bridge is around a sharp right-hand turn. As the riders come around the corner, they put on the power to get up the hill and past the pub. They are so close you can feel the wind brushing your jacket. You can see the whites of their eyes as they come around the corner. Even the marshals need nerves of steel. One guy in the 1000cc race loses the line, goes straight ahead at the bend and then reverts to the track, heading straight for the marshal!

There's a race every second day, so there is plenty of time to catch the Isle of Man sights. But before we can do any sightseeing, we need to confirm the ferry's departure time for Ireland. I can't help but visit the tourist office to gather every brochure of interest. The tourist officer gives me more information on things to do and see, adding that the locals love bikers coming over here; they really don't cause much trouble and are great for the island's economy. 'I'm not looking forward to next week, though,' she says. 'There is a lawn-bowls tournament and they are notorious for being hard to please, whingeing about everything and everyone.'

Who would have thought?

People-watching can be good fun at events like this. The guys sitting next to us have squeezed everything, including the kitchen sink, into a hire van. They're over for the weekend only and will head back with just two hours to spare before they have to be at work. They produce an Esky and a portable barbecue. We feel total disappointment when we notice that the Esky is for storing food, while the beer cans are left to sun themselves beside it.

The island's Purple Helmets are a comic stunt group from the Isle of Man's Southern 100 Motorcycle Club. They started their act to raise funds for local charities. Now they are headliners at bike meets across Europe and a must-see at the Isle of Man. The group comprises about 20 riders all decked out in black (not purple) helmets and wearing long beige padded coats. They ride Honda 90s and do such stunts as The Shit House (yep, a dunny being dragged behind a bike), The Naked Piano Player (doesn't take much imagination to visualise this one), The Rocket, The Baked Bean Powered Bike (picture a man eating the beans and using the methane created to power his bike), The Pyramid (standard gymnastics with bikes thrown into the mix), Jousting, and Walking the Couch. The riders jump over each other, drag each other around in wheelie bins, and take a couch, lounge chair, TV and coffee table out for a ride around the track. One gets into a circle of steel and rolls around the track. And they shoot a member out of a cannon. The act is hysterical.

There is another death, this time a rider in the parade lap. Just over a kilometre from the start line, Peter Jarmann, a Swiss rider who had just competed in the 400cc production race and come ninth, was riding a Bultaco two-stroke race bike when apparently the gearbox seized up. Jarmann had raced the Bultaco the previous week without any trouble. Out of control, he careered into a stone wall. He was on a borrowed bike and the owner was distraught. It seems unreal that you could be killed during a parade.

Our Kiwi friend John, who rode in the parade lap, sums

up the racers' attitude to the high risks: 'You have to die somewhere. This place is not so bad for a pure motorcycle racer to be remembered.'

The fog closes in on the final race day and, after numerous delays, the races are postponed until the next day. The mountain and the town of Douglas are shrouded in fog. We head to Point of Ayre at the very tip of the island where the brilliant sunshine makes the waters look inviting – if you like freezing your bits off!

The Sea Cat ferry is taking us to Belfast, where we are meeting Liam McCabe, a world traveller we met in Melbourne when he was on his four-year motorcycle odyssey. The sailing is a bit rough and we keep checking on the bike. It is, of course, in one piece.

I clutch the directions provided by our B&B as we ride off the boat. So intent are we on finding the right exit that we nearly run Liam over when he steps in front of the bike to attract our attention. We didn't expect him to meet us, as it is after midnight, but that's Irish hospitality for you.

loading the bike

Race day, Isle of Man

Douglas, Isle of Man

Snaefell Mountain, Isle of Ma

THREE

IRELAND

6–19 June 2003

Shirley: I can throw the directions away as Liam leads us to Maranatha Guest House in Belfast. The roads are wet and deserted. It's dawn on Sunday, and Brian and I are pretty knackered. We haven't seen Liam for a while – he's only been home from his four-year motorcycle odyssey for a few months – and find plenty to talk about outside the guest-house, hoping those in the front rooms are good sleepers.

There is something about Irish breakfasts and, despite the intention not to put on masses of weight on our trip, we can't refuse the bacon, eggs, tomatoes and mushrooms on offer. I can't refuse the black pudding either, but Brian does – he can't stand the stuff.

We are staying just down the road from Ian Paisley's church in the heart of the Protestant area. We were booked into the guesthouse by Liam, a staunch Catholic whose childhood home was regularly raided by the RUC (Royal Ulster Constabulary) and the British Army searching for

IRA sympathisers. He tells us about his schoolwork being ripped up by the soldiers. The scars run deep. Belfast is a strange city and we are intrigued by its past, present and future.

Liam and his girlfriend, Catriona, are an indication of the city's future. Catriona works for a youth program that caters for kids from both sides of the religious divide. Liam is keen for there to be peace. When we talk about sights in Belfast, we mention Freedom Corner, but Liam quickly says he won't take tourists there. 'From what I can see, it is a Protestant thing and all they did was kill innocent Catholics,' he says. Maybe there is further to go to achieve lasting peace than we first thought.

Falls and Shankill roads were the heart of Belfast's troubles, with Protestants living on Shankill Road and Catholics living on Falls – divided neighbours. Today, this once-dangerous area is the heart of the burgeoning tourist industry. You have to hope it stays this way.

On our tour the next day, our guide regales us with stories of gruesome yet enthralling conflicts between religious zealots. We hear stories of people burnt out of their homes, shot at funerals and gunned down in pubs. One official of the IRA was gunned down in a hospital bed while waiting for surgery. Others were killed in a fish-shop bombing. One section of the road was known as Murder Mile because the 'Shankill Butchers' roamed at night, killing anyone they suspected of being Catholic.

There are still plenty of murals, razor wire, boarded-up houses and macho displays of support for both sides. The kerbing is painted red, white and blue with Union Jacks flying proudly from windows in the loyalist Protestant sector. The Irish tricolour flies proudly in the Catholic sector.

There is no problem stopping to take holiday snaps, but there is a long way to go before the old hard-headed attitudes die out. We find it interesting that the loyalist murals are still very paramilitary, while the Catholic ones are more historic and look to a brighter future. The murals are illegal but, as our guide puts it, 'Who is going to stop them painting them?'

Like so many urban areas, this part of Belfast has trouble with its youth. The kids go to other areas of Belfast, steal cars and take them on joy rides, sometimes killing themselves and others. Both communities have a summary justice policy to stop this dangerous pastime. If miscreants are caught, they are treated harshly. Kids have been known to be beaten with baseball bats with nails sticking out of them (punishment beatings) or shot (punishment shootings) either in the kneecaps or the 'six-pack' – knees, ankles and elbows. There is a mural about Bobby Sands and the other hunger strikers of 1981 that has a great quote: 'Our revenge will be the laughter of our children'. These kids won't be laughing.

The tour takes us along the peace line, a wall between the Falls and Shankill districts. There are 26 other such walls in Belfast. Some have electronically controlled gates that can be shut whenever there is trouble. They are a graphic illustration of the divide, and the fact they haven't been removed says a lot about Ireland's hopes for the future.

There is no doubt that the city is trying hard to rid itself of this image of division and conflict with many new buildings and community projects, but there are also new graffiti and posters near Queen's University claiming the RUC/British Army was involved in the murder of Pat Finucane, a civil rights lawyer.

The predominantly Protestant RUC is no more. The government is trying to ensure the police force is made up of an equal number of Protestants and Catholics. It is now called the PSNI (Police Service of Northern Ireland) and is trying to recruit more Catholics to the ranks. I wonder how successful they will be when we pass a Sinn Féin office with large posters warning its members not to join the PSNI.

So many tourists avoid Northern Ireland because of its past. But miss it and you miss some of the most spectacular natural beauty you will ever see. This part of the country is green and lush, with a coastline that offers great roads, magnificent beaches and villages, like Cushendall and Cushendun, that seem right out of a storybook. The white-washed homes glisten in the sunshine as it breaks through threatening storm clouds (well, it is Ireland, after all). Narrow roads hug the coastline, taking us up and down steep hills. Even in the rain, Brian and I enjoy this area – stone walls, ruined stone farmhouses, sheep and cattle grazing in pastures.

Like so many other bikers, Brian and I make a pilgrimage to Joey Dunlop's home town of Ballymoney. Joey was the master of street motorcycle races such as the Isle of Man TT. He won numerous trophies, including 26 Isle of Man TTs. A family man, Joey was touched by stories of the orphans in Romania, a country he visited often in order to race. He would smuggle food and other essentials into Romania in the back of his van, wedged between his race bikes and spares. To all who knew him, Joey was an unassuming man with a passion for racing but, above all, a humanitarian. He shunned the big contracts. He died tragically racing a 125cc bike at a small meet in Estonia.

We visit Dunlop's local bar. It's a shrine to Joey. There are two bikes suspended from the ceiling and pictures of him all around. Being a biker-friendly pub, they don't even mind when we only order soft drinks to toast their hero. We ask an old man at the bar for directions to Joey's grave in Carryduff.

With his thick accent, he is virtually incomprehensible, but with some effort we work out the directions. When we get onto the road, it is clear we are heading in the right direction – we recognise the straight road from the video of Joey's funeral. The Irish estimate that 50,000 mourners lined the route to his final resting place, such was the love and admiration for this little Irishman.

We stop for lunch at The Fullerton Arms on the site of a sly-grog shop. A local businessman, Dr Fullerton, bought the building for £20,000 in the eighteenth century to prevent the sale of the alcohol. He'd be spinning in his grave if he knew the venue is now a pub and bears his name!

We continue our journey through the beautiful Irish countryside listening to Luka Bloom, our favourite Irish singer. We head to Bunbeg on the northwest coast at Liam's suggestion. We want to take the smaller country roads, but this isn't as easy at it sounds. Many of the smaller roads, while they appear on the map with a number, don't have a number on the signpost – if they are signposted at all. And further west, the signs are only in Irish. We've read that if you say the Irish names out aloud with a thick Irish accent, you can pick up the English name. It sounds like a reasonable theory, but we can't get it to work. It's only when we meet another travelling couple with a much bigger map that we have a chance of finding our way.

At Bunbeg we discover one of the problems of travelling in Ireland. In Northern Ireland, the pound sterling is the currency. Without crossing an obvious border, we are now in the Republic of Ireland and need Euros to buy a drink in Bunbeg. Luckily, we have some. While at lunch at a small cafe we feel that the locals are talking about us, but we can't understand them. They are talking Irish – another first for us.

Asking the Irish for directions is always a treat. There is

the (possibly apocryphal) story of the man who, when asked for directions, replied, 'If I was going there I wouldn't be starting from here'. We don't experience anything like that but just love the man who, when we tell him we are looking for the road to Cong, tells us we are on the wrong road. Well, we do know that. The Irish also have a unique way of warning motorists about the danger of an approaching corner. Painted on the roadway are three very clear signs: 'Slow', 'Slower' and 'Dead Slow'. We take their advice.

The potato famine of the 1840s claimed one million lives in Ireland and forced mass migration. My family came to Australia during this time. Today, those who died are commemorated by 'famine graves' marking mass burial sites across the country. They are a poignant reminder of the past that helped develop Australia. We wander through one in Donegal. The suffering of these people must have been horrendous and death was probably a welcome release.

We've endured rain most days since arriving in Ireland, so we fear that we will miss the most dramatic piece of Irish coastline – the Cliffs of Moher. But we are blessed with brilliant sunshine the day we visit them. Walking along the coastline, we stop to listen to a busker playing a harp. Ah, this is Ireland! The sun glistening on the water of Galway Bay gives the cliffs a majestic shimmer. It is not that they are particularly high – the highest is just 200 metres – but on a clear day like this one they seem to go forever. Signs warn of getting too close to the edge. The cliffs are unstable and it would certainly ruin a good holiday if you fell into the sea. But, in any case, you don't need to get near the edge to realise this is one of the most spectacular views in Ireland.

In the Cliffs car park, Brian and I create a bit of interest. A man on a bus tour approaches and begins chatting away. He's from Bavaria and his daughter is married to a US captain killed in Kosovo (at least we think that's what he says!). The bus driver is getting impatient and begins blasting the horn to get his passenger back on board, but this man has a mission. He climbs onto the bus and within seconds is off again and heading our way. He has a gift for Brian – a bottle of Bavarian beer, and it is cold!

At Cong, Brian and I realise we're spending far too much time on the road. If we keep up this pace we will kill ourselves before we leave the UK. It's time to slow down and enjoy the journey rather than rush from place to place. Chilling out with the *Irish Times*, I discover that Luka Bloom is playing in Dublin. We can't believe our luck. Well, we'll have to hightail it to get across the country in time to hear Luka live.

Before hitting Dublin, we do have time to visit Sligo for the bikers' rally we heard about on the Isle of Man. Rallies are big in Ireland. Bikers get together, camp in very rough conditions and get horribly pissed listening to really bad music. Not my scene, but you have to experience everything once. Luckily, we don't have camping gear and the local B&B is the perfect spot to build up to a night of headbanging music.

Just seeing the names of the local bikers on the wall of the local hall is worth the journey. There are the Highciders (sic) – a pun on the very common way of coming off a motorbike, the high side. Then there are the Iron Horsemen. They bill themselves as 'One Percentors'. This might be right, but they don't know how to spell, having put out a poster advertising their upcoming rally High Verlosity. And they also get the date wrong, having had to cross out July and scrawl June across the posters by hand.

The rally indeed turns out to be an excuse for too much drinking while listening to really bad, loud music. We guess it helps if you know people because there are certainly groups of bikers having a good time.

The food is served from a takeaway food van, just like the ones we've seen in English movies – you know the kind, where the hero stops on the way home to get fish and chips to soak up the alcohol. The options are limited – we're glad we ate at the Indian restaurant in town before heading out to the rally.

We sneak off when the music gets too much. The next day, when we stop by to say goodbye to the bikers we met on the Isle of Man, there are many sore heads and those with cast-iron stomachs are having just a bit more fried food.

We cross the Shannon on the car ferry, head to Tralee and then to Dingle Peninsula via Connor Pass Road. The views are said to be absolutely brilliant from here: at a height of 456 m, you can see Dingle Peninsula spread out below. Unfortunately, the pass is shrouded in cloud. Our view is of a light-grey mist. Ah, it's Ireland.

Capital cities and motorbikes are not usually a good mix when you are unsure of the roads. We ride into Dublin and battle the heavy traffic to the port town of Dun Laoghaire. We are doing pretty well when a Mercedes pulls in front of us and brakes heavily. Brian does his best and slams on the brakes. Even with ABS, he doesn't avoid a low-speed tumble. Heavy braking makes the bike unstable. One minute we are upright, the next we are sideways. Luckily, we are in the inside lane so we aren't at risk of being hit from the side. The bike lands on top of us and it's heavy. We are half on and half off the footpath. The guy who caused the accident stops a short way up the street and looks back at us in his rear-vision mirror. After a minute of indecision, he drives off! The man in the car behind Brian and me puts his indicator on to move around us without even taking his mobile phone away from his ear. We are okay and the bike is okay. Maybe we have been blessed by the luck of the Irish.

We head to Dun Laoghaire, on the harbour a few ks south of Dublin. We leave the bike at the hotel – everyone has warned us about thieves in Dublin – and get the train into the city centre. After a long day on the road, and our accident, there is just one thought in our minds: Luka Bloom had better be worth it.

The concert is €20 well spent. For three hours Luka plays the acoustic guitar and sings modern Irish folk songs. They are poems set to music telling of love, despair and hope for a better world. In the taxi back to our hotel, we experience our first language difficulty in Dublin, even though we are all speaking English. After several attempts at explaining the name of the hotel and the address, we end up handing over the hotel key.

Finding the road back to Northern Ireland isn't that easy. After circumnavigating Dublin, we end up in the CBD. A motorcycle courier drives up alongside us and asks about the bike, the trip and our destination. Rather than trying to give us directions, he tells us to follow him. Without a thought for his next delivery, he leads us to the highway heading north – motorcyclists are like that.

Heading to Belfast is a little like coming home. We are welcomed back to the guesthouse with open arms and Catriona is there to meet us. Liam is off to Germany for a rally of Honda Africa Twin riders. He will, no doubt, be the star attraction, having punted his way all over the world on his Africa Twin.

Our next stop is Scotland. We board the biggest ferry we can find and make our way to a castle on the banks of bonnie Loch Lomond.

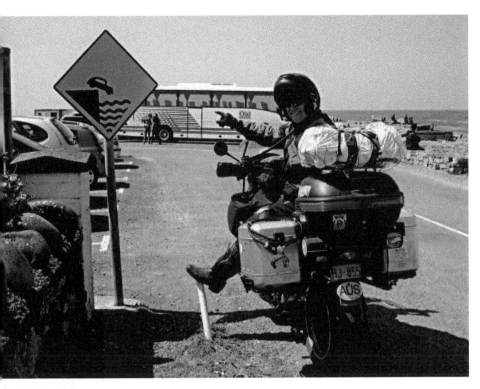

We love the Irish roadsigns

They say the view is spectacular from Connor Pass

Joey Dunlop's B

FOUR

BACK TO LONDON – VIA THE SCENIC ROUTE

19 June – 2 July 2003

Shirley: On the ferry to Scotland, ours is the only bike among semi-trailers and tour buses. We land in Stranraer in Scotland's southwest and the first thing we notice is an improvement in the road surface. In Ireland they seem just to asphalt over the bumps; here they seem to smooth the roads out before laying the new surface. The sky is grey and threatens rain. The wind sweeps across the water, whipping up small white caps on the surface. Grey shrubs, small bushes and sheep dot the roadside.

Brian and I, now used to being lost quite regularly, have trouble finding our way to Glasgow. At a service station, a local tries to give us directions and then offers to lead the way. With very few teeth and plenty of tattoos, he looks like an escapee from the local prison. We follow his little beaten-up Ford Escort through some very dodgy neighbourhoods and, just when we are sure he is leading us somewhere unpleasant, we see the motorway to Glasgow.

Brian: We follow the signs as best we can, but at one stage I get caught in the wrong lane. I indicate, hold up my hand apologetically and move over with plenty of room to spare in front of a 'suit' in a new Mercedes (yep – another Mercedes driver and my thoughts go straight back to the one we 'ran into' in Dublin). The driver gets indignant and blasts his horn, which just goes to show who the nice people are in this world. Give me Ford Escort drivers any time.

Shirley: It is amazing how lost you can get with one small error. On the banks of Loch Lomond, we pass a sign to our youth hostel, but instead of waiting for another sign we take the next turn. The road is the scenic route along the very shore of the Loch, and while we enjoy the scenery we miss the hostel. The dark skies make the deep water of the loch appear gloomy. The surrounding hills look as though they want to get away from the water, but even on the overcast afternoon their reflection adds to the beauty. We ride for another 15 minutes before realising we have missed the place. We ask for directions at a pub and the barmaid is bemused. She can't work out how we missed it. 'It looks like a castle with sheep in front of it,' she tells us.

And it does.

Leaving Loch Lomond, the scenery is breathtaking but it is very hard to enjoy because of the biting cold. This is a mid-summer weekend and it is freezing. It is mid-winter in Melbourne and we learn that it is warmer there than it is here in Scotland. Even Brian has resorted to his jacket, riding-pants liners and waterproofs to cut down on the wind. I've donned thermals and waterproofs. From Firkin Point, where the mountains come to the water's edge, we head across rugged, windswept plains into the Highlands. Here, the wind is biting and strong, and Brian struggles to keep the bike on the road. I begin to lose heart, as well as the feeling in my fingers and toes. Brian is coping well and makes me feel inadequate as I really feel this is too hard. If I find this hard, how will I cope in the more difficult countries? But there is no arguing that this is one of the most picturesque areas we've visited. The steep mountains, rushing streams and green pastures are postcard perfect. Trampers walking through the fields are fighting the blustering wind. What on earth are they thinking?

We plan on venturing even further north, but a quick check with Carbisdale Castle, the haunted castle of choice for backpackers, changes all that. There are no rooms available until after September. Seems everyone wants to share their room with a ghost. In this busy time, however, we eventually get a room at the Letterfinlay Lodge Hotel overlooking Loch Lochy. Not to be outdone by the more famous and close-by Loch Ness, Loch Lochy has its very own monster. She has been spotted a few times in the twentieth century, including once by some staff and guests of this hotel.

A 1997 expedition by the Friends of the Loch Ness Monster, the true believers in the 'Nessy' myth, claim to have got a signal from her at 50 and then 60 m deep before she disappeared into water at least 90 m deep. Well, that's the story, anyway. We decide to have a drink in the bar and see if we can spot her – nothing to report!

After dinner we chat with a couple from England. He races motorcycles and is planning to ride in the Manx GP at the Isle of Man later in the year. He is obviously very courageous or very stupid.

When we check out, the owner tells us that he should have quoted £34 a head for our room, not £32, but as it was his mistake he would let us have the room at the lower rate.

I thank him, adding, 'We are on the road for 12 months so those four pounds might make the difference between a meal and us starving in a few months.'

'Well, that might be the case,' he says in true Scottish style, 'but I need everything I can get to keep a roof over my head.' He seems to forget that we ate in his expensive restaurant last night and drank in his bar!

The ride to Loch Ness is a biker's dream. The long, sweeping corners take us along the banks of Loch Lochy, Loch Oich and, finally, Loch Ness. There might have been a monster or two floating past, but Brian didn't notice – he was too busy concentrating and having a blast. To Brian, a clear road equals freedom.

The touring is getting easier the more time we spend on the road. We've organised the security chain so we can now lock the helmets onto the bike and only have to carry our jackets and the tank bag when we go sightseeing. Unfortunately, because of terrorist threats no-one has cloakrooms any more.

The only other problem we have is sniping at each other every time we get lost – and that is more often than I care to admit. I hate to say it, but it's probably true that women can't read maps. Brian gets stressed and swears, and I get defensive and apologetic – whether it is my fault or not. We can feel the tension rising and we know this has to stop.

Touring castles in the UK is a bit like visiting churches in Europe – you've seen one, you've seen them all. But then we find Doune Castle near Stirling. We walk into the ticket office and souvenir shop and are met by the guard. He produces two half coconuts from under the desk and does a very fine impersonation of a horse riding up to the castle wall. Then, in a very bad French accent, he says, 'I wave my private parts in your direction.' Briefly thinking we have walked into a lunatic asylum, we soon realise this is the castle where *Monty Python and the Holy Grail* was filmed. Before getting to see the castle proper, we have to browse through the photo album of the movie shoot and the guard tries to sell us a couple of bottles of Holy Grail Ale. This is when being on a motorbike has its advantages. 'We have no room' is the answer whenever we are offered something we couldn't possibly want in our wildest dreams.

Brian and I stop to wander through Stirling Castle, Edinburgh Castle and Dryburgh Abbey before heading to the border town of Kirk Yetholm. Spending a night at our hostel is like trying to sleep in the middle of a French farce. The building is tiny and we are the youngest guests. The others are all well into their seventies and are here to walk the Pennine Way, a 250-kilometre walk from the Scottish border to Derbyshire in central England. As the sun gets up, so do the other guests. The first door to slam is the dormitory door. Then there's the door to the men's room, the individual toilet doors and the shower-room door. And when the doors aren't slamming, you can hear the lambs calling for their mothers in the distant fields. But it's impossible to get annoyed in places like this.

Brian: After all the early morning noise, there is no point in hanging around. We hit the road at 9 a.m. and ride along almost-deserted roads. The big sweeping bends and undulating landscape get the juices flowing. Sometimes I liken riding to a form of bizarre dance and, when it flows, it is addictive. This is one of those days. The weather is fine and the road surface good. We play with a few fellow bikers taking in the morning roads. Of course, I have no hope of staying in touch loaded up the way we are, but it is good fun.

Shirley: We have our first sighting of Hadrian's Wall, built by the Emperor Hadrian to keep the marauding Scots out of the 'civilised' world of the south in 122 AD, while stuck in the middle of a field in northern England. We dodge cow pats and the cows that left them to get close to the wall – or what's left of it. Not only have the ravages of time taken their toll, but over the centuries the locals have used the stones to build dwellings and animal shelters. When you are next to something unique and the only people there, it is hard not to be a tourist and take ridiculous photos. We lie and stand on the wall for the camera before we find out at the nearby visitor centre that this is frowned upon.

Brian: Riding around the Lake District, through Windermere to Bowness, we see heaps of bikes out, and no wonder. It's a beautiful day and the roads are something else. As we crest hills, Shirl admonishes me for taking both wheels off the ground. Getting around the tight sweepers, however, I know she is really enjoying this. I'm not doing anything over 100 km/h.

Shirley: Summer has finally arrived and it is amusing to watch the Poms sunning themselves on the shores of Lake Windermere – masses of lily-white flesh that will be scarlet by high tea. On the other side of the lake we stop at Keswick, where there is more white flesh.

This is obviously a popular tourist spot during the summer months and we can understand why. It's hot but the breeze off the water is cooling. The grassed banks of the lakes are dotted with tourists on deck chairs. We expect them to be wearing hankies tied in knots at the corners but they aren't.

Still, many of the men do have their trousers rolled up, making the most of the sun.

People in hire boats row across the water and the colourful sails of the yachts add to the postcard look of the scene. After the ride through the hills it is peaceful to sit here and watch the world go by.

Brian: We head to the Yorkshire Dales. The day is great, with clear, blue skies and crisp air, and the roads flow through laneways with stone walls and hedges along the side. We have become used to the black-faced sheep grazing on the sides of the road, but as we head into the Dales, we cross a cattle grid – hundreds of cows seemingly oblivious to the constant stream of traffic.

At the hostel we decide not to carry our entire luggage up the 52 steps to our room. This time, I leave the panniers on the bike and just take up a change of clothes, our passports and laptop. After all, if a thief wants to steal my dirty jocks from my pannier, good luck to them! Besides, my lower back is really sore. I damaged it years ago, and I can do without lumping the heavy panniers around. Maybe the strain is starting to show up in these little niggles; I resolve to get fitter. Shirley is not all that enamoured with opening up her pannier in the car park and displaying its contents to all and sundry. As she ferrets through to find some clean clothes, I remind her of her father's immortal words, which she often recites, 'F!@#, you're middle class.'

Shirley: Some of the guests at the hostel put us to shame. Two old cyclists, probably in their sixties, are spending a few days riding their pushies around the Yorkshire Dales. After breakfast we meet one of them. He's been for a brisk walk into town and back to see a rock garden! We ponder his sanity. After cycling some 112 km up and down rather steep climbs yesterday, he has enough energy to walk about 4 km to see a rock garden. And he intends to cycle about 160 km today! We get tired just thinking about it.

Brian: The Horizons Unlimited website is the overland motorcyclists' online bible. If you want to know about border crossings, visas, places to stay, fuel quality – anything about travel on two wheels – this is the place to look. When we heard the Horizons Unlimited get-together of world travellers coincided with our trip, we had to get there.

Everything is going very well. Shirley has the written directions from the Yorksire Dales to the meeting in Derbyshire and seems to be following them well. I should have known it was too good to be true – Shirl misdirects me into a major shopping centre. I boil over and snap at her through the intercom. It doesn't take long to get back onto the right road and then I notice it is very quiet on the back seat. There is no answer to any questions. I feel bad when she tells me I made her cry. I know this is testing her comfort zone and I have to make sure I don't do that again. We are in this together and need to work as a team to get the most out of our adventure.

When we at last find the rally site – a vacant block beside a rundown pub outside the small village of Somercotes – we look for somewhere to stay. We check out all the surrounding towns for a B&B but find nothing. Finally we head for Alfreton and come across a Travel Lodge just off the M6, but of course, true to form, there is no-one on reception until 3 p.m. That is one thing we have noticed in the UK – service verges on non-existent. We wait around in a Burger King cafe next door and grab the only available bed for at least a 15 km radius. As we open the door to our room, I see the smile return to my loved one's face. There is a real double bed and a bath!

Shirley: At the rally we meet world travellers and those who would like to be world travellers. There's the man who sold everything and travelled for eight years and the young bloke who spent a month riding through the Moroccan desert. But the people we most enjoy meeting are Kiwis Trent; Jacqui; and Peter, Jacqui's brother. Peter is about to head to Goa to work for a motorcycle tour company taking punters around India on Royal Enfield bikes. Jacqui and Trent plan to ride home to their native New Zealand next year after living in the UK for four years. The more experienced travellers at the rally are happy to pass on their knowledge and some tell us we are too heavy, with too much luggage. They are probably right.

We get the chance to test our bike and load on rough dirt roads well before we had planned to when we ride through some of the local lanes with a guy on a trail bike. I'm a little anxious, but Brian is keen to get going. There is a handful of riders with us, including a Dutch girl on a Yamaha XJ900 road bike with a sidecar that looks a lot like a coffin. She and her boyfriend have taken this machine around the world – twice! We figure that if she is taking this machine, then we will be fine (famous last words!).

Brian: We head off and ride down some great little English country lanes, which are so narrow the bike's sidecar is hitting the overgrowth on both sides of the road. The lanes are gentle and we have time to admire the rolling hills, even when we hit the first dirt section. Then we ride through a farmer's yard where a lot of cow manure has recently been deposited. It flicks up over the front of the bike and us, but we figure this is the country and it's all part of it.

Then the lanes get narrower, the surface turns to deep stones and it becomes a constant battle to keep the bikes upright – that is, of course, unless you are on an out-and-out trail bike like our ride leader. We scramble up a steep, slippery hill and Jacqui falls off in front of us as she slows because the sidecar is stuck with all three wheels off the ground. We manhandle the sidecar up to the top of the track and Trent gets Jacqui upright again.

We take a rest and muse that it can't get much worse – but it does. We get to a steep descent, which disappears out of sight into the undergrowth. There are huge wheel ruts at least half a metre deep, the road slopes wickedly away to the left and there are boulders the size of helmets. To top it off, the surface is muddy. The sidecar bounces its way down the hill, out of control and out of sight. Jacqui falls off again and is assisted down the hill.

Now it's my turn. Shirley wisely gets off and says she'll walk. I start but the weight of the bike takes over and begins to pull me down the hill. I lock up the back wheel but still gather pace, the front wheel falls into a rut and I'm stopped dead in my tracks and topple over to the right, unable to keep my foot on the rear brake and the ground at the same time. It's a heavy landing, with a rock springing the pannier off its mount. It takes three of us to lift the bike back on its wheels in the mud and sloping ground. I sit on the bike and need two other guys to balance and stop the forward momentum as I bounce down the hill with the engine off. Three more bikes suffer a similar fate as it takes us an hour to traverse about 300 m. Our ride leader is a little embarrassed, realising he has chosen a route that is great for trail bikes but not so good for these types of bikes.

Despite a small dent in the right pannier, there is no harm done and, really, it was great to explore the boundaries of bike and rider. Physically, my back is killing me; I think I strained it while twisting. Due to some earlier damage I know it will take ages to come good.

We head back on some more beautiful laneways, through some farmers' gates and onto another loose-stone road. Again, the weight of the bike makes the front wheel act like a plough. It twists sideways and rather than fight it and risk a high side, I run it into the raised grass verge. Those behind laugh but understand it was the safest option. At least we stayed upright this time. I back it out and continue on. We come to a small village, obviously the back way, and surprise patrons of a church fête, who are spread out on the lawns sipping tea and eating scones. They all look alarmed as we rumble through. The road back to Somercotes takes us through a road with signs declaring, 'Slow down, 36 lambs killed last year'.

After four hours we drag ourselves back to the rally site and we find out the other riders didn't even attempt this route due to the slippery road. We certainly took the wrong ride!

Shirley: Our ride back to London is like going from the sublime to the ridiculous. We take to the motorways with Jacqui, Trent and Peter and it is a smooth run. We pull into the service centre to say our farewells, planning to spend Christmas with Peter in Goa and to catch up with Jacqui and Trent when they come through Australia on their way home.

In London we head back to the home of our relatives Bettina and Tim. We need to go to Germany for the BMW Motorrad in Bavaria, the third annual get-together of BMW bikers from Germany and around the world. Bettina is about to give birth, but it is clear that the baby won't arrive before we have to leave. We want to be there when the baby comes, so plan to return to London. Before we leave, I have one job. I know my hair colour will be a problem while we are travelling, as touching up regrowths will be virtually impossible, so I hit the hairdresser to go back to my natural near-black colour.

Brian: Shirl arrives back from the hairdresser complaining bitterly. She hates her hair and thinks she looks like a witch.

The colour is close to jet black and so different from what she is used to. I anticipate this reaction from her (no matter what the colour) and have planned some lines that husbands should drag out on such occasions. Actually, when I open the door and see her hair, I genuinely like it. I'm probably too effusive, because I don't think to this day she believes it looked any good.

Shirley: We've been on the road for nearly six weeks and realise we have way too much gear. We rationalise our clothing and bike spares. With my new hair colour and a lighter bike, we hit the road for the BMW Motorrad in Garmisch, the heart of Bavaria.

axing on Hadrian's Wall

A ride through the country lanes with Horizons Unlimited

The Lake District

FIVE

ON TO THE CONTINENT

2–30 July 2003

Shirley: Six days before Tim and Bettina's baby is due, Brian and I leave for Germany. Avoiding choppy seas at all costs, we decide on the Eurotunnel train from Dover to Calais in France. When we check in, the officials ask the standard questions without looking up: 'Do you have any weapons or animals with you?' When Brian replies, 'Are you kidding, mate?' the official looks up. 'I couldn't squeeze in a flick knife or a flea.'

This gets a laugh. The French official is so uninterested he just waves us through without even checking our passports.

The Eurotunnel is the way to travel. We ride the bike onto the platform and then onto the train. We just stand by the bike for about 30 minutes and then we are in France. When the doors open we ride straight out and onto the roads of Calais. The road is great and we arrive in Brugge without missing a beat. We find a square with lots of activity, but the problem is we don't know where we are. A local gives us directions to the tourist office in the centre of Brugge, a real picture-postcard scene of old houses, magnificent churches and official buildings.

While we avoid taking ferries with the bike, we seek them out in cities. They are a way of getting a good look at a town away from the madding crowds. Brugge is no different. Viewed from the canals, it is an exquisite city and in the shops we buy even more exquisite chocolate – there goes the diet. We visit the Heiligbloed-Basiliek, where they say they have spots of Christ's blood, and the local marketplace. The bells peal the most amazing tune before chiming the hour, which tells us it is time for a beer. Brian opts for the local brew – it's eight per cent proof and packs a punch – while I opt for a French red. It's our first day out of the UK and we haven't moved an inch out of our comfort zone.

Call them autobahns or call them motorways, these roads in Europe make getting somewhere fast and easy. In dry weather the speed limit is 130 km/h. In the wet it drops to 110 km/h. In reality it is anything up to 200 km/h, depending on the car. We crisscross from Belgium into France, France into Belgium, Belgium into Luxembourg and Luxembourg into France. Thank goodness for the EU, and hence no borders. It is a circuitous route, but we find our way despite rain so heavy we can't see a thing in front of us.

The bike comes into its own when we encounter the first of many accidents on these roads. The traffic banks back at least 10 km every time there is a crash. Brian just cuts the traffic, ignoring the black looks from the car drivers who sped past us half an hour ago. We encounter a truck that has careered across two lanes and ended up on its side on the median strip. The most serious accident site we see is a small van having ploughed into the back of a caravan, forcing the car to jackknife.

Heading into Germany, we get a little bamboozled

trying to find our way to the Motorrad in Garmisch-Partenkirchen. We see a group of BMW riders, so we follow them. We drive up alongside the tail rider and in my terrible German I ask if they are going to Garmisch. He nods yes and waves when we ask if we can ride with them. They seem to be heading for Garmisch before they take a turn on to the motorway for Munich. They pull up on the side of the motorway and we follow. A couple of them speak English and we discover they are not going to Garmisch until Sunday. We could have spent a great weekend following them around Germany!

When we finally get on the right road, the scenery is awe-inspiring: the Alps, pine forests, pastures – and the bikes. Garmisch is literally buzzing with BMWs of all makes. We follow the signs to the BMW Motorrad and find a wonderland of tents and bikes. Brian is in heaven.

We walk the cobblestone streets around the village of Partenkirchen nestled under soaring mountains. The church bells toll every quarter hour. The buildings have wonderful murals – walking around is like walking through a postcard. And Bavarian food is a knockout, as long as you only want to eat once a day. The locals don't understand small serves, small appetites or vegetarians. The meals defeat even Brian! But while the food is good, the beer is brilliant and everyone drinks it. In Bavaria, we are told, beer is a food not a beverage. Even the police enjoy a litre or two at the Motorrad. Standing with their guns on their hips and steins in their hands, they are interesting to us, but no-one takes the slightest notice. A policeman having a beer? Of course. This is Bavaria.

Bikes are the common ground here – there are literally thousands – and language is no barrier. Our Australian registration and koala strapped to the bike make it clear where we are from. Everywhere we stop we get talking (or charade playing) with other bikers. A Slovenian dentist even wants us to visit him when we head down the Dalmatian coast.

Today, the ride out is at 2.30 p.m. We are used to Australian rides, which never start on time so nothing prepares us for German efficiency. At 2.30 p.m. the church bells chime and we are told to start our engines. Four-and-a-half-thousand bikes head off for a 70-odd kilometre ride around the Bavarian hills. The police block every cross street – there is no stopping – and the motorists blocked on the side roads sit on their cars and wave. There is no anti-bike animosity here. We ride in a seemingly endless line of bikes around Lake Eibsee, passing through tunnels cut into the mountains and towns with church steeples and cows with bells around their necks.

Catering for 20,000 hungry bikers seems an impossible feat, but no-one goes hungry here. There is an entire ox on the biggest rotisserie we have ever seen, and in a massive oven are hundreds of chickens. No meal would be complete without a heap of potato salad about the size of a small alpine mountain and a huge Lowenbrau. We can feel the kilos climbing by the hour here.

We park our bike in the paddock outside the main tent. When Brian goes to get something from it, he finds it surrounded by officials and photographers. We've been short-listed for The Most Interesting Journey prize to be presented at the party.

Over dinner and more beers we meet Stefan Stoll from Munich. He asks a question in German and answers in perfect English when we apologise for our lack of German. He works as an engineer in Munich and has ridden his BMW here for the weekend. Stefan becomes our surrogate manager when they start announcing the prizewinners. He pushes us to the front of the hall before hundreds of bikers from across the world. When they announce the Most Interesting Journey category, a picture of our Nullarbor crossing sticker from the bike flashes onto a huge screen. Then there is a picture of the bike. We've won!

Stefan pushes us onto the stage. There are kisses all round from the young men and women hosting the party. It is surreal. Stefan has our camera and takes photos, people cheer and clap and Brian is interviewed. We are celebrities. At the bar, people come up and welcome us to Europe and wish us well. When we have a quiet moment I check out our prize pack. There is a Perspex trophy, a T-shirt, hat, badge and a model of a BMW K1200RS – Brian's next road bike (well, the GT version). Brian's Australian accent must have caused a few problems for the officials around the bike earlier tonight. They have written the certificate to 'Brian Wegs and Charlotte'! At the end of the night we exchange details with Stefan and promise to come and visit when we return to Germany.

On our way to Zugspitze, the highest mountain in Germany, our celebrity status continues. At the station we meet Joachim from Monaco. 'You're the Australians,' he says by way of introduction. On the summit of Zugspitze, at 2964 m, there is snow and that warrants a photo. As I take a shot of Brian, a man offers to take a photo of the two of us. 'You are Australian. I saw you last night.' He's Ralf Fritzke, from the Ruhr.

At dinner, we are joined by Bodo and Marion, two Germans Joachim met on a ride today. We have a wonderful evening of good food, good beers and lots of laughs. The Germans make us feel so inadequate, with their bilingual abilities, unlike the Englishman we met last night who wore his inability to speak another language like a badge of honour.

Life on the road is not all beer and bratwurst. There are sights to see and places to visit, like Bavaria's Neuschwanstein Castle. Mad King Ludwig II built this Disneyland-like castle in the nineteenth century before meeting his untimely demise in a lake along with his psychiatrist. His brother couldn't take the throne because he was mad, too. Some family! The castle is testament to King Ludwig's insanity. It was never completed, but the finished rooms are bedecked with religious murals on the ceilings, and massive statues and paintings of swans, his favourite animal.

Brian decides to head back to Garmisch via Austria. I immediately become paranoid about border crossings because our passports are in our hotel room in Garmisch. We don't get stopped and the road was worth it. The Alps tower over us – what a spectacle of nature at its most beautiful, with snow-capped peaks and pine forests. On the outskirts of Garmisch we encounter an in-line skate run, with hundreds of skaters hurtling along the road. The Germans don't do anything by halves.

It is late by the time we return for dinner and we are starving, so we decide to do one of these huge Bavarian meals justice. As we are about to launch into our meal, a familiar voice says hello. It's Bodo, the German biker we met at dinner last night. He and Marion are still in town and thought they might bump into us. Over some schnapps they share with us their local knowledge of good bike roads through the Alps. The Williams Schnapps tastes of fresh pears and could become addictive.

Brian: We have come to expect strangers to strike up conversations with us. At a service station on our way out of Garmisch, we meet an elderly German who tells us he rode an army sidecar during World War II, seeing active service in Africa. He loves living in Garmisch (who wouldn't) and has recently lost his wife. He is obviously lonely, but we leave him with a smile on his face.

We find the roads Bodo recommended to us. They take

us through the southernmost part of Germany, rather than hitting the highways across the border in Austria where, of course, you have to pay for the privilege by getting choked to death on diesel fumes. The switchbacks become sweeping bends with a few mountain tunnels thrown in as we ride around a lake. We cross the border into Austria via a back road and pass a paddock of contented cows wearing stylish bells. We sweep through a forest and come to a clearing and a small hotel advertising 'Bikers welcome' in English. Here, we stop for a lunch of bratwurst and sauerkraut.

When we get back on the road, we have no option but to join the main road to Salzburg, which has its own endless supply of poorly tuned trucks belching black smoke in our direction. Implanted in my brain are the words 'throttle to the kerb, throttle to the kerb' to ensure I stay where I should.

Shirl is a bit quiet on the back after a few more blunders with her directions. I can tell she is getting a little frustrated and upset with herself. I try to be understanding and listen to her like a good husband should, but when I end up off the highway and in the middle of a town called Waidring, I lose it slightly and swear because I now have to get back on the highway and battle the same bloody trucks I passed a few ks back. Shirl says nothing as another bike looms up behind us. I wave him past and then follow to let off some steam. He is setting a quick pace and, being lighter and only one-up, accelerates quicker than I can, but it's still fun. He also takes the turn off the highway to Berchtesgaden then a tight, twisty sprint of around 20 km. I am scraping toes and the undercarriage, and really enjoying myself. In no time, Berchtesgaden comes into view, and I head for the information centre.

Over dinner we decide that tomorrow should be a day off the bike to give my back a chance to recover. It's been nearly two weeks of pain now and the knotted muscles in my left side are still pinching my sciatic nerve. I can feel the pain down my left leg. Despite days of deep heat and gentle twisting exercises, it's not improving. I know it needs rest. Getting on and off the bike and twisting the lower back really aggravates it. The weight of the bike and luggage renders the side stand useless, as it's too short. If I balance the bike on it to slide off the seat, the bike wants to tip over, lifting the front wheel off the ground.

Shirley: We play regular tourists and head down to the salt mines at Berchtesgaden. Contrary to popular belief in our part of the world, this mine was not used by Hitler as punishment for miscreants. In its depths, an underground lake of brine sees us taking another 'water tour'. A punt takes us across the underground lake – a still, inky stretch of water. It is 600 m from the surface and has a dreamlike quality. The surface of the water seems like black marble and tastes so salty you expect it to be solid.

From this underground wonderland we head up to Eagle's Nest, an alpine retreat that ended up a bastion of the Third Reich. It is here that Hitler and Eva Braun shared the house with the famous stone patio seen in so many documentaries of the period. The house and many other buildings of the time, including the SS barracks and headquarters, were destroyed after the war – the German government didn't want any reminders of those days or the chance of people building memorials to the Reich.

The road to Eagle's Nest 1837 m above Berchtesgaden is not for the faint-hearted. Hitler didn't like the retreat because he was afraid of heights and claustrophobic (a 124 m-long marble tunnel leads to a small lift that travels up a 124 m shaft into the building). Hitler only visited 14 times.

The Alps are calling and we ride to the Hohe Tauern National Park, the massive Grossglockner glacier and the Hochalpenstrasse – the High Alpine Road. We begin the climb to the summit with hundreds of other bikes. This is obviously a popular spot for bikes and we can see why. The road is brilliant and the scenery is out of this world – massive peaks topped with snow tower over the roadway. It gets colder the higher we go. At Edelweiss-Spitz we come to the first of many bikers' points. Here there are free lockers for bikers to store their gear while they walk the trails. They actually encourage bikers here – an attitude Australian authorities could learn from.

The road is too narrow for buses and caravans, which is good for us, and the short climb takes us to 2571 m – the highest point on the Grossglockner High Alpine Road. Here you are surrounded by higher peaks and Grossglockner. There is an incredible 'wow' factor up here. Further up the mountain pass we are at Kaiser-Franz-Josefs-Höhe – 2369 m. We are standing in front of Grossglockner and the longest glacier in the Austrian Alps, the Pasterze. It is quite a sight and it is bloody freezing. The wind whistles through the mountain passes. These towering outcrops are covered in snow and the glacier runs below them. It is making very slow progress through the valley. We watch people frolicking on the glacier and think they're crazy.

We head to Werfen and the ice caves. Whenever we stop we tell people that's where we are going, but no-one seems to have heard of the place. We take the road to Mallnitz and look for the road out of town. We take one road that ends up as a goat track. Back in town, we take another, which just peters out. Mallnitz seems to be lovely, but we can't find our way out. We want to ride to Werfen, and our map seems to indicate a train. Yep, there is no road out of Mallnitz, just a car train and we've missed the last one for the night. Still, there are many worse places to spend the night.

Brian: We both sleep soundly and awaken to a half light that shows grey-blue skies and the surrounding mountains shrouded in low cloud. Nothing to worry about in this part of the world – we are assured it will clear into another beautiful day. Shirley admits to feeling the strain of travelling day in day out. She is very tired. I hope she is all right, but fear she has picked up a virus that is running her down. Apart from my aching back, I feel fine. I have not thought of the pressures of work or what might be happening back home for some time now. I am finally starting to get into the routine of being on the road, soaking up the atmosphere and enjoying the different sights, sounds, smells and freedom that only motorcycling can provide.

Shirley: The car train out of Mallnitz is an open-air freight car with a couple of tie-downs for the bike. Brian leaves the bike in gear and hopes for the best. When he meets me in the carriage he chides me for not getting a window seat. What does he expect to see? The whole point of this train is to get through the mountains – an 8 km-long tunnel. In 15 minutes we are out the other side.

Back on the road, we only travel 100 km to Werfen. I am relieved when we discover it does exist and embarrassed when I work out why no-one had ever heard of it – it's pronounced 'Verfen'! The reason we've come to this pretty little town is to see the eleventh-century Hohenwerfen castle, and the world's largest accessible ice cave.

We huff and puff our way up the very steep climb to the castle and realise how quickly we've lost our conditioning after sitting on a bike day after day. This is where they made that classic war film *Where Eagles Dare* in 1968. The background scenery and the interiors are spectacular. This castle's rooms have been restored, giving a glimpse of life in the eleventh century. You can even get into the clock tower and see the mechanism of this centuries-old timepiece. During World War II, the Germans used the castle as a training centre and recently the Austrian gendarmerie occupied it as a training academy. Finally, its money-making potential was recognised and it was made a tourist attraction. The ancient art of falconry is on display at the castle with massive birds of prey swooping just inches above the crowd and then soaring high into the air. Only the surrounding mountains are higher.

Cut high in the mountain is an ice cave. The next day we take a bus up the mountain, the climb a struggle even for the bus, and soon we have great views over the valley and the castle. From the cave's entrance gate, there is a 15-minute steep climb up to a cable car. We struggle up the hill and are sweating by the time we reach the next level. The cable car shoots straight up the side of the mountain. At the top, there is another 20-minute walk to get to the cave entrance. Here, the Austrians are testing the theory of evolution, making sure that only the fittest of the species will survive!

Everywhere there is evidence of rock slides and in places the path is covered with a manmade shelter to stop stones hitting you on the head. In other places, wire netting strung above the path serves the same purpose. The walk up is a real struggle for Brian's back and knee, especially after yesterday's steep climb to the castle. I am worried about him, but in his usual stoic form he carries on regardless.

Our guide hands us a lantern and opens the door to another world. The wind coming out as the door opens is so cold it takes your breath away and all the lanterns promptly blow out. The first thing we are told is that there will be 700 steps up and 700 steps down on this tour. Oh, great news! This is a world where the temperature never rises beyond zero degrees and where the word darkness has a new meaning. Our guide doesn't turn out the lights to show us, but you know you wouldn't be able to see a thing in the cave. He carries a length of magnesium that he lights occasionally to give us a better view of the ice formations. Water has been dripping and seeping into this cave for centuries. It lands on rocks and freezes. The stalactites and stalagmites form the most amazing sculptures when they meet. The walls of the caves sparkle like diamonds, but these are just ice particles on the rock face. The caves' ice surfaces change constantly, which proves a problem for the guides. The 'elephant' ice formation has lost its head and trunk in recent years, the polar bear is still forming and the giant 'ice castle' – where stalactites and flowing forms give the impression of a castle – is easy to make out. We feel such wonder here, 400 m inside the mountains above Werfen. When we come to the highest ice peak inside the cave, we are told the scientists who discovered the cave had to cut 120 ice steps into it. Now we have two very steep wooden staircases to get to the top. From there, our journey is quite level and easy. Our tour comes to an end and we walk back down the 700 steps out of this magical world.

There is a text message when we wake the next morning: 'Max Samuel Harrison was born on July 11 at 5.35. Mother and son doing well – father, shattered!' We can't wait to get back to London to wet the baby's head.

From Austria, the Czech border is our first major border crossing. The open borders of the EU have been a dream, they've been so easy. The border policeman checks our passports and waves us on. He doesn't want to see the carnet. The checkpoint is also just a passport check with a form to fill in. Again, no-one wants to see the carnet. It takes less than 10 minutes and we are through.

The land is flat and uninteresting after the Austrian and Bavarian alps. The farmhouses are plain and we no longer see the characteristic flower boxes on every window. We pass a town filled with large concrete blocks of flats. It's a historically Eastern European feel, and, all in all, very depressing.

On its outskirts, Tabor looks like another town of concrete blocks, not the medieval town of Southern Bohemia we have read about. We head to the town square and walk into a wonderland of Renaissance buildings. The cobblestoned square has an elaborate fountain as its centrepiece, and buildings dating back to the sixteenth and seventeenth centuries line the square. Sitting in a cafe overlooking the cobblestoned square, we try the local Budweiser (the original, not the 'soap suds' made in America). It is delicious.

The old city of Prague is said to be the 'jewel in the world crown', yet the modern city is the pits. Oh for Tabor! Accommodation is expensive and parking isn't easy to find. We opt for a 46-a-night pension that's a 10-minute walk from Wenceslas Square and has parking in the garage underneath. The room is a dump: we have to climb over a couple of bags of sheets to go to the laundry; a vacuum cleaner and a few crates of empty beer bottles to get to the door. From here, there is another door that opens onto a small corridor with very cheap carpet that leads to two rooms – the toilet and the shower. The end of the corridor forms the bedroom. It has twin beds, bars on the window, two chairs and a shelf in the corner. Pipes run around the wall and there is a heater under the window. To say I am gobsmacked is an understatement. I look at Brian and we both laugh and then I feel like crying. It is a real dump, but then what can you expect at this price in the heart of a city. Brian puts it all in perspective: 'There will be times in Pakistan and India when you will be pining for a room like this.' I reckon he might be right!

The old city isn't the only attraction in Prague. There is Laundryland. Here you not only get your clothes washed, dried and folded, you get some street theatre thrown in. Instead of watching the wash go round and round, we watch young backpackers playing out the mating ritual. I never thought of a laundry as a pick-up joint, but Prague's Laundryland is just that.

Wenceslas Square marks an important place for my

father. In 1968, Soviet tanks rolled into this square as part of the Warsaw Pact invasion of Czechoslovakia. My father was Australian author Frank Hardy. He joined the Communist Party of Australia at the end of World War II. In the late 1940s he wrote the controversial novel *Power Without Glory.* He was an outspoken communist at a time when the Australian government was trying to have the party outlawed. His belief in the pure theory of communism never faltered but his belief in the Soviet Union was badly shaken during his visit to Czechoslovakia in the 1960s. The invasion shocked him and he left Prague disillusioned. He went straight to London, where he wrote articles condemning the party for what it had done. Overnight he became persona non grata. All his mail from the Soviet Union stopped and there were no more free tickets to the Bolshoi Ballet, Moscow Circus or other visiting artists. Party members in Sydney turned on him and Mum, also a party member. She was the first to tear up her membership card and Dad stopped going to meetings. Soon the horrors of the Stalin years would be revealed, changing many people's minds about communism. Dad, however, was always a believer in it in theory.

Today, the broad boulevard that carried the tanks sweeps down towards the old part of the city. Instead of Russian tanks, now there are gardens in the middle of the roadway. And there are people everywhere – even though it is 5 p.m. the crowds are thronging and the traffic is a nightmare. For us, it's a culture shock after visiting the small towns in Bavaria and Austria.

The old square takes our breath away. There is the astronomical clock, St Nicholas Church and the very gothic Tyn Church. There are crowds around the clock, as it is heading towards 6 p.m. We join them, ever conscious of the pickpockets who are said to work in the area. At six, the clock does its stuff. Faces pass by the windows and a skeleton rings the bells. It is very impressive. So are the bells from the gothic church across the square.

After dinner we sit in the pews of St Nicholas Church, under its massive crystal chandelier, and hear the music of Mozart, Bach and Vivaldi, with solos from a soprano and a trumpet, by the Consortium Pragenses Orchestra. What an aural delight!

Brian: On the road to the spa-resort town of Karlovy Vary, we encounter a police roadblock, which isn't unusual in this part of the world. We have been keeping pace with the rest of the traffic, letting some of the crazies scoot past us, so we are surprised when we are pulled over. In very broken English, the constable tells us we have been speeding. I think to myself, 'No faster than the other motorists who have sailed past the roadblock'. Their aim becomes clear very quickly. 'You must pay me 300 koruna, now.'

'No, that is not right. I want to see your supervisor. I am a police officer in Australia and this is not right.'

The young constable blanches visibly and mutters something to his superior. The more senior man looks very nervous and uncomfortable. Before I can get my licence out and well before they call their supervisor to come to the road-block, the senior officer says, 'Okay, you can go'. He waves me on and his offsider takes a step back and salutes me! As we leave, I am left wondering if this was a legitimate interception or a blatant attempt to extort money from a tourist.

At Karlovy Vary, we leave the highway and wind down a lovely valley that follows the course of a river. I stay by the bike as Shirl goes off to find a room for the night, with strict instructions not to go downmarket from the pension in Prague.

Shirley: Karlovy Vary was discovered when King Charles IV was on a hunting trip in the region and found the warm thermal springs. He built a hunting lodge here and the soothing effect of the waters became common knowledge. Soon after, a town was built on the site and the commoners were able to enjoy the waters. Everyone from Peter the Great to astronaut Yuri Gagarin has come here.

At the local spa we again step back into the Eastern Bloc of the 1960s. The stern-faced female attendants wear white surgical coats. The one taking the money has so much makeup on we wonder how she can hold her head up. She is eating a cream cake and doesn't stop chomping away when she takes money with an expert lack of interest. She has perfected the art of non-service! We must take off our shoes and hand over our valuables to another woman in a long white coat. After seeing our identification, she takes our stuff and puts it into a locker. We get one key, she keeps the other.

Finding the changing rooms isn't too difficult, but the location of the pool is a bit of a mystery. After wandering around for a few minutes, we find hidden stairs at the back of our changing rooms. Once outside, the pool is magnificent – just what the doctor ordered on such a hot day. The water temperature is said to be 29.5° Celsius and is surprisingly refreshing. Kids play and older people simply wallow. There is a grassed area and kids' pool, plus a sunbathing deck, which is covered with large and small Czech women and men. After our swim, we retrieve our valuables and walk back into the twenty-first century. To top off the afternoon, we have a couple of very refreshing large Czech beers.

Brian: As we head west from Karlovy Vary, the topography gets more interesting, with some hills and forested areas. I must be enjoying the ride too much and take a wrong turn towards an inviting winding mountain road just out of Ostrov and, sure enough, we go through Klinovec and there is the border crossing!

I stupidly pull up in sight of the border and discuss with Shirl if we should turn back or go through. I get the passports out of the tank bag and decide to head into Germany. As I ride up to the barrier, I can't help thinking how suspicious this must have looked. There is no-one at the first window. We wait for a while and then move on to the next window. The officer on duty is uninterested. He takes a cursory glance at the paperwork and waves us through with a dismissive flick of his wrist. This is too easy.

Shirley: Berlin is a bit like one big construction site. Not much was left after the war and they are renovating and rebuilding, particularly in the east where little was done during the separation of the country. It is a very old city, having celebrated its 750th anniversary, yet it looks new in most places. But there are some hints of its dark past. At the Brandenburg Gate we are reminded of President Kennedy's address to the West Berliners in which he said those famous words '*Ich bin ein Berliner*'. To make sure the East Berliners didn't see such an historic event, authorities put curtains over the gaps in the Gate.

The Checkpoint Charlie museum is proof of the determination of Berliners not to be separated from their fellow Germans. Their attempts to cross this no-man's-land separating East and West Berlin were as ingenious as they were dangerous. They used balloons, tunnels, hollowed-out surfboards and even a gramophone to hide people and smuggle them out of the country.

The Berlin Wall was 155 km long. More than 5000 people attempted to escape into the West and 176 died in the attempt. Not much of the wall remains after that historic night in 1989 when the people began tearing down the divide. One small section is now home to a group of spaced-out hippies. It is covered in graffiti, some good and most not so good. Techno music blasts out. It just doesn't seem right to have squatters in what is a piece of history.

Around the corner there is a much bigger piece of wall – about 150 m long. It has been preserved and makes up one side of the Topography of Terror. This chilling outdoor exhibition of the Nazi era is set up in the remains of the foundations of the old SS headquarters, the Gestapo headquarters and the Reich Security Office. It was in these buildings that the genocide of the Jews and the persecution and murder of others was planned and put into action. The Gestapo prison was here and prisoners were regularly interrogated and murdered. The horrific tales of survivors and those who died are portrayed in pictures and personal accounts. The city seems determined not to let people forget the horrors of the past so they won't be repeated in the future.

Stefan Stoll, our friend from the Bavarian Motorrad, is true to his word and opens his Munich apartment to us. My accent kicks in again when we try to explain we would like to visit Dachau. Stefan thinks we are talking about visiting 'Decker', a town he has never heard of. When they realise we plan to visit the concentration camp, Stefan and his girlfriend, Gabi, become very defensive. They can't understand why we want to visit the camp. The locals get a hard time because of the town's past. They are insistent that if we must go we should visit the castle and gardens in the old town centre, not just the scene of a gruesome past.

Gabi is right. The old town is about to celebrate its 1200th anniversary, something we find hard to comprehend. We eat lunch under a tree that is probably older than white civilisation in Australia and surrounded by buildings equally as historic. It seems a thousand miles and light years away from the horrors of Germany's concentration camps. The Dachau Castle is more like a small palace. The manicured gardens are a welcome respite from the heat and there is even a pear tree trellised along a wall like a vine. We can't work out how to get inside the castle until we see a tour group come out a side door. There is no-one inside so we just wander around at leisure, without another person in sight.

The Dachau Concentration Camp is now a memorial to those who were imprisoned there. Our first sight of the electrified, barbed-wire fences, gravel rollcall yard and long, drab buildings is disturbing. Dachau was the first camp and the only one to be used for the entire 12 years of Hitler's power. It was always a concentration camp and not an extermination camp, yet 46,000 people died here.

The cruelty of the Nazis is legendary and the tales our young American guide tells us as we walk through the memorial are harrowing. Men were forced to stand in the parade ground for hours on end for no reason at all. They were punished for bringing a small stone into the barracks on their shoe or losing a button from their uniform. The wire was electrified and some men threw themselves on it to commit suicide. If the guards saw that this was about to happen they would shoot them so they suffered a long, slow death rather than a speedy one. Some men were chosen to be worked or starved to death – again for no apparent reason. As the years passed and war began, different nationalities were brought here as well as priests, Jehovah's Witnesses, Jews, intellectuals, political activists and anyone else who stood in the way of the 'master race'.

While Dachau wasn't an extermination camp, it did have a gas chamber. It may have been used for testing to ensure it worked before being replicated at other camps. There were fumigation areas for the clothes – the holding rooms and the shower block – where the pesticide used to fumigate the clothes was also used to kill the prisoners. The camp's original crematorium was deemed too small in 1942, and a larger one built to cope with the number of bodies. When the Allies liberated the camp on 29 April 1945, they found piles of bodies waiting to be cremated. The Nazis hadn't enough coal to use the crematoriums, and even if they had run 24 hours a day there were still too many bodies.

A film presentation using documentary footage shows the camp in operation – filmed by the SS themselves. They were so proud of what they were doing to create and protect the master race. After their liberation, the footage – now shot by the Americans – shows men crying with disbelief that it is all over. But how would they ever come to terms with what they had seen and lived through? Some of the final shots show bodies piled high and local people from the town of Dachau being led through so they could see what had been happening. As even today residents of Dachau get a hard time about the camp, some women go to Munich to have their children so the birth certificates don't read 'Dachau'. Many younger Germans just wish everyone would leave the past behind, yet 800,000 visitors come to the memorial every year. Even though it should remind us of the horrors of the past, all over the world similar atrocities are being carried out every day. We haven't learned a thing.

It is time for the bike to get the full BMW treatment at the home of the company in Munich. The service manager pushes us to the head of the queue, instead of making us wait the usual couple of weeks. It's a bit embarrassing, really. The workshop is pristine – you could eat off the floor. Every piece of chrome and stainless steel shines. There isn't a drop of oil on the floor and no bits and pieces lying around. Our bike is filthy. We wonder if they will let it into such a rarefied environment, but when we collect it, the bike is washed and shining like new. It's impossible to know if they washed it before or after the service!

Stefan is Hungarian and shares a local delicacy with us on his terrace. With a chilled beer, the homemade salami his mother made, a mild horseradish sauce, onion and paprika on white bread with strips of yellow paprika on the side is delicious! At a local bar we have a 'ratler' each – half beer and half lemonade. A shandy isn't usually our drink of choice, but this one is extremely refreshing.

You can't go to Munich and not visit the local tourist mecca – Hofbrau House. This beer house is hot, crowded and noisy but a must on the tourist trail. The oompah-pah band belts out Bavarian beer-drinking songs and show tunes, which seem incredibly incongruous. Locals are dressed in jaunty Bavarian hats and lederhosen. It is summed up by a saying emblazoned across the wall: *Durst ist schlimmer als Heimweh* (The thirst is worse than the homesickness).

We are not homesick as such, but just when we feel comfortable in a city and have formed a close bond with Stefan and Gabi, it is time to move on. I am close to tears when we say farewell. There are promises to see each other again but we all know that is probably unlikely. Stefan and Gabi opened their home and their hearts to us. We sat together on the terrace talking into the early hours of the morning. They are kind and generous people, and we will miss them.

Now it is time to move on and we have a baby to meet in London.

Brian: We follow the signs to the autobahn and get up to cruising speed. I feel relaxed and happy to be back in the saddle. The bike is sounding sweet and the two new tyres feel good. It's not too hot, so we make decent time. We cross the border near Saarbrücken and into France, and almost immediately come to a motorway tollbooth. I feel this is a rip-off after using perfect roads for nothing in Germany. We get off the motorway onto the secondary N3 road near the town of Metz. This is more like it – winding roads through farmland and quaint French villages. It's been a long day, nearly 700 km, so we find a nice little hotel in Verdun for the night.

Shirley: Verdun is marked on our map as a town of interest, but we didn't realise just how interesting it is. In 1916, during World War I, half a million young men (mostly German and French, with some Americans) lost their lives on the battlefields of Verdun. The French have dedicated the battlefields to the north and west of the town as memorials to the brave souls who never came home from what the historians describe as 'the bloodiest battle in history'. Less than one kilometre from the town centre we discover a sea of white crosses. It is just one of many war cemeteries that dot the hills around the town.

The battlefields are now peaceful wooded hills where the playing of sport and loud music, picnics and camping are banned. This entire area is a memorial to the dead. The battle was almost 90 years ago but the bombardment by both sides has left the countryside pitted with craters that still bear testimony to the destruction today. What a futile waste of life – 500,000 lives (the equivalent of five Grand Final crowds all dead). It gives us something to think about as we ride off towards Calais and the Eurotunnel to England.

We get the usual warm welcome from Tim and Bettina, and a special hug from Bettina's mum, Carole, who has come from Melbourne to see her new grandson. We meet Max Samuel Harrison for the first time and can't stop cuddling this much-loved bundle of joy.

It is now time for yet another farewell. Bettina and Tim have been so good to us. Tim has nicknamed us 'The Boomerangs' as we just keep coming back, but this time our farewells will be for the long haul. We don't know when we will see them again. We won't be in Australia when they come home in January for a quick visit and who knows when we will return to London. There are tears all round as we say goodbye.

We hit the road with just one look back from the corner. I wipe away the tears and look to the future. We are now beginning our journey home – the real journey. Brian gives me a comforting pat on the leg. We will keep heading east now.

Grosslockner

Zugspi

BMW Motorrad — Garmisch

SIX

WESTERN EUROPE

1–17 August 2003

Shirley: History calls and we head to the D-day beaches on the Normandy coast. International flags – French, Canadian, American, British and even German – fly at all the beaches along this stretch of coastline. Monuments pay homage to the soldiers who came here to free the French. Gun placements stand alongside ice-cream stands and cafes along the waterfront. Tanks still stand guard over the beaches.

Almost 10,000 American servicemen are buried at Omaha Beach. The cemetery has the aura of a holy place, even though there are scores of tourists here. It is one of the very few places in France where dogs are banned. The chimes from the carillon echo through acres of pristine lawns. There are row after row of white marble crosses. Written across the monument are the words 'This embattled shore, portal of freedom, is forever hallowed by the ideals, the valour and the sacrifices of our fellow countrymen'. No matter how many war cemeteries we pass, no matter how many white crosses or headstones we see, we can't comprehend the enormity of the loss of human life.

Pointe du Hoc, 13 km west of the Normandy memorial, brings the reality of war home again. Here the Germans held firm on the cliffs about 30 m from the beach. They believed their position was impenetrable until a team of 220 US Rangers climbed the cliffs using grenade-propelled grappling hooks. The pitched battle lasted days before a tank division came to their aid – by then only 90-odd Rangers were left in combat condition. This area has been left pretty much as it was on that day in 1944. The bomb craters are more than 3 m deep. The remains of the German bunkers are twisted piles of concrete and reinforcing. The monument built by the French is now perched on a cliff that is crumbling and surrounded by barbed wire. It is hard to imagine, as the sun shines, the mayhem of 1944.

The European summer is proving to be a killer – literally. People are dying from the heat in Paris and we are finding it difficult in our riding gear. After a long day following wrong roads and missing the scenic routes, we are delighted when we come across a sign reading *piscine* or pool. After a swim, a steak and a bottle of good red the heat and the foibles of the last nine hours are a distant memory.

Brian: Breakfast at our B & B in Le Sabeau near La Rochelle poses a previously unthought-of obstacle. There is a delectable platter laid out with a lovely quince jam and a baguette. That's no problem. There is a plate. That's no problem. And there is a large bowl. That's the problem for us travellers from Australia. I am 'Captain Grumpy' without a coffee first thing, so observe the only other couple in the room at the time. No clues here as to what to do, so I take a chance and pour coffee into the bowl and hold it as though it were Chinese soup. I feel stupid as another couple come in for breakfast, but better when they do the same. Either I've got it right or I've started a new trend for coffee-drinkers in France.

Shirley: We plan to get the car ferry from Royan to the Atlantic beaches of the Bay of Arcachon. It's starting to get hot. We follow the signs to the car ferry and find ourselves in a queue that must be more than 100 cars long! This is not looking good. We sit in the queue for a while watching it inch up closer to the ferry terminal, which is on the other side of a lovely little bay and white beach and beach club with a couple of pools and sun lounges. It looks very inviting while we swelter on the bike in all our gear.

Finally Brian cracks it and rides to the front of the queue and pushes in. No-one bothers about this. Unlike us, they are aware bikes get put on the ferry in their own spot and don't take up a car space. We get through, pay the €15.30 one-way fare and are ushered to the front of the loading area. There is another bike here – a 150cc scooter loaded up with even more luggage than we are carrying. The rider has two huge bags, a tent, sunbaking mat and a backpack. Crikey!

The next day begins with clear blue skies and it is quite obvious it is going to be another scorcher. We stop to buy water and the shopkeeper tells me it will be 40°C today.

We head into the hills, crossing the now-non-existent border into Spain, towards Pamplona. We thought it might be cooler in the hills, but the weather is getting hotter. Riding further into Spain, it is hot and desolate, but the roads are good and twisty. At the end of the day it takes several cold showers to get my core body temperature down. The Spanish eat their main meal in the middle of the day and often late into the afternoon. We have a snack, more wine and then lie down for a while. At 9 p.m., we have a pleasant meal outside on the terrace, but it is still too hot. Back in the room, we shower again and try to get some sleep. Little wonder we feel washed out – the top temperature today has been 52°C! After a fitful sleep in hot and sweaty conditions, we watch the dawn rise over the surrounding olive trees and vineyards.

The good roads continue through pretty little Pyrenees villages, especially once we cross back into France. We decide to stop in Eaux-Bonnes at a friendly looking two-star hotel. We have only travelled about 200 km today, but it is good to get away from the heat of the road.

In the cool of the evening we stroll around the town square and watch the locals playing a very serious game of boules. At the completion of each end, there is always a very animated discussion, with several people talking at once and lots of gesticulating. Every time it ends with smiles, a few shoulder shrugs and on to the next end. Some of the men are quite skilful; playing on an uneven gravel surface cannot be easy. We join the wives and family groups on the sidelines until another French meal calls.

Brian: Pic du Midi de Bigorre, at 2872 m, is the highest peak in the Pyrenees in this part of France. The road starts out tight and twisty and gets tighter and twistier the further we go into the national park. We hope that the higher we go the cooler it will get. We pass cars as they wheeze up the steep hills with ease, and we settle into a steady rhythm using the bike's low-down grunt to effortlessly overtake them. Occasionally, we come to villages and as we slow down the heat builds up and becomes almost intolerable. We battle on and the road gets so narrow that cars must stop and crawl past each other. In places it's only wide enough for a single car. I take care and hug my side of the road. Up here there are few safety rails. One slip off the paved surface would see you plummet hundreds of metres into oblivion. I slow to second gear and ensure I leave plenty of room for oncoming traffic around blind corners. At one point a car hurtles towards us on our side of the narrow road, the driver lighting a cigarette. I get closer to the edge and prepare to take evasive action as he sees me at the last minute and swerves violently back to his side of the road.

I hear Shirl's shrieks over the wind noise and my own intake of breath. We continue on and I notice something like graffiti on the road – all brightly coloured messages in French and other foreign languages. Finally, the penny drops; this is one of the dreaded hill climbs used during the Tour de France. Fans have painted messages to their heroes on the road surface. In places it is difficult to see the black asphalt underneath. Of course, any sort of paint on the road surface is a hazard for motorcyclists, so extra care is needed.

The temperature is now well into the high thirties, but we see lunatics on racing bicycles emulating their heroes, trying to climb up this steep hillside. At the top of the mountain there is a parking area with dozens of parked cars baking in the hot sun and hundreds of cyclists resting in whatever shade they can find. There is also a herd of cows. I try to ease past a cow standing on the road, only to become embroiled in a Mexican standoff. The beast refuses to move out of the way, much to the amusement of the onlookers, so we have to back down and move around it.

On the way down, I overtake a serious-looking cyclist who then proceeds to keep pace with me down the mountain. I am impressed at his cornering skills and give him a wave as we scoot off.

Shirley: In this heat we are fading fast and finding a hotel is our priority – a hotel with air conditioning. When I spot an Ibis sign, it feels like a blessing; we know they are good, reasonably priced and should be air conditioned. When I take off the helmet I know I am not looking my best, but put on a brave face and head into reception.

The young woman behind the counter is very friendly and says yes to all the right questions. 'Yes, we have air conditioning. Yes, we have a vacancy. Yes, we do have a bar that has cold beers.' The only thing she doesn't have is an ice machine, but bustles off to get a jug of ice for us to take to our room. When I look at my reflection, I work out why she is so friendly. My face is puce and my hair is stuck to my head with sweat. She clearly thought I was going to drop dead in their foyer, which isn't good for business!

An old friend from Melbourne, Sue Souchaud, now lives in France with her French husband, Vincent, and is keen for us to visit them at their home in Gex on the French–Swiss border near Geneva.

We check out the map and it is about 700 km. It's a long way on a bike in one day and even longer with the debilitating heat wave. Bugger it – we'll give it a try!

We make it. We haven't seen Sue and Vincent for about eight years and have never, of course, met their children – six-year-old Alexandra and the four-year-old twins, Oscar and Isabelle. Sue speaks to the kids in English and Vincent speaks to them in French. The children are bilingual and change over from one language to the other with no problem. As Vincent puts it, 'At this age, it is like burning a disc. We are just burning two discs at the same time – one in English and another in French.'

Over a glass or two of French wine, we sit in the garden

and catch up on all the news. The sun goes down and the air remains warm – it is unseasonably hot here too. We watch the lights of the nearby villages and listen to the distant tinkling of cow bells.

The next day promises to be another hot one. There is no end in sight to this European heat wave. We ride into Geneva for the day. To combat the heat, we wear only jeans and no jackets. It's a short ride but of course we have to take our passports as we are making another border crossing. I make sure the carnet is there too, just in case. We needn't have bothered. When we get to the Swiss border we are just waved through by indifferent border guards.

We need a bit of local currency and find that there are banks everywhere in Geneva. But they are private banks with doormen, numbered accounts and, probably, dodgy histories. What they don't have is ATMs. After wandering aimlessly – which we tend to do – in very bad French I ask a girl. She does some pointing and mentions *droit*, so we wander down to the right and find a hole in the wall.

Lake Leman (not Lake Geneva, we are told) is the best place to be on a hot day, as the waterways are utilised to their best advantage during the heat wave. There are several areas roped off with pontoons for swimming. With a great deal of envy we watch the people frolicking. Around the lake is some amazing real estate – a mansion donated to the city by Baron Rothschild, Josephine's home before marrying Napoleon, and other mansions that have been converted into museums or other public buildings.

Back in Gex we share some Champagne under the trees in the garden as the sun goes down. But it is now time for yet another farewell.

Brian: Petrol seems to be leaking out of the bike, so before we head to Chamonix and Mont Blanc we must find a bike shop.

There are no BMW dealers in close proximity, and we head to Sallanches. We find a Honda motorcycle dealer and there are guys working on a bike on the apron outside. Shirl tries to make herself understood with little success. We need a fuel-hose clamp – not a phrase to be found in guidebooks.

The bikers are now intrigued by our bike and after a quick game of charades they understand exactly what we need. They take me around to the workshop, where I find Shirl hunched down with the mechanic rummaging through his store of fuel-hose clamps. What a girl. We get two, including a spare, for 3 and I proceed to pull the bike apart with the aforesaid audience. I replace the clamp with no difficulty and use the choke. There's no leak of petrol onto the hot exhaust – that's a good thing. The problem is that the bike seems to be running on only one cylinder. After much head-scratching, one of my audience notices the throttle cable is not seated properly and, voilà, the problem is solved.

Many bikers are heading to Chamonix so we tag along. They set a cracking pace along the motorway, which is fun, but we have to slow down. The scenery is breathtaking, with Mont Blanc and the accompanying mountains a brilliant white, dominating the skyline.

Shirley: In Chamonix, the Mont Blanc mountains tower over the village, shimmering in the summer sun. As it cools, we open up the balcony of our B&B, and sit outside sipping red wine and watching the changing colours and cloud formations over the mountains. We talk about our journey and the dangers we face. I remind Brian that I always knew there was an element of risk, which is why we spoke to police chaplain Jim Pilmer about looking after things for us and left a note with my brother, Alan, expressing our final wishes and updating our wills.

After pondering life on the road and patting each other on the back about how well we are doing so far, we notice it is almost 10 p.m. so we head out for something to eat. We choose a creperie around the corner and eat *crepe citron.* I have a glass of Champagne and Brian has a local cider. It is the perfect end to a great day. Tomorrow we go to Mont Blanc.

We leave the bike at the hotel and head into the mountains. The cable car is jam-packed with hikers, climbers and sight-seers. Some have tents and sleeping bags. We have our camera. The ride up is spectacular and, before long, the village of Chamonix disappears as we skim across a pine forest. After about ten minutes, we reach Plan de l'Aiguille at 2317 m. Some hikers get out to start their trek through the foothills. We swap to another cable car and complete the journey to Aiguille du Midi at 3842 m. Most people disembark and rush to the viewing platforms. We head for the much smaller *telegraphique* gondolas that will take us across the glacier into Italy. The gondolas are grouped in threes and stop frequently across the glacier Dent du Geant.

The sky is the bluest of blues today, making a stark backdrop for the towering peak of Mont Blanc. The snow shines in the bright sunlight. Below us the glacier is severely cracked and it is clear the European heat wave is taking its toll. The crevasses below us are wide and appear bottomless. Parts of the area are closed to visitors because of the danger of avalanches and more crevasses opening up.

After about 30 minutes we reach the border of Italy and France. We are at 3466 m and have a crystal-clear view of Mont Blanc only 1400 m above us. We enjoy strolling around, but find we are short of breath and I am getting a headache. Brian talks about Paul 'Possum' Carr. He was at

7000 m when he died, and we can't imagine what it must have been like for him.

Our last sight of Mont Blanc is a mighty one as we take the road to Tunnel du Mont Blanc – 11.611 km through solid rock under the tallest mountain in France. We have to pay €18.60 for the privilege and there are rules to follow. The top speed is 70 km/h and every vehicle has to leave 150 m to the one in front to reduce the chance of accidents. It is amazing to spend so long under that amount of rock. For the next 50 or so kilometres, we encounter tunnel after tun-nel. Some are more than 3000 m long, others are just a few hundred metres. In 50 km of travel, we spend up to 40 km under mountains. The big bonus is that the air was cool in the tunnels.

There is no let-up in the heat. The lakes are tempting and we both feel the need for a break off the bike. I suggest we follow the signs to Lago di Garda, our planned destination, and this puts us on the wrong side of the lake and the wrong side of good humour and friendship. After snapping at each other, I ask for directions and we are only two or three kilometres from the lake – but on the wrong side.

Food always calms us down, so we find a cafe on the lakefront. After a great seafood meal, we ride around the left bank through picturesque towns perched on the edge of the lake. We get closer and closer to the Dolomites. The roads are twisty and hug the coast. We ride through tunnel after tunnel, cutting into the Dolomites. The twists and turns are a biker's dream and put Brian back in a good mood.

We ride to Riva del Garda, the town at the top of the lake where the Dolomites meet the water and their sheer rock faces seem to burst out of it. Here, one night turns into two and we alternate between swimming in the pool and the lake.

The lake offers a rocky foreshore and our rubber thongs become the footwear of choice.

Lunch is a bread roll on the foreshore. I order in my best Italian and the girl behind the counter answers me in German. That doesn't say much for the year I spent studying Italian a few years ago.

After dinner it is still 29°C and a good night's sleep is proving to be difficult. We opt for the 'Coolgardie safe theory' and lay a couple of wet towels over our bodies as the warm breeze comes through the window. This cooling method works – sleep at last.

Brian: With a fair degree of regret, we prepare to leave Riva del Garda. We have enjoyed two days rest here and can see why so many people rave about the Lake District of Italy. But it is still unbearably hot – at 9.30 a.m. it's already 30°C.

We take the road to Trento and wind our way through vineyards reminiscent of my home town near Mildura in Victoria. We see water being sprayed on the vines and this keeps the ambient temperature down to a bearable level.

We continue on and find ourselves on the main road to Bolzano, which we want to avoid, so we backtrack a little and find a road to 'Ora Auer'. As soon as we get off the major road, the mountain road is alive with motorcycles. We have found what all bikers talk about in the Dolomites – corners, corners and more corners. The road is also in good condition and motorcyclists are obviously very welcome. There are signs everywhere advertising hotels, restaurants and even viewing spots for bikers. We get off the beaten track and find some of the windiest roads. We traverse at least four valleys – Passo Rolle, Passo di San Pellegrino and Passo Valles and Passo di Cereda – and get some cool air at over 2000 m.

I can feel the skin peeling off my left big toe as I constantly go up and down the gearbox. I'm wearing hiking boots rather than bike boots to see what they feel like. They are a lot cooler and may be a better bet in hotter climes. They appear to be okay until we start to hook into some corners. I start my usual routine of scraping boots on the ground just before the foot pegs hit. But when I examine the boots at a stop I can clearly see that these will not last as long as the bike boots; the rubber is a lot softer.

We ride through some wonderful scenery – from cool pine forests, woods and meadows, to valleys and mountain streams. There are bikes of all makes out for a ride. Most of the people on them are good riders and handle the challenging roads with aplomb. I can't say the same about some of the car drivers who see a bike and want to race you.

Shirley: Finding a hotel in the Dolomites isn't easy. It's holiday time, but we press on and eventually come across a hotel overlooking the mountains. There is also a nice one opposite our lodgings and we go to the rather upmarket restaurant at its rear. Tables are set on the open balcony and we enjoy a candle-lit dinner overlooking the setting sun on the spectacular Dolomites, which turn a stark red. We sit sharing a bottle of Trentino chardonnay and admire the view. I query our fun-loving waiter over a word in the menu, *stang*. He can't come up with the English word, and then it hits him in a flash. 'Bambi. It is Bambi,' he says. Thanks, but no thanks. I don't think I can eat venison when it is described as 'Bambi'.

What a difference 24 hours makes. The next day we can feel the humidity in the air and there are greyish clouds over the peaks of the Dolomites. We think we might get a little rain today. We're wrong – we get a lot of rain. We have to take every hairpin bend slowly due to the wet and slippery roads.

The weather clears and the cooler temperatures make riding very pleasant. Then we head further into the Dolomites and black clouds loom ominously. We take the road out of Padola heading generally east and then turn south for one last mountain ride. We stop at Rigolato for lunch and I encounter my first hole-in-the-floor toilet – crikey, I don't expect this so soon! I manage to have a wee without peeing all over my shoes, clothing or myself. So far, so good!

After lunch we ride down through more twisty roads following the course of a river. The Dolomites look very different outlined against grey clouds – truly magnificent. The dark skies bring out the silver in the rocks, giving them an eerie glow. Several times we decide to take a road heading out and come to an intersection that leads us back – as though the Dolomites were pulling us in. Brian has a route mapped out, but the road that appears on our map doesn't appear on the road itself.

We are still on the edge of the Dolomites and enjoying our last ride through them when we come across the town of Longarone. Forty years ago, a huge flood swept through Longarone, killing 1900 people in 10 minutes. The flood occurred at 10.40 p.m. – no-one in its path stood a chance. While we check into the Hotel Posta, four Harleys pull up outside. These Italian bikers are on their way to spending two days riding in the Dolomites. Lucky bastards!

Brian: Reluctantly, we turn the front wheel away from the Dolomites and its great motorcycling roads. As I find the highway and head down the valley south from Longarone, I visualise 9 October 1963, when water burst through the dam and washed away most of the town. The topography is just like a big funnel and I can imagine the force of the water pouring through here.

On the highway there is a constant stream of traffic going towards the mountains. Double lines are no reason to be complacent. I am now used to the sight of cars and motorcycles overtaking at every opportunity and cutting in at the last moment. Some don't even bother to cut in for a motorcycle coming the other way. We are expected to get out of their way. I obey the 'might is right' rule to survive.

Outside of Trieste we get talking to an Italian biker and his wife. They are heading into Slovenia for the long weekend. He informs me that accommodation will be tight as most of Europe is on holidays – tell us something we don't know. He has a tent and other necessary gear and is heading for the islands off the Dalmatian coast. I rue not having some form of emergency accommodation, but Shirl is sick of hearing about it.

I manage to avoid saying anything remotely like 'I told you so' when we try to get a hotel room in Trieste. The first hotel Shirley tries is on a cliff overlooking the water and looks great. She comes out smiling, saying they want €150 for a room. It's a good view but I don't want a title to the room.

Shirley: We decide to seek food rather than a hotel and meet a couple of Italian guys who take a huge interest in the bike. One says he has no car and only rides his two motorcycles. His father rides an 1100GS BMW – the predecessor of our bike. He is impressed with our setup and says it is his dream to ride the world like us. He is off to America next year to ride Route 66. As we eat, he rings his father and talks about us excitedly.

With a belly full of food we start room-searching all over again. We head away from Trieste, and find the small suburb of Sistiana and another Hotel Posta. There is a beach just down the hill where locals arrive on their tiny scooters packed with sunbeds and huge beach bags. The footwear of choice is the Japanese safety boot (thongs). No-one has heard of protective motorcycling clothing in this part of the world. It is such a good spot we decide to stay for another day.

At the beach there are plenty of interested bystanders who want to talk about the bike and our journey. Two bikers have some advice for our trip through former Yugoslavia. 'Don't go beyond Dubrovnik on the Dalmatian coast. It is too dangerous.' Everyone seems to agree that banditry is a problem when you get past Croatia. Brian is keen to take the road as long as it's not too dangerous. I'd rather have a pleasant sea voyage – and that is saying something, considering I dread ferries!

aiting for the Eurotunnel train

World War II bomb crater at Pointe du Hoc

Love the roads in the Pyrenees

Col d’Aspin, Pyrene

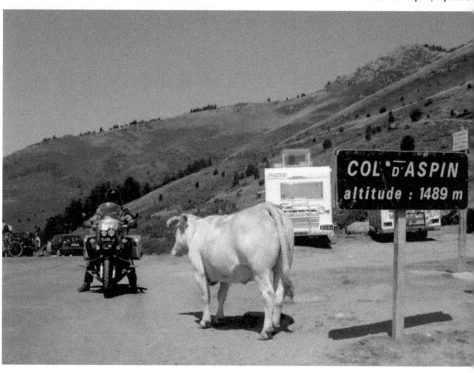

SEVEN

THE DALMATION COAST

17–27 August 2003

Shirley: The autostrada takes us to Slovenia. The freeway goes from three lanes to two and then slows to a virtual standstill near the border. Brian cuts the traffic and no-one shakes an angry fist or yells abuse. At the border there are two very bored guards checking passports. We prepare for long delays but it is not the case; they glance at our passports and couldn't care less that we are on a foreign-registered bike.

Brian: Back on the highway we round the corner and come across a toll booth. Great, the Slovenians have picked up one of the worst traits of European governments: tolls on public roads. I don't mind supporting national parks, or some great feat of engineering in a road's construction, but not a standard piece of bitumen.

Shirley points out some caves in this region (not once, but at least three times), so I take the hint and turn off to Skocjanske Jame. We find the road well signposted and in no time are parking near the entrance. The next tour is in a little over an hour, so we chill out in the shade.

Shirley: Inside the caves, it is instantly cooler. After about 100 m we glimpse our first stalactites and stalagmites and marvel at the different shapes and colours. As we go deeper into the cave, the air is even cooler. The walk through the caves is 3 km long and goes to about 164 m below ground. There are two main caverns – the silent cave and the water-whispering cave where the river Reka flows underground. These are classified by UNESCO as a World Heritage site and you can understand why when you're inside.

The exertion of walking to and from the cave in the heat wearing all our bike gear is telling. We both struggle with the temperature, which is even more oppressive after the cave visit. We both shed our jackets for the ride to the coast. At least it isn't far and I am grateful to Brian for taking the time out to visit the caves.

We arrive at the small town of Fiesa, right on the water's edge. Our hotel doesn't boast a beach, it boasts its own private concrete ramp into the water. The water is cool and refreshing and not too salty – just the ticket after a hot walk into the caves.

At the Slovenian border with Croatia we are again disappointed in the lack of interest in the Carnet de Passage for the bike. We begin our journey down the coast and are horrified by the standard of the roads, which show a distinct lack of maintenance. Trucks have made huge ruts in the asphalt and road gangs have gouged the surface to provide some grip in the wet on the well-worn surface. This isn't the best thing for motorcycles, as the wheels track in the gouges.

Brian: The countryside consists of rolling hills and farmland. There are many roadside stalls selling everything from vegetables to wine and grappa. I've tasted Croatian grappa before, when a supporter offered me some for my efforts after playing a good game of football. That was more than 25 years ago, but the memory is vivid. It is so potent, I could run the bike on the stuff if necessary.

The going is slower than expected with the poor road surface and an out-of-town speed limit of 60 km/h in most places. The infernal trucks are spewing black diesel smoke and motor homes get in the way of more spirited progress. All of a sudden the temperature drops markedly and we are on a clifftop overlooking the Adriatic Sea some 300 m below. There are no safety rails, just concrete bollards to stop bigger vehicles taking the big jump. They won't do much for us.

The sea is an iridescent blue and ferries between the ever-present islands leave a phosphorus wake for a kilometre. We are now hugging the coast and traversing a road similar to the Great Ocean Road at home. The going gets slower as we get into the suburbs of Rijeka. It seems like the whole population has made its way to the water. There is plenty of flesh on show, with some people showing far too much.

Shirley: On the island of Krk we find another seaside town with a foot-punishing stone beach. We really don't know how lucky we are to have sandy beaches in Australia. We notice the water isn't as clean as in Italy or Slovenia and there is a lot of rubbish on the foreshore, which you don't find in Italy. People seem just to leave their rubbish anywhere and everywhere.

It is a long ride to Split – about 355 km – and it is hot again. While the cool change has hit northern Europe we seem to be staying one step ahead of it! We leave Krk via the massive bridge and pay our toll. The man in the tollbooth sticks his head out the window and looks at the bike. He asks where we are from and shakes his head when we tell him.

When we explain we are riding home to Australia, he says we are crazy and laughs. It is a pleasant reaction!

We turn right to Split – hugging the coast for a while. The traffic is very heavy in both directions and the road, in part, really bad. The surface is ground-up in places. Overtaking is necessary wherever and whenever possible to get past the trucks, caravans and motor homes. A couple of times we come around the corner and find a car coming the opposite way on our side of the road. Brian certainly has to keep his wits about him. A couple of times he has to do some quick accelerating to get around cars. We both ride without our jackets, trying to deal with the heat, until we come around the corner and find an accident. A motorbike has smashed head-on into the front of a car. The guy on the bike is just nursing bruises. This is enough for me – the jacket goes back on.

We take a wrong turn and end up on the inland road to Split, which turns out to be fascinating. We ride past completely deserted towns, as if the townspeople have just walked away en masse – and they probably have. One with about 60 houses has been abandoned. Some towns look as though they have been hit by an earthquake, but it is more likely mortar fire and may be the aftermath of the ethnic cleansing. When we hit the coast again the road winds past bay after bay of crystal-clear blue water and sunloving beachgoers.

Split is amazing. There are Roman ruins inside the palace walls and marble streets that meander through a maze of laneways and squares. We opt not to pay to see the treasures inside the cathedral, instead taking the time to listen to five young men in shorts and T-shirts singing in the square – a cappella. They are singing Croatian folk tunes and it is very stirring stuff. They get lots of applause, but we don't buy a CD. They might not sound so good in the loungeroom at home.

People still live in the old town behind the palace walls and it is incongruous to see washing hanging out of the windows. We walk through one gate in the palace walls and find a huge statue of the tenth-century Slavic religious leader Gregorius of Nin. He is quite a fellow and it seems that rubbing his foot brings luck, as it looks like polished brass and is much brighter than the rest of the statue. Gregorius bears an uncanny resemblance to Merlin the magician, or the headmaster of Hogwarts in the Harry Potter books and movies.

We ask at our Split hotel about riding through Albania. '*We* go there [meaning Croatians] and we have been at war with them!' is the answer. Fair enough.

For still more advice I ask a radio audience during my weekly interview with Red Symons. Should we go to Albania or take the ferry to Greece via Italy? In the morning there are lots of emails and the advice is pretty much the same: Don't go to Albania. My brother's email is short and to the point: 'Take the ferry'. One Albanian now living in Australia says he wouldn't go to Albania, and he speaks the language and of course looks Albanian.

We head south along the Dalmatian coast to Dubrovnik. We come to a border crossing into Bosnia. We have no visas and begin to panic, but the guards just wave us through without stopping. Fourteen kilometres later we hit another border crossing, but again we don't even get a sideways glance. We are now back in Croatia.

Of course, it is the height of summer and when we hit Dubrovnik, the city is booked out. We head out along the bay, stopping at little beaches. Alas, there is no room at the inn. Eventually we end up in Zaton, about 18 km out of the city. The first guesthouse we try has no rooms, but the owner's sister has a place on the next bay. It is basic but clean and the window opens out onto a small part of the bay over the rooftops from the third level. At €30 for the night, it's cheap. We don't have many options, so we take it.

We strip off and dive into the cool water from their small jetty. You can almost see our skin sizzle and the steam come off our bodies. We then walk to the beach bar and sit and take it all in.

Brian: All of a sudden I notice Shirl is crying behind her sunglasses and I wonder what I've done. She assures me it's nothing. A stray cat and her kittens at the hotel in Split have upset her and sometimes a girl just needs a good cry. No-one cares for the abandoned animals. We sit in silence for a while. Shirl is okay but quiet. I wonder how she will handle depressing sights when we really hit the third world. She assures me she will be all right . . . I'm not so sure.

Shirley: Our accommodation might not be the best, but it is a great location, and we decide to stay another night. There is a good feel about the place and the other guests. We head into Dubrovnik to look around the old city. We can't find it until Brian has a look at a map on the wall. I still can't get this navigational aspect of the trip right.

First things first, and we head past the gates to the castle and for breakfast go to a restaurant overlooking the wall. Before we even get to order we hear a cat miaow. Brian can't believe it; a cat has walked around the edge of the wall, has somehow managed to get itself into an alcove high above the water line and can't get back out. I immediately want to ring the fire brigade, but ever-practical Brian says that the cat will find its way out. Its cries are mournful and echo around the small bay under the walls.

During the war with the Serbs in the early 1990s, Dubrovnik was devastated by a bombing campaign that left the city separated from the rest of Croatia. The Dubrovnik Freedom

Fighters Memorial elucidates the enormity of the battle. Staring out from the walls are faces of young, middle-aged and old men who fought to save their city and their freedom. No matter how hard they tried, the Serbs couldn't destroy the peoples' will or the city walls. The desire for freedom is reflected in the name of the local motorcycle club, *Liberatas* (Liberty).

Our little B&B has some interesting guests – David and Carol, an English couple, and their children, and a Croatian couple living in Sarajevo. David works with the UN and is based in Sarajevo. Zoran is in a wheelchair after a horrendous car accident. Brian, David and Zoran spend hours discussing the conflict with the Serbs and the terrible atrocities that occurred. Their advice about the next stage of our journey seems to match just about everyone's: don't go to Albania. They say that if the bad roads don't get us, the bandits will.

On our last day we take up our host's offer of a boat ride up the coast to Dubrovnik. Brian and another guest help Zoran into the boat in his wheelchair and we all clamber in around him. The breeze off the water is cooling and we get a completely different view of the city from the water. Along the way we pass the homes of the wealthy and luxury hotels. They look special but we are sure the guests are not having as much fun as we are.

Back at the house, we spend the afternoon sipping beers and wines, including the homemade wine Luca's father makes mixed with water. We eat cheese, meat and bread. Zoran adds some melon, prosciutto from Zagreb and good parmesan to the mix. What a life we are leading!

Moving further along the coast, we realise we need maps, but you can't buy a map for Serbia, Montenegro, Kosovo or

Albania in Croatia. The tension is evident when we are told, 'You can buy the map there, not here'.

We head into Montenegro, following the coast down to Budva, and then ride around the bay rather than taking the car ferry. Montenegro is trying very hard to attract the tourist dollar and it does have its fair share of natural beauty, but we are not impressed with the locals, who seem to dump rubbish beside the road despite big dumpster-style bins provided for them. We see one man take all his domestic rubbish in a wheelbarrow to the edge of a small cliff and just dump it over, while 20 m down the road there's a dumpster bin.

There are not many Western tourists in this part of the world and the locals have more than a passing interest in us. We come across police checks everywhere. These are normally just one or two police standing in the middle of the road with a little paddle saying, *Stop Policije.* We are not doing anything wrong, so we don't worry too much, but they pay us a lot of attention.

Brian: We get waved to the side of the road by one rather arrogant-looking young policeman who has already pulled up a car with German registration. From my vantage point on the bike, I see the young car driver fumble and then hand over his papers and a cigarette packet. The policeman looks inside the pack, nods and puts it in his pocket.

This seems to be the way in this part of the world and, quite frankly, it disgusts me. He sees me looking at him and gives a confusing signal. Is it to wave me on or to stay where I am? I decide I don't want a car chase, so I wait. The policeman comes up to me and we can't understand each other, but clearly I have done nothing wrong. I decide to show him my police identification and put on a friendly face, despite my strong desire to straighten this thief out. He nods a more familiar greeting, pats Shirley on the shoulder with his paddle and lets us pass.

We pass more police checkpoints. Sometimes I disguise us by sitting close behind trucks and buses. This way, we pass too quickly for the police to see the foreign-looking bike. Near Berane we find ourselves in the rain with no 'cover'. An old Mercedes is chugging along so I overtake him when I can. There are no lines marked on the road and I'm only doing about 80 km/h. Around the next corner we are pulled in by yet another solo policeman. Again I cannot understand him. I keep asking if we have done anything wrong. After a few minutes it becomes clear I am not going to offer him any money and he hears another bike coming, so he waves us on.

The scenery is spectacular up in these mountains but the roads are treacherous. The fact they are wet makes them even worse. At one point, we follow a tilt-tray tow truck down a steep hill. The driver touches his brakes and instantly goes sideways. Undoubtedly, there's something on the road, and the driver holds out his hand to warn me to go slowly. Down the hill there is a policeman standing on the side of the road. I immediately think it's another police check, but then see a semi-trailer on the side of the road and we smell diesel. That is a lethal combination – a diesel spill and a wet road. A car is approaching from behind too quickly. He brakes and instantly spears off the road and into an embankment, nearly taking out two cars chugging up the hill. The bike tyres want to go in two different directions at once. I'm down to walking pace and preparing to cop a slow-speed fall. We get through okay, to the amazement of the police officer and the tow-truck driver.

Shirley: We pick our way through the hills. The going is very slow and it's getting late. We come across signs advertising hotels, but when we find them they are burned out or bombed. Roadside traders are pushing their bottles and jars of goodness knows what in our faces. Some are very aggressive, shouting at us as we pass. We are very close to the Albanian border and we aren't stopping for anything.

Brian: Further on we find a tunnel with a green light showing on our side of the road. As I enter, it is black. I put the lights on high beam and am horrified to find the road is mud and the air thick with smoke and dust. We are slipping all over the place and can only see about 20 m in front of us. The tunnel curves around, but there are no markings or reflectors to help guide us. I warn Shirley to hang on – we are bound to hit the deck in here. I get ready for a slow-speed tumble. A truck appears out of the gloom so I pull over to let him pass. We slip and slide for about a kilometre underground before emerging out the other end. The workers are standing around smoking. They all smile and wave. Shirl is terrified and my arms ache from the effort of holding us up.

Shirley: About 10 km down the road we find a grand-looking ski-resort-style hotel in the middle of nowhere. We've had enough so we pull in. It seems we are the only guests, with the waiters outnumbering us at dinner. After a fairly ordinary meal we sit out on the balcony with a bottle of the local red – very good and served chilled.

The still night air is disturbed by the distant rumble of engines. Over the hill come some of the local farmers on their tractors. This must be their 'local' and they are obviously intrigued by the tourists sitting in their domain.

After the beauty, friendliness and peace of Dubrovnik and Zaton, Montenegro has been a real culture shock. And tomorrow we head into Kosovo.

I am nervous about today, as we are not sure what Kosovo holds for us.

There is no traffic on the road except yet another police checkpoint. We've passed through about 20 checkpoints since entering Montenegro yesterday. Around 10 km down the road we come to the UN-patrolled border post for Kosovo. The distance between the two is indicative of the tensions in this part of the world. Most border posts between two countries' checkpoints are usually just 100 m apart.

The UN police and Kosovo customs agents are friendly. They check our green card and, as we are already aware, we are not covered for the old Yugoslavia. All that is required is to pay the minimum of €30 for 15 days of insurance cover at the border. That's not a bad earner for the authorities when you consider we hope to be in Macedonia tonight!

After checking the paperwork we have to ride through a 'disinfectant pit', which is just a concrete pit full of water, to wash off the Montenegrin germs. As a parting gesture they warn us not to wander off the road. 'There are still many landmines out there. It will probably take us 100 years to clear them all,' we are told.

The road conditions change from excellent to goat tracks. When we see a sign announcing an EU-sponsored project we know the road will be good. We thank Germany for the road out of the mountains.

Brian: We head for Peć in the heart of Kosovo. It is a big provincial city and today is market day. The road is clogged with traffic – everything from horse and cart to Mercedes Benzes. We crawl through the town and, as we pass, men in the coffee shops all stop what they are doing and stare at us. Shirl is disconcerted by the attention and stern facial expressions. I tell her that this is just the way these people are and we should start to wave at them. As soon as I do that, there are smiles, waves and shouts of encouragement. This eases Shirl's fears somewhat.

Shirley: It is slow going. We are within 10 km of the Albanian border and we start to notice army trucks and well-armed soldiers patrolling the streets and countryside. The road takes us within sight of Albania and, as we climb higher, the traffic reduces to just army and UN vehicles. As we head down a road through beautiful countryside, an Armoured Personnel Carrier (APC) comes barrelling down towards us, complete with gunner in position. The pine forest and rolling fields had looked like a good place to picnic. The APC gives us a quick reality jolt.

We have to stop twice at army checkpoints. The soldiers position one man to stop the traffic (us). About 50 m down the road is their APC, providing covering fire in our direction. Next to the APC are more soldiers with guns at the ready. We wait with the first soldier until they wave us forward. The conversations at both checkpoints are the same:

'Passports.' We hand them over. The soldier looks at them with interest. 'What are you doing here?'

'We are tourists.'

'Tourists?'

'Yes, tourists.'

The young soldiers shake their heads in disbelief. Why would anyone be here voluntarily? They wave us through.

I find it comforting to have the army and UN presence on the road. As well as the mobile patrols we come across two 'camps' surrounded by barbed wire and sandbags. Brian finds it unnerving because it clearly indicates we are close to Albania and in a very dangerous part of the world.

Brian: The buzz of travelling through Kosovo is exciting, if a little dangerous. But, due to the presence of the UN and the army, I do feel there's a greater chance of being harmed by the poor road conditions than getting hijacked.

Shirley: We hit the Macedonian border and there is a thorough check. I guess they don't want people sneaking out of the country. We have to pay for our visa despite the guidebook saying they are issued for free. We decide that arguing with the young female official wouldn't be a good career move and hand over the cash. We are granted a five-day transit visa. That's fine with us. We just want to see Lake Ohrid and chill out after the last two fairly stressful days on the road.

After a long day – two border crossings, two fuel stops and more than 400 km in more than seven hours – we arrive in Ohrid. All the restaurants on the edge of the lake boast barbecues with every form of meat you can imagine.

Lake Ohrid puts on a superb light-and-sound show for us, with lightning, thunder and the most incredible downpour. It is magnificent. We stand on the balcony of our room in a hotel overlooking the lake and watch everyone running for cover in the streets. The thunder is deafening and the lightning illuminates the sky. We hear girls scream with fright.

Outside the old town, Ohrid is like many other provincial cities. It has Western services, but the people are poor by Western standards, if monetary wealth is a guide. But they have a rich culture and close family ties, which is obvious from the number of families wandering the streets. There is not the hustle and bustle of a modern Western city.

A 900-year-old plane tree gets our attention, as well as eleventh-century churches and a Roman amphitheatre. Perched on the clifftop overlooking the lake and town is a basilica. An archaeological dig here has uncovered floor mosaics dating back to the fifth century. A roof has been erected and a walkway a metre above the tiles has been put in place, so we can take in the magnificent workmanship without damaging the mosaics. The intricate designs feature animals and fruits. We are careful not to step on the tiles close to the edge of the cordoned-off area. To our horror, one man walks all over this treasure taking close-ups with his video camera.

We end another idyllic day by spending a lazy afternoon on the balcony watching rain showers drift across the lake.

We head to Greece and manage to get horribly lost in the last Macedonian town before the border. Instead of finding the borderpost we end up in a lumberjacks' marketplace. They all seem to be driving funny little petrol-driven devices with the flywheel where the radiator should be and massive timber cutting saws whirring away as they putter down the street. From the minute we drive into the market area there are two possibilities: we will find the friendliest people we've met to date, or we will be bashed and robbed of the bike.

The lumberjacks are tough but incredibly friendly. In his inimitable style, Brian rides up to a group of young men, opens his visor and says, 'G'day, fellas. We're looking for Greece'. It is a great line. From here on we are everyone's friends and these young men are pleased to try out their English and help us on our way. Brian has a natural flair when dealing with people and it is coming to the fore on this trip.

lmatian coast

Dubrovnik

An impressive statue in Split

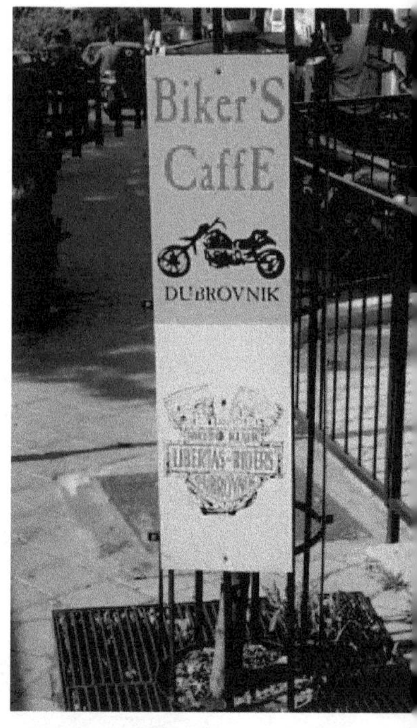

Bikers' hangout in Dubrovnik

Overlooking the city of Dubrovn

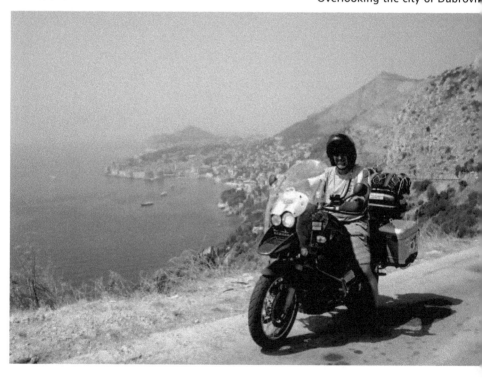

EIGHT

GREECE

27 August – 20 September 2003

Shirley: Greece is getting ready for the 2004 Olympics. We notice it as soon as we cross the border. The roads are good and there are roadworks and other infrastructure works under way. There are signs praising the EU for its sponsorship. We add our own praise – it's a pleasant experience to be on good-quality roads again.

The mountains of northern Greece offer up narrow and twisty roads through picturesque villages and contented sheep grazing in the fields. There are no guard rails here to spoil the view or stop you from plummeting into oblivion. Seeing all those sheep, it seems appropriate that we should enjoy some Greek lamb and salad for lunch at a delightful restaurant on the shore of a lake. Here we meet a Greek man from Sydney who's come home to see his grand-children. He doesn't class himself as Greek – he's Australian and proud of it.

Brian: We head back into the mountains and there are some traps waiting for us on the roads. The EU hasn't been working on the roads here. Occasionally we come around a blind corner and find a narrow and poorly maintained bridge just wide enough for one car. On some corners, gravel and dirt have been washed onto the surface, making the wheels slip sideways. But overall we get into the corners. The hiking boots I'm wearing take a hammering as I occasionally scrape my toes on the road whenever we swoop low into the corners. The ride ends too quickly when we arrive in the Meteora region. As we enter the village of Kalambaka, the towering rock formations rise dramatically 450 m above the town. This is what we came here to see.

It was probably hermits in around 950 AD who first settled in Meteora. Then came the monks who built the monasteries, mostly in the twelfth century. These monasteries are perched atop the rock formations, which gives them breathtaking views and seemingly impossible access. It must have been, and probably still is, a harsh life for the religious zealots.

Shirley: Tonight is ABC Radio night. I call in and Jen, Red's producer, sounds genuinely relieved. They've been worried all week about our route through to Greece and wondered if we made it safely. She is relieved to know we avoided Albania and made it to Greece without an ounce of trouble.

Meteora exceeds our expectations. The road up the side of the pillars of rock is a good one and there is very little traffic. There is a lot to be said for staying the night and hitting the road early to see the sights. Most of the monasteries are still difficult to get to, as access is via incredibly steep steps. We ride past a couple of the hard-to-get-to ones before stopping at the Monastery of St Stephen, which is actually an 'open' convent of nuns. Some of the resident nuns must be getting on in years, because there is a metal chairlift-type contraption on wires to the convent for the residents.

My bike gear is hardly revealing and it certainly isn't sexy, but there are rules to be adhered to before you can visit the convent. Women in pants are not permitted and you can't show your arms. To get in, I must wear a dress and long sleeves. I put a skirt on over my bike pants and do a minor strip on the side of the road. My only long-sleeved tops are right at the bottom of the pannier, so I wear my bike jacket. I must look a picture in flowing skirt and cumbersome bike jacket. We leave the helmets, my pants and boots on the bike with the tank bag containing our passports, Minidisc and other valuables. Brian's theory is that it is a religious site and therefore safe.

The nuns here wear the old-fashioned habit, with just their faces and hands showing. But this clobber doesn't stop them from their daily duties. We pass a young nun sweeping the floors with an old-fashioned birch broom.

The chapel is incredibly ornate, with brightly coloured religious frescoes and intricately hand-carved wooden doors. The nuns have individual stalls for their daily prayers. The wealth here is overwhelming. The vestments and priests' stoles are embroidered with gold; solid silver shines out in the darkness as do golden icons. Many of the pilgrims kiss the pictures of Christ. We are a little more circumspect.

The gardens, with their spectacular views of other monasteries and the valley below, feature roses with exquisite perfumes and large Greek-style urns.

We leave the convent and ride around to the Monastery of the Great Meteoron. This is the largest of the monasteries, reasonably accessible by foot and very popular with the bus tours. This makes it very unpopular with us. We just admire it from the outside, noticing a net on the wall, which was used to winch visitors and other monks to the monastery from the valley below. Today, it is just used to bring up supplies. I must say, if you knew you had to travel in this net you wouldn't bother visiting!

We head off the beaten track to visit Vikos Gorge. The road to the gorge was once asphalt and is now broken-down and gravelly. As we ride higher the road gets worse and worse. The only other soul up here is an old goatherd and his flock, guarded by two old dogs. The dog up front decides to show us who is boss and barks at the bike. When the bike ignores him, he wanders off, leading his flock. The goats pay us no heed. The goatherd gives us a wave and continues on his journey.

Back on the highway, the peace and quiet of the gorge is shattered by a near-death experience. We are stuck behind a semi on a very twisty part of the road when from behind I hear a horn toot. A white Peugeot hurtles past us and a semi on a blind corner as a refrigerated truck comes around the corner. The truck brakes and the Peugeot slips in front of the semi, just millimetres from a fatality. It is the closest we have come to something truly dreadful. We catch up to the kamikaze driver further down the highway. We expect to see a young buck behind the wheel, but it is a 60-something man with his wife in the front seat and a woman who could be his mother in the back. He may have preferred death to the nagging he is probably getting. Serves him right!

We've been on the road for 100 days. Sitting overlooking the water in Igoumenitsa on the west coast with a cool drink, we talk about how well we are going so far. We have issues about directions and navigating, but they are minor in the scheme of things. The constant travel and minimalist living are taking us out of our comfort zone. Being together all day, every day, is proving to be the highlight of the journey. The separations might be the hardest thing to deal with when we get home. And there is one thing we agree on without hesitation: we miss Connie, our bitser dog, more than anyone and seeing her will be the best part of getting back.

Brian: I often think about the beginning of this adventure, how the loss of a good mate and work colleague in Possum Carr, a man with a similar adventurous spirit, has affected me. The sadness has strengthened my resolve to experience everything even more, because life is too short to sit at home and brood it away. We have sacrificed a lot to get this far, but we are learning something new every day. Each turn of the road, each new country, each new friend we meet on the way gives us a deeper understanding of the world we live in. We all sit at home and watch the news, where you might get 30 seconds' coverage on the troubles in Kosovo, but to be there, to talk to the people, see their daily hardships and glean an understanding of the religious and ethnic divides that the international community is trying to deal with is enlightening.

Shirley: Riding along the west coast, we pass little coves with crystal-clear water lapping on the shore. It's hot and these beaches are inviting – it is time for a seaside holiday. The locals tell us that Lefkada is the place to go, even though there was an earthquake there last week. Lefkada is an island connected to the mainland by a bridge and a tunnel the locals describe as the 'immersible tunnel'. With a name like that, we have to try the tunnel! It is magnificent, brightly lit and with a good road surface. It is so much better than the tunnels we had to deal with in Montenegro.

At Lefkada, we are keen to get out of our bike gear and

into the water, so we don't check out our hotel options as thoroughly as we should. Our room, however, is wonderful and overlooks the water. The pool has a delightful bar, plenty of sun lounges scattered about and lilos for anyone to use. We change quickly and dive into the pool. After a few minutes, something dawns on me. 'Listen to the voices,' I say to Brian.

'What about them?' he asks.

'Notice something?'

'No.'

'They are all English.'

We have lucked into a destination that is a favourite with the British package tourists. There are no Greeks at the hotel apart from the staff. The restaurants in the town advertise 'full English breakfast' and 'English football live'. There is an upside to all of this – our hotel offers a huge collection of English-language novels to swap. That's the real drawback of bike travel; there's no room to carry enough reading material.

We have news from home and it is not good. It is with trepidation that we open the first of several emails from friends. A friend from our motorcycle club, Wayne Flemming, has died. He was a good bloke. It is very hard being so far away from home at a time like this. So many of our friends are hurting and we aren't there to share their grief. We both shed a tear for 'Flem'. Replying to the emails is emotionally draining.

We figure that arriving in Athens on Sunday will be easier than in midweek and we are right. On the outskirts of the city it is madness, but once we hit the city centre, the traffic is not too bad. And that is just as well, because finding our hotel is not easy. While we are standing on the side of the road looking very lost, a local comes to assist. He points up a street and tells us we can nearly see our hotel, but getting to it is a completely different story. We even find the street but can't find the hotel. When we finally find another hotel and get their map and directions we realise where we have been going wrong – we should have ridden down the one-way street the wrong way. Silly us.

Traffic, heat, time spent hopelessly lost, and even an intermittent problem with the bike's battery are all forgotten when we take a dip in the hotel's rooftop pool. We can view the Parthenon in the distance. It's probably the best known site in Athens and the pillars atop the hill are so easily recognisable. It's hard to believe we are so close to this ancient monument.

Dealing with bureaucracy is a nightmare at the best of times, but in foreign countries it is worse. Here in Athens we must get our Indian visas and renew our visas for Pakistan and Iran, so we call the relevant embassies. The Iranian embassy wants to see us to discuss our expired visas. The Pakistani embassy fobs Brian off with vague promises to call us back and the Indian embassy point-blank refuses to entertain our application, because we are not Greek. We try to explain the Indian officials in Australia insisted we apply for our visas in Greece. We even get Canberra to contact Athens and they still refuse. We decide to re-apply in Turkey.

When I originally applied for the Iranian visa in Canberra, my status as a journalist was queried. The visa was issued after I assured the Australian officials that I would be travelling as a tourist and not as a working journalist. At the Iranian embassy in Athens, the consular official photocopies our passports and gets us to fill in another application just in case. He says he will cable Iran and we can ring him back in a week! I put 'journalist' on my form again and Brian isn't happy, but I feel that a change of occupation might cause even more problems.

Sick of the over-the-phone fob-offs, we go to the Pakistani embassy. In the foyer there is a throng of men, pushing and shoving and shouting. It's back to the phone for us and this time it works. We make a time to come and meet the consul.

With all the new applications, Brian and I need some more passport photos. There is a photo shop across the road from our hotel. Brian throws on his BMW T-shirt – a favourite after our prize-winning journey to Bavaria. The T-shirt starts a conversation about bikes and a friendship with the shop-owner, Nikos, and his Dutch wife, Judy. They decide to shut the shop early on Wednesday and take us for a ride into the countryside. We can't knock back such an offer.

Back at the embassy, it is Brian's occupation that is now raising questions. The Pakistani consul is concerned about a policeman visiting their country. He wants to know if Brian is working, if he has a gun and why we allowed our original visa to expire. Thinking on his feet, Brian explains we had to head back to London. This does the trick. With assurances there is no gun on the bike and no police work to be done, our paperwork is signed. Once we deposit money into the embassy's bank account, we can get our visas.

We thought rural Greece was one big construction site. It pales into insignificance next to Athens. The roads are being dug up, the underground railway is being built and monuments are being spruced up. It's a real pity the tourist brochures don't mention that this is causing some closures, including that of the National Archaeological Museum. We are pissed off, to say the least, when, after walking in the heat and through a park littered with used syringes and a large population of junkies and deros, we find the museum is closed until April next year! It is being renovated for the Olympics.

Nikos rides through the city traffic with the ease only a local can muster. Brian follows with me fending off the crazy car drivers and people on scooters who want our bit of road as well as their own. It is nerve-racking. Brian does a great job in getting us through it all while keeping Nikos in sight.

Out of the city, the traffic disappears and we can enjoy the scenery. Whitewashed churches stand in olive groves that must be hundreds of years old. Goats graze on the craggy mountainside and don't even look up as we ride past. We head to a small bay, where the beach is virtually deserted, which is just as well – Brian and I can't get changed into our bathers under a towel nearly as well as Nikos and Judy can. After spending more than an hour floating around in the water, we reverse the procedure and change back into our bike gear under the towel.

The sun sets over the still water, and Athens seems a million miles away as we eat magnificent fresh whitebait and local fish with some octopus and fresh salads, all washed down with retsina and local beers.

It is time for another boat journey – the ferry to Crete. Nikos leads us out of town and puts us on the road to Piraeus. When we get near the port a young man on another BMW GS rides alongside us. He wants to know where we are from, where we are going, and asks a thousand questions about the bike. When we get to the ferry terminal, he admits he wasn't going our way – he just wanted to talk to us!

On the ferry we leave the bike in the lap of the Greek gods. It is tied down with a nylon rope. The ferry hands assure us it will be fine. Brian's not so sure. The entire way to Crete he feels every roll and pitch. Just as well it isn't rough.

It is well after 10 p.m. when we arrive at Crete. We've been warned that the road is bad, but we want to get to our resort tonight, even though it is on the other end of the island. Brian rides hard and fast to get the ks behind us. The deserted roads are in our favour – no-one else is crazy enough to ride at this time of the night. We finally get to our room in the early hours of the morning and, gratefully, find that the hotel manager has left our room key in the door.

Makrigialos, on the southeast corner of Crete, is billed 'where agriculture meets tourism'. Our studio apartment is set in a communal garden filled with fruit trees, frangipanis, flowering vines and hedges and a small olive grove. It is heaven. There is a swag of mail waiting for us, including some books from Bettina and Tim in London. Dear Tina includes a bag of our favourite Sainsbury's chilli-flavoured chips. The only problem is the bag has burst and there are chips through everything, but they are still edible. We don't have to take the chips with us when we go to the pool to read – they come with us in the books.

The town of Makrigialos has everything we need. There are several small supermarkets, a butcher, greengrocer, wine shops, souvenirs and several tavernas and fish restaurants. The sandy beach stretches for a kilometre, offering plenty of chances to get away from the crowds. The local fishermen sit in the sunshine untangling their nets, preparing for another trip out to sea tonight.

We stock the fridge with local cheese, olives and Cretan wine before taking a spot beside the pool. There are books to be read, food to be eaten and that's just about it for the next week. I didn't realise how tiring a bike holiday can be! The biggest decision we will make in this town will be where to go for dinner.

We meet a one-legged doctor from the UK and his wife, who is nursing a very badly gashed leg after tripping over one of the sun lounges. She has 20 stitches. Lying by the pool can be dangerous.

We feel guilty when all the guests announce one morning they are going for a hike through the local gorge. We drag ourselves off the sun lounges and join them. The 1000-year-old village of Pefki is at the top of the gorge. The history of these old villages is fascinating. One thousand years ago the seas around Crete were occupied by pirates. The locals built three villages to protect themselves. The primary village was up in the hills out of sight of the sea, just as Pefki is. While the hills are hard to farm even now, in those days they would have been impossible, so a secondary village was built through the gorge on flatter country, but still out of view of the sea. The men would come to this village to work the fields and their women would come twice a week on donkeys to bring provisions and 'comfort'. The ocean was a good source of food, so the men built a third village of shacks to shelter in after fishing the coastal waters. It was mostly left deserted to avoid confrontation with pirates. This is where the present-day Makrigialos stands.

There are constant reminders of past civilisations. Minoan and Roman ruins still exist in the heart of town. A rusty gate in a dilapidated fence is all that protects the ruins of one Roman villa. The mosaic tiles of its once-decorative floor, as well as slabs of magnificent marble in what was originally an entrance foyer, are still visible. Some of the mosaic areas measure 30 square centimetres or more, while others comprise only a dozen tiny tiles. There are water courses, a grinding stone of some kind and an area that was probably the kitchen of the villa. But more surprising than all of this are the pieces of pottery and clay tiles that are everywhere. You can pick up pieces that once formed the rounded edge of an urn or pot, circular pieces that may have been pottery tiles, and cornices that could once have adorned the outer or inner walls of the villa. It is mind-boggling to think that it is all just lying there, unprotected.

Whenever there is a storm, the seas wash up pieces of pottery and other odds and ends from boats that came to grief off the coast around 2000 years ago.

Many of the houses in Makrigialos are made from remnants of old ruins. To some, this is a desecration of ancient sites, but Brian and I begin to understand the reality of a harsh existence where, to survive, everything is used. Even today, old Grecian urns are used as chimney pots, their shape providing the perfect vortex to draw smoke from the fires below.

Crete's recent history is littered with tragedy. During World War II, it was occupied by the Germans. The entire population of Ano Viannos was executed on 4 September 1943. Today, there is a sign that says the town is only a few kilometres away. When you arrive at the spot, there is no town, just a memorial to the dead:

Bypasser, stay guarded
Here lie dead
Who never betrayed
Who never lied
Tyranny never worshipped
Bypasser, stay guarded
And with a lucid spirit
Study them
What if you enjoy the light
And if you walk full
Of courage
And if you love
And are loved
And whatever good
You have in life
Was offered to you by those dead.

What could possibly have been achieved by killing every man, woman and child? At the end of the war, locals destroyed the village and erected the memorial over the mass grave.

Brian: The journey is starting to take its toll on my body, so I book myself in for a shiatsu massage. The masseur was formerly a photographer with an advertising firm in Europe; he got sick of the rat race, learned the ancient art of shiatsu and relocated to Crete. He takes one look at me and asks, 'How long ago did you break your right leg?' (I was not even a teenager when it happened.) I tell him that my right hand is going numb through constant throttle and brake use and the old knees aren't what they used to be. He spends a full hour stretching tendons and manipulating my hands, shoulders and legs. I am surprised at the tingling sensations. At first I am sceptical, but when he finishes there is no doubt the massage has been beneficial. We talk about Tai Chi and the benefits of Eastern remedies and lifestyles. A good mix for a balanced life would no doubt be a blend of Mediterranean diet and Eastern lifestyle. Am I turning into something other than a hard-nosed copper?

Shirley: The Cretan olive oil is said to be the best in the world. Stories abound in this area of the residents' longevity and the absence of heart disease. We are told that at the end of World War II, the Americans arrived to re-establish the infrastructure. They asked where the heart ward of the local hospital was. There wasn't one because heart disease was so rare. Unfortunately, with the advent of junk food and a lack of physical labour, that is not the case now.

Brian: Greeks love to party and Cretans are no exception. Our last night on the island is spent singing, dancing, eating and drinking with the locals. The men dance in lighted rings of raw alcohol. The women sing and we all eat.

One of the local olive farmers entices us to try the local raki, guaranteeing that it won't give you a hangover. 'Raki doesn't leave you with a soft head in the morning.'

He lied. I awoke with a soft head.

Shirley: We're finding it hard to drag ourselves back to Athens, so we take a ferry to Santorini for a few days. The Greek gods will need to take good care of the bike again. This time we are only offered string hanging from overhead water pipes to secure it.

Santorini is a great place to chill out and watch the sunset, and we do just that. I doubt if we can get more relaxed. Donkeys graze in a field at the back of our hotel. Just after dawn they are dressed up in their best saddles and taken off to carry tourists from the wharf to the town – all except one. He spends the day alone in the field; his braying is mournful. There is a definite change in his tone when his mates return from their day's toil.

Local wine, seafood and the sun setting over the water is as close to perfect as you can get. Until you see Oia. Think of every photo you've ever seen of whitewashed churches and houses against a backdrop of blue water – it's as though they were all taken in this tiny village. The narrow, cobblestoned lanes wind between the beautiful buildings. We glimpse the sea between the structures set atop steep cliffs. There are art galleries, restaurants and bars dotted between the churches and houses. It's peaceful up here – despite the tourists.

Brian: We arrive back in the real world with a thump when we collect our Iranian visas in Athens. First off, the officials relieve us of €120 for the privilege of issuing a new visa. Then the real trouble begins.

A consular official queries Shirley's profession as a journalist, saying that it is not possible for a journalist to travel to Iran due to the problems some Western nations, including Australia, are making for them. Luckily he wants to help and tells us to fill out a new application form without declaring Shirley is a journalist. I assure him we are just tourists travelling through, and he says she should be called a writer or publisher. I get a fresh application and think I impress him by getting her to fill it out while I stand over her!

Shirley: It is another emotional farewell when we say goodbye to Nikos and Judy. Nikos embraces Brian and kisses him on both cheeks – the traditional farewell for good friends.

We take a detour to the Temple of Poseidon – one of the wonders of Ancient Greece. It is impressive, standing on top of a cliff 60 m above the sea. The temple has stood there for more than 2000 years, a credit to the talents of the original constructors. The peace is shattered by the noise of American tourists – and by gunshots coming from the nearby hills. It is duck-hunting season and they take it seriously here. We see many middle-aged men in army fatigues wandering along the road toting shotguns.

We head back towards Athens and our last stop in Greece – Delphi. The road skirting Athens isn't finished yet and we wonder if it will be before the Olympics. We travel 20 km in choking dust and diesel fumes before finally clearing the industrial zones of Athens. As we climb into the hills the road narrows and gets steeper. Long lines of cars bank up behind struggling trucks and the bike comes into its own as we overtake the traffic with ease. Slowly but surely, we leave it behind us and crest the mountains surrounding Athens. We find ourselves travelling through lush farming country with fields of vegetable crops of all description stretching as far as the eye can see. The fields are interspersed with small villages eking out an existence supporting the local primary crop producers.

We get off the highway and go into Livadia for lunch, and find natural springs and a stream dissecting the town. Two water wheels turn lazily as the stream tumbles down small waterfalls. We park under the shade of the trees overlooking the small town square and share yet another salad, a small meat dish and delicious grilled peppers in olive oil.

Eventually we drag ourselves away, mount up and ride towards Delphi. Rounding a corner, we are knocked out by the view of the Temple of Apollo high on a hill, and the smaller, yet no less impressive, temples to Athena nestled among the olive groves just below the road. The marble columns are in stark contrast to the dark cliffs behind. Delphi quite rightly lays claim to being the heartland of civilisation.

Even up here the Delphi Museum is being refurbished, presumably for the Olympic Games. Only one room is open and the main display is the cast-bronze *Charioteer of Delphi* made in 470 BC. He is incredible. You can see his eyelashes, the curls in his hair, and the folds in his tunic. He looks as though he was only cast yesterday. He still holds his reins. Unfortunately, all that remains of the rest of the sculpture, believed to be four horses and two servants holding the outside reins, are a couple of horses' legs, more reins and the leg of one servant. There are also the remains of a silver-plated bull that was held together with leather strapping on a wooden frame, and an exquisite bowl featuring Apollo playing the lyre and making an offering to the gods. It is beautiful and I am enchanted by it. There are also a couple of statues from the same period and Brian and I can't help but notice the first toe on each foot is longer than the big toe. (I mention this to Red during our next radio chat. His wife is Greek and we laugh at the image of her sticking her foot out from under the doona to see if her first toe is longer than her big toe!)

The original Temple of Apollo isn't as ancient as the *Charioteer of Delphi*, dating back to 330 BC. What we see today has been reconstructed from the ruins by archaeologists. The Ancient Greeks deliberately built structures to withstand Mother Nature, taking earthquakes into account. They inserted wood inside the marble columns so they would sway in a quake and not break.

Alongside the columns, blocks of marble still show ancient inscriptions. Apparently, in the museum there is a block with the words and music to a poem in praise of Apollo, but of course we didn't see that because the museum is partially closed due to refurbishment for the Olympics. We walk along the Sacred Way and pass the treasury erected by the Athenians as an offering to Apollo after a victory in 490 BC. It is said to be the most impressive building on the site, but it is covered in scaffolding because it is under restoration for the bloody Olympics. We hope the visitors next year enjoy all this work!

At the Temple of Athena stands an olive tree with a gnarled trunk probably 3 m in circumference. It is anybody's guess how old it is.

After a meal overlooking the lights of the bayside towns, we go shopping and find a replica of the Apollo bowl from the museum. It is a ridiculous thing to buy when you are on a bike, but the shopkeeper wraps it in plenty of bubble wrap and pops it into a box. We keep our fingers crossed that it will be whole when it gets home and not in a thousand pieces like the original.

Nikos recommended we take the road through the mountains on our way to Turkey and we can see why. The road surface is extremely good and the traffic light. Even when we do come across slower traffic we get around it quickly. I can tell that Brian is having a terrific time. He seems to be scraping his boots on the tarmac on both sides. I guess he is convinced he can wear them out because he has decided to buy some new ones in Turkey.

Before we get to Lamia in eastern Greece, Brian is tearing down a hill into the town of Gravia when he pulls up in a big rush. A bee has got inside his T-shirt and stung him twice – once on the chest and once on the tummy. It must have hurt for him to stop and then put on the Stingose cream to ease the pain!

We could head straight to Turkey but another day on a Greek beach is much more appealing. We head down a side road to San Panteleimon Beach. The season is over, the beach is deserted and the water looks inviting. After a quick change, we swim in the warm and incredibly clean water. Once out of the water, we both end up having a snooze in the late afternoon sun.

As Olympic Games preparations have dogged us the entire time in Greece, it seems appropriate we visit Mount Olympus before crossing the border. It is an 18 km ride to the viewpoint. The road conditions are poor at first and then get worse – the surface is cracked and narrow, providing no room for error. There is a sheer drop down the side of the road. Small rocks, which have fallen from the cliff face, litter the roadway. About 2 km from the viewpoint the road turns to very rough gravel and there are some points where it is completely washed away. When we get to the end the car park is so rough and pitted Brian nearly drops the bike turning around to get a parking spot. We take a couple of photographs, but the sights aren't what we expect – nothing to indicate this was the home of the gods, just a ticket office and a gravel car park. In bike gear, a hike to the top wasn't an option.

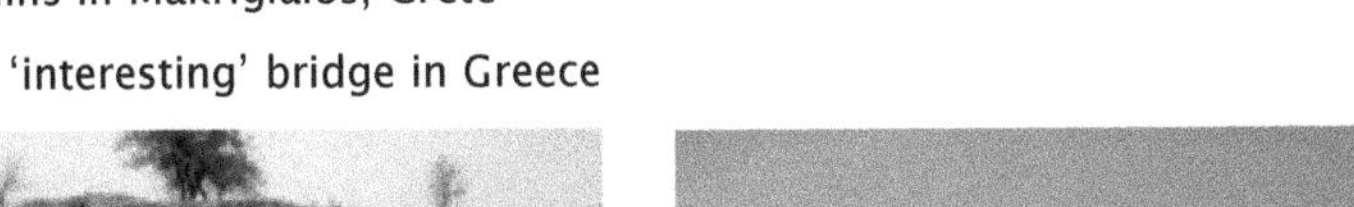

cient Roman ruins in Makrigialos, Crete

An ‘interesting’ bridge in Greece

Santorini

Some of the locals on the road to Vikos Gorge

The road to Mt Olympus was in very poor conditi

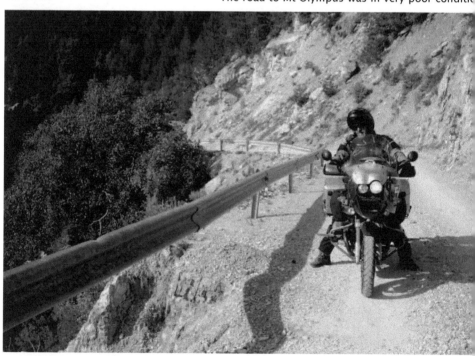

NINE

TURKEY

20 September – 25 October 2003

Shirley: Greece has been marvellous but it is time to move on and we are looking forward to Turkey. The beauty of the morning just adds to our good mood. And when I change some money at the border, our mood lifts even more. Imagine having 357 million in notes! Okay, it is 357 million Turkish lira, and there are 900,000 lira to the Australian dollar.

Arriving in Turkey is like returning to a friend's home. It is a country we have visited in the past and loved. And Turkey also holds a special place in our hearts. A relative lies buried on the Gallipoli Peninsula, a victim of the brutality of war.

At the border, there is an obvious military presence, with Greek and Turkish soldiers armed with machine guns facing each other. They look frightening until they smile and wave as we pass.

I don't know why, but we presumed our visas would be free. Wrong. We have to pay €20 or $US20 in cash. The millions of lira in my wallet are going to do us no good here. We need foreign currency to pay for the visas. Luckily, Brian has a stash of Euros and we are able to get the visas. After a total of 120 days on the road, we finally get to use the carnet. The officials just fill in the forms and slap a few stamps in our passports and the process is over.

When we walk outside we hear the highly unusual sounds of an Australian accent: 'G'day. Are you on the bike? Is that really an Australian rego?'

The owner of the voice is a very lanky hippie with an unusual assortment of tattoos. He wanders over with his hand outstretched. 'Dean, the name's Dean.'

Dean has been travelling for months and is only crossing over to Greece to get his Turkish visa renewed. His German girlfriend is sitting in their clapped-out car just outside the border. Dean is interested in our journey and assures us we will meet again somewhere on the road.

We plan to stop first in Canakkale and the Gallipoli Peninsula, but first we must fuel up. The bowser shows 123,000 and I hand over a 500,000-lira note. We don't speak Turkish and the man doesn't speak English, but we don't need to be linguists to work out we haven't handed over enough money. The decimal points and the zeros disappear off the counter on the bowser – we owe 12,300,000 lira for the petrol. This currency is going to take some getting used to.

The ferry to cross the Dardanelles costs 2,300,000 lira for us and the bike. This seems like a fortune until we realise it is a bit less than $3. On the ferry are several busloads of soldiers, some of whom look barely old enough to shave, but they have machine guns slung across their backs. A couple of them come up to check out the bike, but one quick order barked by a senior officer and they disappear to the other side of the car deck.

Canakkale is very much a tourist town. The Australians

and New Zealanders who come to visit the battlefields of Gallipoli stay overnight. The local youth hostel, ANZAC House, even shows a 1988 documentary of some of the diggers and the movie *Gallipoli* every night.

The journey to Gallipoli is an emotional one. In 1915 my great uncle, Allan Noble, was killed on the battlefields. He lies in the Embarkation Pier Cemetery, such a long way from the mines of Australia where he worked as an engineer and diamond driller before taking up the call to defend king and country. Allan was my grandmother's favourite brother; my brother bears his name as a tribute. His death was the great tragedy of the family and led my grandparents to become pacifists. Allan didn't enlist until late in the year and was only on the peninsula a few weeks when he was hit in the face and chest by shrapnel. The medical officers couldn't save him. The timing of his death just magnifies the enormity of the tragedy. If the generals had realised the error of their ways in the early days of the battle, Allan and thousands of others would have lived. They may have gone on to other arenas of war, and later been killed, but they would have lived through Gallipoli.

When we arrive at the cemetery we know where to look, but even then we have trouble finding Allan's grave. The weather has worn down the engraving on the stone slab that marks where he is believed to be buried. Even when we pour water over it, the inscription is hard to make out. I find this very disappointing and upsetting. The Commonwealth War Graves Commission does a great job, but I guess they can't stop the ravages of the weather.

As I kneel over the grave, running my finger over the faded engraving, Brian, dear Brian, gives me an olive branch to place on the grave and then moves away to allow me some quiet time to reflect on my ancestor who lies here, so far from home.

Australians seem to forget that Gallipoli is the scene of a great victory for the Turkish people and the turning point in Turkish history. This nation became part of the modern world at the end of World War I thanks to the leader of this military campaign, Mustafa Kemal, known by the Turkish as Atatürk.

On ANZAC Day, this area crawls with Aussies and Kiwis. Today, there are busloads of Turkish visitors wandering through the battlefields. At ANZAC Cove the water is calm and the sun shimmers on the surface – vastly different from the dawn of 25 April 1915 when the troops landed here. Even seeing it for the second time it is breathtaking. How did they get so far on the first day and keep such a hold on the place for so long? The leaders of the battle had a lot to answer for, given the number of needless casualties. This feeling is reinforced as we ride past cemetery after cemetery.

From ANZAC Cove we move to the monument inscribed with Atatürk's immortal words to the families of the dead: 'Those heroes that shed their blood and lost their lives . . . you are now lying in the soil of a friendly country. Therefore rest in peace, there is no difference between the Johnnies and the Mehmets to us where they lie side by side here in this country of ours . . . You, the mothers, who sent their sons from far away countries, wipe away your tears; your sons are now lying in our bosom and are in peace. After having lost their lives on this land they have become our sons as well.'

No matter how many times we read these words, we are moved by them. What a great man Atatürk must have been to care so much for the invaders of his country. He was the epitome of graciousness in victory. Many other leaders have something to learn from Atatürk, known as the father of modern Turkey.

Riding through the Turkish countryside, we wend our way amid olive groves and fields of tomatoes. Our strongest memory of Turkey from when we visited in 1995 is the tomatoes. They are brilliantly red and taste like tomatoes used to taste. It is picking time and the women, wearing the traditional Muslim scarf, toil in the fields under the burning sun. The men sit back on tractors smoking and watching the women work. Occasionally, they hand out a bucket but don't bend their backs or get their hands dirty! This becomes a very common sight in Turkey – women working and men overseeing.

At the end of the day, the farmers rumble past on their tractors with huge trailers loaded with fresh tomatoes, and their women are perched precariously on the end.

Over dinner, we are delighted to discover that the tomatoes are as good as we remember them, if not a little better. We dine on pizza with a huge salad of tomato, cucumber and onion.

Riding into Istanbul, we see the Blue Mosque with its six minarets towering above the city. It is a wonderful sight and gives us something to aim towards on the roads. The closer we get to the city the crazier the traffic becomes. While we have a vague idea of where we have to go to find the hotel and we do have a map, this city, with its population of more than 12 million people, is bedlam. We pull up to check the map and eventually ask a cab driver for help. A passing policeman knows a better way – he orders the cabbie to take us to the hotel. The cabbie's not too happy about that, but does take us through the streets to find the hotel, leaving us on the side of the road with just one illegal turn between us and the hotel. No problem.

Well, there is one problem: the 'parking area' promised in the hotel guide is just a space on the street protected by two brightly coloured cones. The hotel staff bend over backwards to be helpful, putting the bike in a lockable area out the back at 10 p.m.

Brian: The gutter is about 20 cm high and I need to take a run up. I get the front wheel up, no problem, but the road cleaners have been through and the road is wet. When the back wheel hits the gutter it spins and slips sideways. Because the bike is cold, it has slipped off the choke cycle and stalls. How embarrassing! I have a fairly big audience of men watching from a footpath cafe and I know the hotel staff is watching through the window. I have another go and on the second attempt we are on the footpath. The glass doors at the back of the hotel are open, but it is a tight squeeze. There is another gutter so I have to gun the bike again to get it up. This extra speed means I narrowly miss going down a flight of stairs just inside the door. With a bit of manoeuvring I get the bike next to the stairs. It's tight but we manage. I'm happy that the bike is secure.

Shirley: I like shopping, but the Russian women staying in this hotel must be in their country's Olympic shopping team. They stagger back burdened with huge parcels and followed by men with trolleys piled high with even more parcels the size of wool bales. At breakfast these women sit with a rugged-looking man with a tattoo on his thumb . . . the trademark of the Russian mafia. It's like being in the middle of a Cold War movie.

A cup of tea with the hotel manager, Ali, answers my questions about what these women are doing. Ali tells us that people from Russia, Kazakhstan and other Eastern European countries come here and buy cheap clothing in bulk. He promises to show us the real story, leading us around the side of the hotel to the back door, past the bike. There is a covered truck being loaded with hundreds of big white bags secured with duct tape. The place is a hive of activity. We go down the stairs under the hotel to a cellar with four huge rooms, each full of more white bags. Men are checking off each one as it goes up into the truck. Brian's antenna is up. He spies the Russian mafia-looking guy from breakfast and a heap of other tattooed men of Eastern European extraction. Ali tells us that when they are in town they fill the cellar three times a day and then load the stuff on trucks. These people are taking out masses of things – clothing, linen, leather. This has got to be a rort, tax-avoidance or money-laundering scheme. It certainly makes bus shopping trips to factory outlets in Australia pale into insignificance.

One of the 'must do' jobs in Istanbul is organising our Indian visas. Finding the consulate in the traffic is a headache. We cross over the Bosphorus Strait and head into the right general area but can't find the side street. I jump off the bike to ask a young soldier for directions, and he flinches and looks more than a little nervous when this mad-looking woman with a flip-top helmet approaches. A couple of illegal U-turns later and we finally have to ask police for directions and eventually find the consulate. The policeman guarding the entrance has no problem with us parking on the footpath and is last seen checking the bike out as we head into the building. It's certainly going to be safe under his watchful eye. The consulate staff are friendly and helpful. We fill in the forms and are told our visas will be ready in 10 days.

Our other necessary job is to get the bike serviced. The BMW dealership in Istanbul is surrounded by a high fence with armed guards. This isn't that unusual, really, but having an armed guard patrolling the showroom is a little more unusual, and security-conscious to a fault.

The ride back to the hotel is horrendous. We see only two bikes other than those of police motorcyclists. The motorists are not biker savvy or friendly and they don't move over to allow you to cut the traffic. It is a death-defying experience.

Our discussions at the BMW dealership and with Ali

have shown one thing: even in the supposedly progressive city of Istanbul, women count for little and their opinions count for even less. I am becoming invisible and that is not a very comfortable thing for me. Brian thinks it is very funny, he's used to me always speaking my mind. I know I will have to get used to it, but it won't be easy.

Turkey is famous for its carpets and infamous for its carpet sellers. We are in the market for a carpet and don't mind when the friendly man giving us directions to the Blue Mosque tells us he owns a carpet shop. He can't believe his luck when we readily agree to meet him after our tour of the mosque to discuss the serious business of carpet-buying.

For more than an hour we sit and sip tea as Cengiz shows us carpet after carpet. We see kilims, wool carpets and blends. We see old carpets and new ones, plain carpets and elaborate carpets, small and large carpets. It's enough to give you a headache.

Then I stand back to let Brian see to the very serious business of bartering the price down from the ridiculous starting price of US$3200: 'Twelve hundred dollars for the two carpets, shipped to Australia,' he says.

'Oh, Mr Brian, that is impossible. I cannot feed my family at that price.' But then Cengiz comes down to $2200 immediately.

'No, $1500,' says Brian. 'We are travelling east. We will see many carpets.'

I stand in the corner. I love both the carpets, but know it is time to shut up. I hate bartering and just chew my lip to make sure words don't slip out, words that would stitch up the deal and make Brian furious.

Cengiz leaves us for a few minutes with another cup of Turkish tea and comes back, holds out his hand to shake and says, 'Eighteen hundred dollars.' He grabs Brian's arm to shake on the deal, but Brian isn't ready to close it.

'Sixteen hundred.'

'All right. Half way – $1700 and I will ship them to your home and you can pay with a credit card.'

'Deal,' says Brian, and they shake to confirm.

Walking away, we both feel dread that maybe no carpets will turn up at home and that if they do they won't be the ones we paid for. Fingers crossed it will turn out okay. After all, you have to trust someone.

As well as the local tomatoes, Brian and I have strong memories of Doy-Doy restaurant near the Blue Mosque. Wandering the back streets, we find it and treat ourselves to a magnificent lunch of oven-baked kebab with pistachio nuts cooked into the bread and the special Doy-Doy plate of cheese pide, meat pide and four different kinds of kebab. Both come with couscous and salad. What a feast.

I might not be able to shop like the Russian women but I thoroughly enjoy picking up a few trinkets in the Grand Bazaar. When we walk into this Aladdin's cave of silk, gold, silver, pottery, leather and tourist junk, a voice rises above the hubbub: 'You look like Yul Brynner!' With that, the trader comes up and rubs Brian's bald head. 'I love your hair!' Cheeky bastard!

There is an unwritten rule when travelling and shopping in places like the Grand Bazaar: think about how silly the item will look at home and remember that it will probably look even sillier than you imagine. I can't help but break this rule when I spy the silliest pair of brocade slippers. They don't have a pompom on the toe but are over the top all the same. I love them and must have them. I promise Brian I will wear them all the time at home. I get the feeling he doesn't believe me.

Shopping in Istanbul isn't just trinkets either. The Spice Bazaar is the place to get Turkish delights and dried fruits that send your taste buds into a spin. The smells are only surpassed by the bright yellows and deep crimsons of the spices. One of the delicacies on sale is 'Turkish Viagra' – figs stuffed with pistachio. The shopkeeper is keen for us to buy and laughs when I tell him Brian doesn't need it. I don't mention that I don't like figs!

You can't walk through here and not buy something – it's impossible to be so strong-willed. A young Turkish woman tells us the best Turkish delight is a scrumptious-looking concoction laced with double nuts. She is right. And the dried apricots we buy are another winner.

We walk out of the Spice Bazaar and are right on the waterfront. Here, there is another aroma to deal with – barbecued seafood. Bobbing about in the water are floating fish restaurants selling a fish sandwich which is famous. For just 3,000,000 lira we get two of the sandwiches served with more of those wonderful Turkish tomatoes and the biggest chunk of raw onion they can fit into the roll. I have to ditch the onion; the flavour detracts from the delicious fish. Brian loves the onion and is happy to eat mine as well. We sit on the concrete steps and watch the world go by while eating our delicious meal. If the food is going to be this good all the way across Turkey, we will certainly stack on the weight and have to crank up the suspension on the bike.

Brian: It's Grand Final day at home and I am keen to hear the game – after all, the Pies are playing. With Shirley's help I try to get online to listen to the football via the Internet but there is no broadcast. The website tells us we need to subscribe to hear it. I hate using credit cards over the Net but pay my $4.95 to hear the game. However, I still can't hear the bloody thing. The AFL website is complicated. If this is the best they can do to help spread a great game internationally, there is no hope. I am desperate to watch the game, so I call the Australian embassy: 'Hello, I am an Australian citizen on holiday in Istanbul and I want to watch the AFL Grand Final. Do you know where I can see it?'

'You know, you are the third caller in the past hour. I'm sorry, but I don't know anywhere in Istanbul that is showing the game. If the AFL is serious, they should send out this information. Maybe the Australian Prime Minister should do something about it.'

Maybe she has a point!

Shirley: There are so many things to do in Istanbul, we have to work out a priority list. High on it are the Dolmabahce Palace and the Whirling Dervishes – Turkish history from two entirely different viewpoints.

The Dolmabahce Palace was home to the sultans and has such 'can't live without' features as a French Baccarat crystal balustrade on the sweeping main staircase and massive chandeliers. But the pièce de résistance is the Throne Room's chandelier. Weighing 4000 kilos, it hangs 36 m from the ceiling and is festooned with 750 light globes. If that doesn't throw out enough heat, there is an underfloor heating system that takes three days to heat the room.

Part of the country's religious history is the Whirling Dervishes. Outlawed by Atatürk at the birth of the Turkish republic, the group became a folkloric dance troupe. Today they seem to have become a religious group again. Once a month, at the Whirling Dervish Hall or Galata Mevlevihanesi, in Istanbul, this group of devotees whirls in a trancelike state for the tourists, and you get the feeling there is much more to it than just the performance itself.

The haunting music of the Mevlana orchestra and choir sets the scene. Even without knowledge of the Turkish language you sense the tunes are hymns of praise for Mevlana, the founder of the religious group in the thirteenth century. The young men and women play and sing in the main hall before adjourning to the upstairs orchestra stall wearing their tall conical hats and black cloaks, the traditional garb of the Whirling Dervishes.

The chatter dies down when the spiritual leader walks into the prayer hall followed by men and women wearing cloaks and hats. They become absorbed by the music and seem to drift into a trance. Chanting, they circle the floor and then slowly begin turning in circles within circles. They are oblivious to the people taking photos and whispering in numerous languages. The chanting continues and the pace quickens. Slowly the cloaks drop to the ground revealing gowns of white, red, pink and green swirling across the floor.

It seems impossible that these young people could whirl like this without being in a trance. They look into space with their heads to one side. Their arms are outstretched with one palm facing up and the other down. They seem unaware of everything around them, yet they have an inbuilt awareness of where the others are. They move gracefully without a stumble or a bump.

The swirling colours create a wonderful kaleidoscopic pattern. Then the pace slows and the whirling ends, and the pace picks up again. The sweat glistens on their brows, yet they aren't out of breath and they certainly don't seem the slightest bit giddy. Within minutes the whole dance movement begins again.

For most of us, it is a tourist experience, but for two local women in the crowd it is a religious one. They sit with their hands on their hearts, absorbed by the encounter.

We like nothing more than a boat trip and the Bosphorus is calling. The ferry takes us past the Dolmabahce Palace, embassies and mosques. The scenery is brilliant but the ferry is a rust bucket that wouldn't pass a seaworthiness check in Australia.

At the top of the Bosphorus we check out the seafood restaurants for lunch. The fishing village Anadolu Kavagi is home to a fleet that assures the best seafood around. The fleet also feeds a large group of stray cats. It is breeding season and some kittens are doing better than others. I still can't get used to the fact that no-one really cares about the animals in these countries. They just tolerate them. But as we walk through the heart of old Istanbul, a man appears from a restaurant with a carton of milk. When he appears, so do the cats, which lap the milk with relish. While the younger cats are drinking to their hearts' content, the man picks up the largest one and produces a small parcel of meat. This cat gets the special treat. Pleased with his good deed, the man goes back into his restaurant. At last there is someone who likes cats!

Then I feel guilty for worrying so much about the stray animals when I see a young Muslim woman sitting on a footpath nursing a young baby and begging. These young women seem to be abandoned by their families and forced onto the streets to feed their children. It is sad to see them compelled to stoop so low.

All the time we've been in Istanbul, we believed the bike was safe in the back of the hotel. How wrong we were. Brian goes to check on it and comes back in a filthy mood. People have been mucking around with the bike. All the switches have been flicked, a cover from the injector inspection outlet has been stolen and the cigarette-lighter cover has been ripped off. The damage was probably done by the people who take the parcels into the basement for the Russian shoppers. It is not major stuff, but a hard lesson has been learned. No matter where the bike is, it must be covered and we certainly can't leave it on the street without keeping it within sight.

But Brian doesn't notice the worst of the damage until we get onto the bike to collect our Indian visas. When Brian gets to the corner all I can hear is an amazing spray of colourful invective. 'The bastards! The lousy bastards!' Before he tells me what is going on he is riding around the block and pulling up outside the hotel. His blood is really up. The indicator control has been snapped off.

'Not only is it dangerous, it is going to cost me a lot of money to fix,' he tries to explain to the guys at the hotel. They are embarrassed but, quite rightly, say it is not their fault.

I can't soothe Brian, so it is easier just to let him calm down on his own. We don't believe it was anyone from the hotel or even the street. We still think it's most likely the Russians who have been going up and down the stairs to their business operation. There is nothing we can do, so we head off to the Indian consulate and find it with only one slight wrong turn. We find we have visas until March. At least something has gone right today.

Brian: It is time to move on. The bike has been in one place too long and we didn't handle its protection well. I was lulled into a false sense of security because of the friendliness of the Turkish people. And just when our spirits are low we meet Kemal, who reinstates our faith in the Turks. He drives up to us in a car and indicates we should pull over. Kemal is a motorcyclist and just wants to say hello. He also gives us some contacts for tyres, as well as his email and mobile number, just in case we need a hand.

Shirley: When in Turkey you should do as the Turks do – and that means taking a traditional Turkish bath. And if you are going to have a Turkish bath, why not in a restored Roman bathhouse in Bursa? This is a new experience and I am not sure what to do. The attendant tells me to get changed and gives me a cloth towel. I do so and she informs me I should go into the pool room. In there all the women have their bathers on. I go back and ask about this and she looks at me as if I'm crazy. Of course you wear bathers! Oops.

The marble pool room is steamy with hot water overflowing from basins around the walls. In the centre is a plunge pool and two marble slabs. Two women are washing themselves and each other with their own soap and loofahs. They are really giving themselves the once-over. I feel very out of place and just douse myself with water, and then sit and then douse, and then sit and then take a plunge.

After a few minutes, a large Turkish woman wearing cotton briefs and bra comes in and tells me to get onto the marble slab. This woman takes to me with a rough mitt and rubs me all over. There isn't a dead skin cell left on my body when she is finished. There isn't much of my tan left either. After a douse with hot water to wash off the dead skin, she soaps me everywhere and gives me a wonderful massage. I laze in the pool for a bit, then wrap myself in a large, soft towel and rest for a while before meeting Brian.

Brian: I want to put the wanton vandalism behind us. Shirley is right – a Turkish bath will soothe the savage beast. When she disappears into the women's section, I go down a small corridor, past the shoeshine man who has now taken me under his wing. I am directed to a separate room to strip off and given an oversized tea towel to wear. Unlike the women, men are not expected to wear bathers. Apart from the tea towel, it's au naturel. I am given some soap and head to the bathhouse. You can see the original brickwork laid by the Romans, and there is no doubt that even though it's refurbished, this is the original bathhouse used 2000 years ago. It is all marble and old Roman columns, with running taps in small alcoves around a large circular pool. I sit down next to one of the taps running into an original Roman oversize basin. I am provided with a small tin basin to scoop water out and pour it over my body. I watch the other men and follow suit. Next I take a dip in the pool. It's hot, 42°C, and has two levels so you can ease yourself into it. This feels good and I can feel the tension leaving me.

Just as I am about cooked, a strapping Turkish man comes in and beckons me to follow him to another room with similar marble benches, basins and taps against the walls. In the middle is a round raised marble bench. My Turk is dressed in just a tea towel similar to mine. He grabs a bowl of hot water and pours it all over me. Next he takes a loofah and scrubs my body. And he puts his back into it, too. I can feel my skin prickling. I feel pressure on the back of my thigh. He is using his foot to massage my hamstrings and at the same time giving my feet a workover with his hands. The process is repeated on my arms and then he starts on my back, using his full weight to work every muscle and sinew. I feel him working extra hard on the knotted shoulder-blade muscles. He mumbles something and I think he feels I am tense. He finishes with a more relaxed massage and a soapy rubdown, and then splashes more hot thermal water over me.

I stagger out, all light-headed but very relaxed. I lie in the first room like a piece of pummelled meat.

After we've been pampered, it is time for the bike to get some pampering – and new tyres. Kemal gave us the name of a dealer in Izmir, but I am not sure we will ever find the place. With about 150 km to go, we pull into a Shell service station. I ask the people there if they know Serhat Kilavuz's shop that sells Aprilia motorcycles. They don't have any idea but are happy to help. An attendant makes a phone call to the local operator, with no luck. He then rings Kemal and gets more details before making another call. Ten minutes later the phone rings. After a lengthy conversation in Turkish, he hands the phone to me and I speak to Ömer Ölcer, who works with Serhat and speaks very good English. We arrange to meet and get tyres for the bike.

I offer to pay for the phone calls, but the service-station attendants refuse politely and wish us well on our journey across the world. What wonderful people.

We come to the outskirts of Izmir and promptly get lost. It's a city of two million people. The roads have numbers rather than names and go off in all directions. Exasperated, I pull into another service station. No-one speaks English, but one guy knows a little German. We work out we have gone too far and have to backtrack. The owner motions me to follow him. He walks up an off-ramp (against the traffic) as I follow on the bike. Shirl closes her eyes and seems to be praying, but we end up going the right way.

Shirley: We finally find Ömer at a service station and follow him back to his office, where he has some work to do. It is 5.30 p.m. before we finally get to the bike shop. We've just organised the tyres when Serhat finally arrives in his racing leathers. It turns out he was a motorcycle champion and has been practising for a race meet at the weekend. He and Ömer are very keen on the idea of Brian joining in the race on the BMW. I don't think so.

When finally the bike has two new tyres, it is time to see ancient Turkey. We are heading to Bergama and to get there we have to ride through heavy traffic on a very bad road in the dark, something we try to avoid. The road is sealed but the heavy traffic has rutted the surface, leaving holes about 30 cm deep. Brian uses the driving lights, much to the annoyance of the traffic coming in the other direction. I mention this to Brian.

'I don't care about blinding the oncoming traffic. This is all about survival,' he says.

We talk about finding somewhere to stay the night and

pressing on in the morning, but there is nothing out here. We finally get to Bergama in time for a late dinner and a couple of Turkish red wines.

Ancient Turkey is an amazing place; marble colonnades stand like sentinels against the clear skies. But no matter how hard we try, our imaginations won't kick in and bring the past to life – it is so far beyond our world. Bergama must have been a most astonishing city in its day. The 10,000-seat theatre is one of the most beautiful and unusual of ancient times. It is also one of the steepest. The walk down to the bottom looks treacherous and the walk back up would be heart stopping. Brian takes the 162 steps to the bottom, turns and says hello. I hear every word as if he were sitting next to me.

At the bottom of the hill is the Asklepieion, an ancient health resort dating back to the second century BC. This sacred place still bears the symbol of the snake and staff of Asclepius, the god of medicine. It is now the modern symbol of medicine. The Turks recognised the need to heal the soul as well as the body. Historians say the resort's small theatre, with only 3500 seats, was the scene of concerts for the patients. There is even an enormous plunge pool and a 'holy tunnel' used by the patients as protection from the cold when they came out of the healing warm waters and mud baths or as a cooling area before treatments in the hot weather.

Ancient Turkey gives way to modern Turkey when we hear a loud rumbling outside the hotel. Heading down the street are scores of tanks and armoured personnel carriers. It takes more than 15 minutes for the convoy to pass, taking hundreds of soldiers and their machinery to who knows where.

During dinner, the poverty of Turkey hits home. A small boy, no more than four or five years old, comes up to us at the hotel restaurant selling small packets of tissues. He might only be a baby in our eyes, but he picks us as English-speaking tourists and tugs at the heartstrings. 'Money. I am poor. Thank you.' It breaks my heart.

Kusadasi is the Turkish shopping experience for cruise-ship tourists who spend only a few hours in Turkey. They shop till they drop. Just a handful of them jump on the bus and head to Ephesus, which is probably the 'top of the pops' in the ancient world. From our hotel window, we watch the passing parade of ships coming and going.

In Ephesus, the remains of an ancient two-storey library are awe-inspiring. It is the image that sums up Turkey. This ancient city, which dates back to 600 BC, is mind-boggling. The fountains, temples, mosaic pathways and Odeon conjure up a once majestic life of sophistication and style. When the water dried up, the town died and the residents moved away, leaving their legacy in marble.

It is cotton-picking time and getting past the farmers taking crops to the market is an art. They overload their trailers and trucks to such an extent the cotton bales hang a metre over the edge, putting up an impenetrable shield. You can't see over them and you can't see around them. Brian veers the bike onto the wrong side of the road to get past. Once past the farmers we encounter their families. In a barren field there is a group of very grubby children running around. Their humpy village is made from heavy-duty plastic strung across poles. To keep out the chill and give them some privacy they hang kilims over the plastic. In between the makeshift homes are fires on which the old women cook in huge pots, preparing for when the men and younger women come home from the fields. It is a hard life.

The Turkish coastline has offered up many treasures and the best place to see them is the fifteenth-century Castle of St Peter in Bodrum. The museum is set up in the towers, rooms and courtyard of the castle. The main courtyard – complete with peacocks – has an incredible collection of amphoras dating back to the sixth century BC. In the chapel is a reconstruction of a Roman ship discovered off one of the islands near Bodrum in the 1950s. It is scary to think these tiny vessels sailed the wild oceans and seas. The display is so complete it even has cooking implements and the bones of small animals cooked in them. But the most amazing display is an array of glassware found on a ship that sank off the coast in 1025 BC. It is astounding that this stuff has survived through the centuries.

We've been on the road for 142 days and it is time for another holiday within our holiday. We decide to spend some time meandering along the Mediterranean coastline and lazing about in the sun before heading inland to Cappadocia. The Turkish coast is a favourite area for British tourists, who can jump on a charter flight and be here in a matter of hours. The larger coastal towns, like Marmaris, are more English than they are Turkish. There we can't find a pide shop to get a Turkish pizza, but we can get an all-day English breakfast and watch the English football live in a number of bars. Overweight men with very pale skin walk the streets with overweight women wedged into tight shorts and skimpy tops four sizes too small. Their pale skin is red-raw from the sun. We move on.

Fethiye is more to our liking. The centre of the town has a village-like atmosphere and in the heart of the waterfront area is an ancient amphitheatre. Even though it is not restored it is still incredibly majestic. We stop here for a few days enjoying the water, sun and fantastic food. The highlight of the hotel is the 'swapping library' and we stock up on new reading material.

Just down the coast is the town of Oludeniz, where people throw themselves off large cliffs strapped to the chests of almost equally large Turks. Paragliding in Turkey is something we saw on television years ago and it became a 'must do' on our tourist wish list. Our guidebook says it is a dangerous pastime and visitors should research the company they are intending to use. We get talking to the guys at one tour company, Eurogliding, about our journey before we decide on taking the tandem paraglide. They are very confident about their safety record.

'We only use very experienced pilots. They have done the jump thousands of times.'

'But we've been told it is very dangerous and people die every year,' I say with a little nervousness.

'You are riding across the world on a motorbike and you talk about dangerous . . .'

Good point. We sign up for a jump.

At Oludeniz we meet Alp, a keen biker who has travelled the world ahead of us, ending up in Australia and working on Phillip Island. Like all the bikers we've encountered, Alp is generous with his time and knowledge. He even lends us his maps of the roads through Iran and Pakistan. They are boomerangs – we'll have to return them – but will be an enormous help to us.

We have a bit of time to fill in before we fly with Eurogliding so we head to the Blue Lagoon national park beach. We pay 3 million lira to get in and park the bike. (After the vandalism in Istanbul, we now cover the bike whenever we leave it unattended.) Blue Lagoon is the most beautiful beach in Turkey. It has water of the deepest turquoise, so blue you would think it had been enhanced if you saw it on a postcard. There is no pollution here; you can see the beach's sandy bottom. The lagoon is separated from the Mediterranean Sea by a narrow beach. It is so clean we don't mind paying for the privilege of visiting it. The very fine rocks on the beach are more like sand than anything we've encountered to date. The sun is shining and the water is cool. We lie on the sand and watch the tandem gliders and single pilots soaring above us. They are just dots in the sky and then drift closer to the beach. We marvel at their grace and know we will regret it if we don't fly.

Getting to the top of the mountain is the hardest part. We are loaded into an open truck with all the parachutes packed on the roof – along with some of the pilots. The drive to the top is scary. The twisting road is more like a track, complete with potholes and boulders to avoid. There is no way I'll back out of jumping. I couldn't imagine coming back down in this truck voluntarily.

We stop at 1800 m. Because the wind is so strong, we won't be making the climb to the highest outcrop 200 m above us. There is no time to muck around. The wind is making things difficult and there are so many people wanting to fly we have to be quick. The tandem jumpers – that's us – will go first, followed by the solo jumpers. There is no time to change our minds now. Our pilots give us very unattractive boiler suits, helmets and a harness. My pilot, Gonay, is barking orders: 'Just stand up and don't fall backwards when the wind takes the chute. Don't hold on to anything and don't sit down.' It all seems like a lot to remember. The wind is really blustering and I can't help but wonder what the hell I am doing here. I look over to Brian and he is deep in concentration, listening to his pre-flight briefing. A Frenchman stands in front of me to help my pilot. He has orders of his own to give: 'When you take off don't grab on to me.'

I almost laugh at the thought of the three of us taking off with me clutching the Frenchman's suit!

At the first attempt to lift off, we are pushed backwards. Within a minute or two we are in the air and soaring upwards. Gonay tightens my harness and I sit back in his lap. I begin to relax almost immediately. Once we are up in the air he takes my helmet off and clips it to the harness. 'You won't need this,' he says, 'and to be honest if something happens up here the helmet won't help you at all.'

The feeling of freedom is amazing. We sail above the water and the town, and can see Fethiye and the island of Rhodes across the water. It is the most incredible thing I have ever done. I can't believe I am up so high, yet I don't feel scared. Gonay shows me how to steer the sail, pulling down with one hand to make us turn left and the other to make us turn right. All the while he is videoing and talking to me. We can see Brian and his pilot way across the bay. There is only the sound of the wind and Gonay's voice. When we begin to head to the beach Gonay asks if I would like to spiral. I am not sure, but what the heck, I'm here, I may as well. We turn and turn. I don't know how many times but it seems like a few and it's fast. The 'G' forces push me back into the harness and the wind rushing past my ears hurts, but it is great. I scream and at the end use that familiar expression: 'Oh shit!'

We come in to land just behind Brian on the beach and people scurry to get out of our way. In two steps we are stationary. Twenty-five minutes has passed like seconds and I can't wipe the smile off my face. I would do it again in a minute! What a blast!

From the skies above Turkey we head to the Dalyan Delta, the river where *The African Queen* was filmed. Floating past the reeds, we expect to see Mr Allnut and Rose appear. The boat trip takes us from the ridiculous to the sublime: first stop the mud baths, second stop the Lycian tombs carved into a rock face around 400 BC.

At the mud baths you pay for the privilege of covering yourself in stinky mud, letting it dry to a hard crust and then washing it off under cold running water. While it seems disgusting, there is a certain amount of fun involved. Brian gets right into the swing of it and covers himself from head to toe before turning his attention to me. The covering is the easy part. The washing off is harder. It takes some scrubbing and a concerted effort to end up white again.

Back on the boat, we cruise through the delta to the Lycian rock tombs. They are from the ancient city of Caunos and date back to between 900 and 400 BC. The townspeople abandoned their city when the mosquito plague brought with it malaria, stopping traders from coming. The wealthy carved temple-like tombs into the rock face. The bodies were placed inside and the tombs sealed off until the next member of the family died. Tombs for the middle-class were shaped more like houses, while the working class had rectangular tombs with no elaborate markings.

We have stayed in Fethiye for four days and we only planned to stay for two. Now it is time to move on, but first we must check out Kayakoy, a ghost town a few kilometres away. This was once a bustling settlement inhabited by Greeks. In 1923 the Greek and Turkish governments organised an exchange of nationals, sending Greek nationals back to Greece and bringing Turks back to Turkey. After the Greek people from Kayakoy went back to Greece no Turks moved into their homes – the town was left to fall into ruin. It is an eerie place.

We take the twisty road along the coast to Kas and find ourselves a waterfront room at a hotel with a private 'beach' – really just a concrete platform built over rocks with an old, slippery ladder into surprisingly chilly Mediterranean waters. The restaurant and bar are on the top of the cliff.

Kas is not a tourist haven, which is great. We wander the streets and check out the stalls in the bazaar without being hassled. Everything is reasonably priced, except for a day-old copy of *The London Times* which, at 8 million lira, is incredibly expensive, but I am hankering for a newspaper.

At the back of the local school there is a nest of mausoleums cut into the cliffs. Taking what looks like a public pathway through private gardens, we can clamber up the rocks and look inside. A rock-slab bench where the dead were laid to rest is the only thing in the tomb. The intricate designs carved onto the outer wall have stood through the centuries. It is fascinating to see this piece of history up close.

Back at the hotel, the chef puts on a special treat for dinner – leg of lamb cooked for eight hours with peppers, beans and other vegetables, and flavoured with garlic, thyme and rosemary. We can't resist this and it is as good as we expect. The meat just falls off the bone. Served with a good local wine, it makes an excellent meal. The table is decorated with garlands of flowers and candles. We share it with two girls from the Netherlands (not Holland, as they are quick to point out) and Malcolm, a Scot who arrives with a bottle of single malt and a guitar.

After one of the best meals we have had on the road, we sip Scotch and sing along to Malcolm's renditions of songs of the sixties. As the evening should be drawing to a close, the Turkish staff takes over the music selection, and while we should be sleeping we dance to traditional Turkish music and share lots of laughs. And when you dance to Turkish music, you must have a sip or two of raki.

Little wonder we are both a bit foggy and slow to get

started when it is time to move on in the morning. Everyone turns out to say goodbye, and there are lots of hugs and kisses. Well, not quite everyone. One of the girls from the Netherlands is in her bed, nursing a very sore head. Apparently, the last raki was the one that did the damage.

Brian: The coastal road from here on is nothing short of spectacular. Think of the Great Ocean Road in Victoria, the really twisty bits, multiply the distance and corners by about 20 and you have something close to it. The corners that hug the coast are neverending. There are no safety barriers and in places the asphalt is laid right to the edge of the cliff. We have to be careful and hang wide on blind corners. The road is narrow and tour buses ply their trade here, with more than one liking both sides of the road. I signal to one to get back on his own side of the road. He returns the gesture with the time-honoured one-finger salute. Might is right in this part of the world, so he wins – and doesn't bother moving over. If we had been in a car, it would have resulted in a head-on collision, or, with evasive action, a flight over the edge to the sea below.

Shirley: It is time to turn away from the coast and head inland to the Goreme Valley in Cappadocia. Coming down a hill, we see a *Polis Trafik Kontrol* point. We get waved in. We expect them to check our papers and the carnet for the bike and then wave us on. Not today. The very officious policeman tells us we were speeding. 'Do you know,' he says in a very thick accent, 'you were doing 87 kilometres?'

'But it is a 90-kilometre zone,' Brian says.

'Yes, and you were doing 87 kilometres – that is a 64-million-700-thousand-lira fine.'

'But it is a 90-kilometre zone.'

'Yes, and you were doing 87 kilometres'.

This conversation is getting us nowhere. Eventually we work out that motorcycles actually have to travel at 20 km/h less than the posted speed limit. This is the first we've heard of it. When we crossed the border from Greece, we were told the speed limits were 50 km/h in towns, 90 km/h on the roads and 120 on the freeways. Brian does his best to explain this, but the police just keep quoting the road rules. They are interested that he is a policeman in Australia, but don't see that as a reason for leniency. There is no way we are going to get out of this one. After arguing the point to no effect, we hand over 65 million and don't get any change, but we do get a receipt. Lesson learned.

Brian: We hate riding at night, particularly here, where the drivers don't bother turning their lights on. Night also brings with it the slow-moving tractors and huge trailers piled high with produce. Most have no lights and in the fading light, meeting one travelling in either direction could prove fatal. Cars, trucks and buses regularly swerve violently onto the wrong side of the road to avoid the tractors and, being the smallest thing on the road, motorcycles are expected just to get out of the way. Being in the right and dead is no consolation, so I hug the jagged shoulder of the road.

We decide to try the town of Nigde for a bed for the night and leave the remaining 80 km until the morning. Towns in Turkey are usually big and Nigde is no exception, the sign declaring it has a population of 47,900. It's also dirty and for the first time kids run along beside us, shouting, 'Money, money' as they hold out their hands. I don't like the idea of trying to hunt down reasonable accommodation here, so we decide to push on.

Light is fading fast and I am once again thankful for the

driving lights. I just manage to dodge a large sack of something on the road, which could have had disastrous results for us. Oncoming trucks are regularly trying to overtake each other and more than once I have to hold the lights on full beam to get them to pull over and give us enough room to get past. Cresting a rise with a right-hand bend in it, I see what looks like two trucks bearing down on us on our side of the road. I feel Shirl tense up and hear her scream, 'Oh shit!' I brake hard and prepare to take my chances off the road before realising that it is just a trick of the light – the road turned and the trucks hadn't been heading towards us.

Shirley: Volcanic eruptions centuries ago created Cappadocia and the Goreme Valley. Wind and rain have eroded the volcanic tufa, leaving the most amazing towers of rock. Some, dubbed 'fairy chimneys', have boulders perched precariously on top. Christian communities made these rocks their homes, carving churches and living areas into the soft rock.

For centuries many people lived here to avoid religious persecution. Underground cities were home to thousands, living underground with their animals. Today, the elaborately decorated churches and homes comprise an outdoor museum.

We stay in a motel built into caves. Our bed is in an alcove that was once a church and the bathroom is also hewn out of rock. It is unique but just a little cold at this time of the year. The owner doesn't seem to think he should turn on the heating system yet. He's not cold. No wonder – he spends all day in the office crouched in front of the electric heater!

A walk in Pigeon Valley takes us through a lush vale filled with ageing fruit trees and grapevines. The walking track leads us up and over hills, clambering most of the way.

We find gaps in the rocks that lead us to the caves. They appear too small to have been homes, but there are stone ledges inside that make them a perfect spot to sit a while and look down on the valley.

Swords Valley must once have been home to a large community. There are churches with fading frescoes, burial chambers and homes. We haven't walked more than a couple of steps into the valley when a man appears from nowhere and begins showing us around. He beckons for us to follow him and takes us to wonderful churches and incredible land formations that resemble animals carved by Mother Nature. When we indicate we have no money, he loses interest and wanders off to find some other unsuspecting tourists. He must be used to rejection if he tries to abduct tourists off the pathway.

The Rose Valley is a little further away and we take the bike. The sandy soil makes it a bit of a rally. We ride it for a few kilometres, slipping and sliding along the track before we find a church carved into the rock – just at the point where the track gives out! We climb into the cave and find wonderful frescoes painted on the walls and an incredible carving of a religious symbol in the ceiling. It is the most wonderful sight. Unfortunately, some of the visitors over the years have carved their names over the pictures of the saints, but on the whole it is incredibly well preserved – and free.

The owners of Chez Galip in Avanos, the home of pottery in Cappadocia, have a most unusual collection in their back room – hair. Thousands of long and short tresses are pinned to the walls and ceiling of a cavernous room at least 6 m long. I have to add my tresses to the collection. Each year they select 10 locks off the wall and put them into a draw. The winner gets a 10-day holiday in Cappadocia. They have to make their own way to Turkey, of course.

We get an email from Alp, the biker we met in Oludeniz. He apologises for not mentioning the fact that the speed limit for bikes is indeed 70 km/h. He has some sound advice for travellers: 'Don't pay any fines. Just get the pink slip, which says you must pay in 10 days, and then don't pay. Just leave the country.'

The restaurants of Goreme have a local speciality – the pottery kebab. Meat, vegetables and herbs are cooked slowly in a pottery jug sealed with bread. After about 20 minutes the burnt bread is removed and the delicious stew tipped onto your plate. Served with the local wine made from grapes grown in the fertile volcanic soil and a yoghurt dip, it is a taste sensation that is right up there with Turkish tomatoes, pide and lamb!

There aren't many things worth getting out of a warm bed for at three on a cold morning, but the stone monuments on top of Nemrut Daği (Mount Nimrod) are. Dawn and dusk are the best times to see the massive heads and bodies created by a megalomaniac King Antiochus.

We hit the road to Mount Nimrod, and what a road it is. First, it is just tight and twisty through a couple of very small towns. Then it becomes steep, tight and twisty and full of potholes. Finally it is steep, tight, twisty and made from uneven basalt pavers. The road is narrow and falls away to very steep valleys. In the dark it is a bit of a nightmare. Can't imagine what it would have been like on the bike. Yes, we have to admit that we took the soft option – the tourist bus.

It is freezing when we get to the top of the road. We huddle in the cafeteria waiting to begin the climb to the summit and I am obviously looking like a frozen waif. The owner goes to his home and gets me a warm blanket. Brian thinks this is ridiculous, but is happy to share the blanket.

The pathway to the 2150 m summit is rough with very loose stones and, in part, very steep. I am breathing hard as I am so unfit after five months of virtually doing nothing but sitting on the back of the bike! Brian strides out enjoying the bracing air and exercise. There are times I could hit him!

At first it seems like it is going to be a fizzer. It is freezing and we both huddle under the blanket waiting and waiting and waiting. Dawn breaks and we see the statues in the awesome beauty of first light. Then, slowly the sun appears and it is a truly wonderful experience. King Antiochus built a 50 m high rock tomb and then placed huge rock statues of himself and the gods around the base. He thought so much of himself, he considered the gods his relatives. The statues depict Apollo, Hermes, Fortuna, Zeus, King Antiochus and then Heracles. There are also eagles and lions. Over the centuries, the heads have toppled from their original positions atop bodies seated on thrones. On the eastern temple, the heads stand below their bodies and the bodies are pretty much intact. The sun shining on the statues gives an eerie light – all well worth the lack of sleep and the long trek to the summit.

There are times you just wish you weren't Australian – like the morning we meet a guide, Sahin, used by Mike Ferris, an Australian running motorcycle tours to Turkey. We check out of the hotel near Mt Nimrod and Sahin asks Brian if he knows Mike. They discuss motorcycle travel for a few minutes, but Sahin's tourists are keen to get going and so are we. As a parting gesture, Sahin repeats a favourite expression learned from Mike: 'No Wucken Furries.' Ferris has a lot to answer for.

Our time in Turkey is coming to an end. Our journey is now taking us to the east, towards Iran. To get there we must cross the Tigris River. The 'feribot' is a dilapidated flat-top hulk with a ramp of sorts winched by hand. There's a wheelhouse and an open deck for passengers on foot and that's about it.

We have to wait while the buses and trucks load on. Then the cars reverse up the ramp. Each of the bigger vehicles threatens to tip the boat over at the front. The feribot is well settled in the water and there is very little room for the bike. Brian eventually gets a run up and bounces along the ramp, scattering curious passengers. We are perched so close to the edge they can only wind up the ramp about 15 cm. We cross our fingers and set sail across the lake.

Thank God there is no swell or we would be knee-deep in water. Brian can't get off the bike, so he sits there balancing it. When the ferry docks, with the help of some passengers we push the bike back off the ramp and head on the road for Siverek. Here the landscape is incredibly barren, like a moonscape with huge boulders scattered about and not a tree or shrub in sight. We do, however, see shepherds tending flocks of sheep and goats and cattle eating goodness knows what. There are no fences and they all wander aimlessly across the road – humans included.

Dotted through this inhospitable landscape are rock walls that look like housing without roofs. We watch a shepherd stringing plastic over some walls to form a temporary roof. It's ingenious and so suited to the nomadic lifestyle.

The outskirts of Siverek give us another surprise. There are piles and piles of 'fresh' manure on the road being moistened with water. Village women dunk them in a bucket and shape them into rounds and set them in the sun to dry. The finished product is piled high all around. Brian and I presume it will be used as fuel for their fires.

We are now fairly close to the Syrian border. There is a

constant buzz of fighter jets above us. Their engines whine in protest as they simulate low-level runs and what look like dogfights. The closer we get to the border, the more military activity there is on the roads and in the sky. And here in the east the Muslims are more devout. We pass a small van pulled up on the side of the road with the doors open. Three men are praying in the nearby field.

We didn't intend to go to Hasankeyf, but fate seems to have brought us here. We are first told about it by the manager at ANZAC House in Canakkale. Alp tells us it is a must-see and an elderly woman at dinner the night before said her guide insisted on taking her to see it. When the police advise us to go, we decide this is an omen. We are close (and have taken a slightly wrong turn to get this close), so we should go. This is confirmed in the town of Batman (yes, Batman). We ask the police for directions, but when we come to the end of the road we seem to be off track, so we ask another carload of police. The young driver starts to explain in Turkish with sign language when the boss in the back says something. The driver then grins and makes some more gestures. When I ask if he wants us to follow him, he says, 'Yes – follow me!' He then leads us through the back streets and marketplaces of Batman and on to the road to Hasankeyf. He pulls over and we pull up alongside. 'Go straight for 30 kilometres to Hasankeyf,' he says. The boss in the back even writes down the name of the town and '30 km' on a piece of paper and hands it to us. Now we know we are meant to go to Hasankeyf.

The road there winds its way alongside the Tigris River. The trucks beep their horns as we pass. A young man on a smoky two-stroke with a huge sidecar smiles and waves as we come up behind him. It is a fun ride and everything is right with the world. Then we see the ruins of a castle perched high on a cliff above the river and an old tomb on the riverbank. As we cross the river into the town we can see where people once lived in the rock caves, and we spot the remains of an ancient stone bridge.

We end up on the riverbank under the towering cliff and castle. On the river is a cafe with dining platforms over the water. These are decked out with carpets and huge cushions. Brian and I decide we must stop here. We take off our boots and stretch out on the carpet, propped up by the pillows. The sound of the river rushing below is very soothing. It lulls us both into a light snooze after a delicious meal of local river fish and it isn't long before Brian is snoring in the dappled sunlight. It is a blissful place to stop and take a break from the road, but we opt to move on after lunch.

The military presence is increasing the further east we head. Every 500 m or so there are concrete blockhouses decked out in camouflage with one or two soldiers on guard. They all watch with interest as we ride by. And there are tanks on the road. We pass about a dozen during the afternoon. On the last stage of our journey for the day – Baykan to Bitlis, the main road to the Iraqi border – we come across at least 20 jeeps filled with soldiers. They watch as we ride up behind them. As we get close, they react to Brian's big smile, and by the time we pass most wave and smile back. They all have such young faces. Turkish boys are only 20 when they do their 15 months of national service.

We ride into Bitlis, which has a star on our map indicating a town of interest. It is incredibly busy and dirty. I have my visor open and Brian tells me to close it. We are riding through the business area of the town, and among the hundreds of men on the street there are only a handful of women. We are creating more than a bit of interest.

We continue on to Tatvan on the banks of Lake Van. It is getting dark and we are going no further. We find a three-star hotel in a side street. Rather than do a U-turn to return to the side street, Brian pushes the bike back.

Brian: As I walk the bike backwards the ground slopes away on the left and I lean the bike into the gradient on the right. When my foot disappears down a drain, which has had its metal grate removed, the weight of the bike takes over and I have no chance of keeping it upright. Fearing a broken leg, I kick my foot out, collecting Shirl on the shin as she falls off the back.

Shirl's up on her feet picking up the pannier. I know she's all right. I don't only care about the bike!

I pick the bike up and there is no damage to speak of. The right-hand pannier has sprung off its mount, the crash bars have protected the engine and the handlebars didn't even touch the ground. I remount the pannier and get angry as I look at the grate with its gaping holes. In the dark, dimly lit street I had no chance, but still chastise myself for not being careful enough. I hate dropping a bike in any circumstances and have gone 10 years or more without doing it, while on this trip it has been dropped three times.

Shirley: There is a magnificent egg growing on my shin – my worst injury to date! Brian is very worried, but I am fine. Mind you, he really shouldn't throw me to the ground and then kick me while I am down!

Before we head to the border town of Doğubeyazit, we must get to the post office and send home a rug, pottery and other odds and ends we've collected.

This has to be Brian's job, as this country is a man's territory. He speaks to one man, and then another, who seems to be the boss, comes up. They decide it will be okay.

A third man approaches. He drags out manila folders filled with photocopied letters and begins flicking through them. He seems to be looking up the rate for postage to Australia. Now it is time to make sure we are not exporting anything we shouldn't be. The rug and scarf are unwrapped. They are okay. They eye off the mini-tripod for the camera Nikos gave us, so Brian opens it and demonstrates how it works. We can't get it to close again! Then they try to work out the pottery. We say 'pottery' and 'Cappadocia' and eventually they give this the go-ahead after we hold the packets up to the light. Now there is the plastic bag of receipts, a booklet from customs and some photos. One of the men goes through every receipt separately, opens the CD and gives this the okay.

Now the fun begins. They fold up the rug and the scarf and jam them into the plastic bag. They go to put the pottery on the top, but Brian convinces them to put it in the middle. This all then goes into a white canvas sack. The two men get string and tie the sack up. They tie the neck about 10 centimetres above that. They get a pointed screwdriver-type instrument and stick that through the canvas and pull one piece of string through this and then pull it through again. A metal tag is placed on the parcel to make sure it isn't opened along the way. All very ingenious, I must say. When it comes to paying we discover air mail is the only option, so we are 38 million lira poorer for the experience.

Outside our hotel a small boy tries to raise money by weighing people on his ancient bathroom scales. What he clearly doesn't realise is that women don't want to be weighed in public and certainly not when they are wearing bike gear and boots! We give the small boy some fruit. He glances around furtively to make sure no-one is watching and then runs away, presumably to eat it.

Riding along the shores of Lake Van, the scenery is spectacular. For the first time we see green pastures with goats and sheep grazing well off the roadway. The leaves of poplar trees are showing the colours of autumn. We glimpse Mount Ararat with its snow-capped peak across the lake and stop to take a picture.

We climb up into the mountains and it gets colder. I don't even bother asking Brian to stop, because I know once he is riding there is no stopping for something as stupid as putting on extra clothes. As we ride higher, we see Mount Ararat close-up for the first time. It is massive. The guidebooks tell us it's 5137 m and the peak is usually obscured by cloud. We are obviously blessed today, because the sky is as clear as a bell and the most amazing shade of blue.

Brian: I am surprised to see villages up here. They look very poor, but the people all wave and give us big smiles. I see a small boy running along the road without shoes or pants and with not a care in the world. They must be a tough breed.

Shirley: There aren't too many reasons to stop at Doğubeyazit. However, it's a handy rest stop before crossing the border into Iran and it is our last chance for an alcoholic drink for a while. The shops sell fetching coats suitable for Western women venturing into the land of the hijab but best of all there is Ishak Pasa Sarayi, the partly restored palace of an eighteenth-century Kurdish chieftain. It once boasted 366 rooms, and is still impressive today. The doors and door frames are adorned with intricate carvings and Persian script. There is a mosque inside the palace with frescoes still clear on the dome, and the chains that once held lights still hang from the ceiling. Many pigeons have taken up residence in this room but they don't detract from the beauty. The library that leads into the mosque is also amazing, with decorative carvings, and recessed shelving. You can stand in the fireplace, it is so enormous. Throughout the palace are more fireplaces, and nooks and crannies bedecked with carved stone. The dining hall is incredible, with columns, archways and carvings. It no longer has a roof, but it takes little imagination to see what it would have looked like in its heyday.

When we walk outside, a minibus filled with young Turkish students pulls up. They say hello and then two of the girls whisper to each other. They come back and ask me my name and where I am from. Then the real reason for their interest emerges: they want their photo taken with the bike. Brian is delighted and before he can get off they are trying to clamber on. He is swamped by young, beautiful Turkish women and some young men all keen to be photographed with the world traveller. I get dragged in for a photo amid lots of smiles and laughs.

We ride down the hill and see a bike with Touratech panniers and two four-wheel drives parked in a camping ground. We pull in to say hello. There is a friendly face among the crowd – Dean the hippie we met at the Turkish border. There is a couple from the Netherlands travelling to Iran and a German couple on their way home. The bike looks like a BMW 80GS that has done 400,000 km. It's owned by a young man from Singapore, Max Ng. This is quite the world travellers' meeting. We all chat about where we are going and where we have been, and swap English novels with the Dutch couple and Dean – a three-way swap that gives us two new books to replace the two we have each read!

Brian: Max is an interesting guy, who spent 12 years in the Singaporean Navy before beginning his round-the-world motorcycle journey. He has basically come through Nepal, India, Pakistan and Iran, the reverse of what we are doing. The left side of his bike is damaged. He tells us that on the stretch of road near Quetta in Pakistan there are bandits, and he believes guys on motorcycles were chasing him there so he took off. He got away, but kept going hard and lost the front end on a bad stretch of road. I'm not worried about the road, but the bandit story is a concern. Still, there is no other way – we have to go through Quetta. Dean also tells us that Quetta is lawless, with everyone carrying weapons, mainly Russian AK47s.

We meet Max for dinner and he brings along another traveller, Pek, a Finnish PhD student. We have a great discussion on travelling in this part of the world, and comparing notes. Max offers us an Iranian map he'd been given by two Germans he met in Pakistan. They didn't need it any more. He felt it was only fair to pass it on to us, as he too no longer needed it.

We have enjoyed Turkey immensely, having explored new sights and reacquainted ourselves with old ones. This land is much misunderstood by travellers too frightened to venture out of their comfort zone. We found the people friendly and accommodating, the sights spectacular, and the country's opportunities seem to be endless. I hope the people achieve their aim of joining the EU – it may be the first breaking-down of that invisible barrier between East and West, Christian and Muslim.

Now the real adventure begins. With scarf and coat, we head off into Iran.

Pergamon

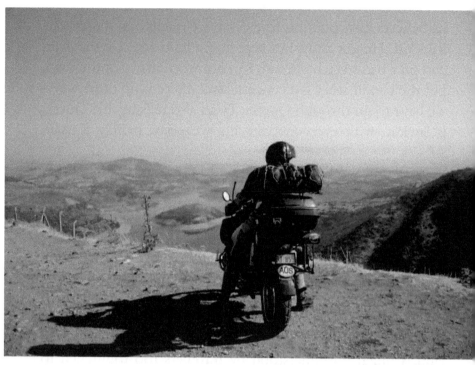

Spice bazaar, Istanbul

Getting my boots cleaned in Istanb

esus

Gallipoli

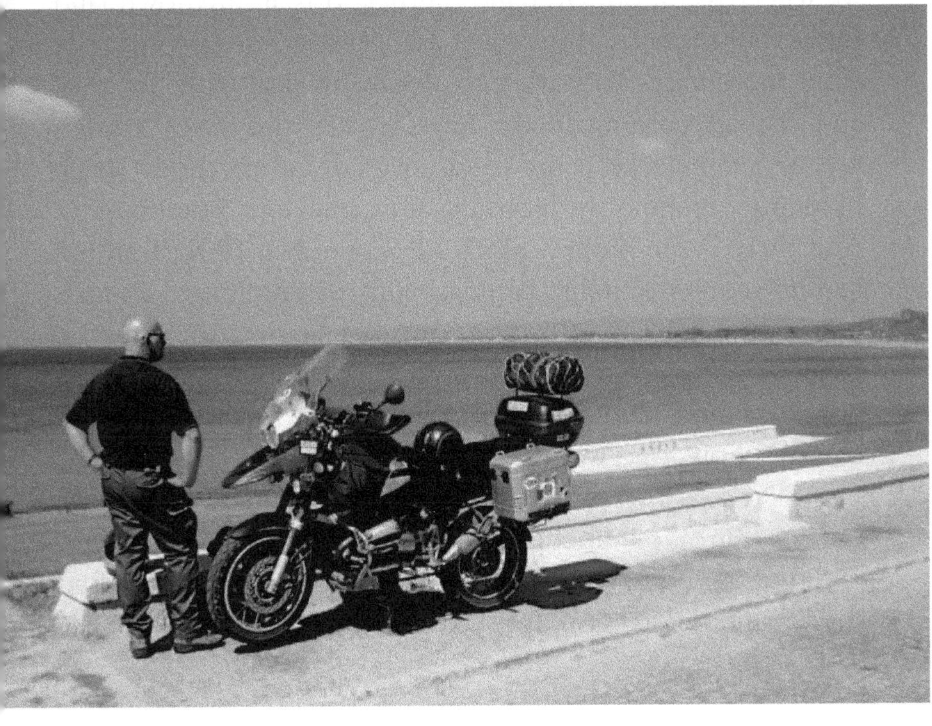

TEN

IRAN

25 October – 7 November 2003

Shirley: We presume Iran won't be the easiest of countries we will cross on our overland journey. It is an unknown land for us, but there are differences and problems we are aware of from the outset. To start with, I have to deal with the scarf and coat. According to the hijab laws of this strict Muslim country, I must keep my head covered and my body shape hidden every time we leave the privacy of our hotel rooms. And there is the money. Since 11 September 2001, Iran has had no access to foreign bank accounts or credit card companies. You can't get cash from an ATM or over the counter. When we cross into Iran we must have enough US cash for our time there. Not knowing exactly how much things will cost and how long we will stay makes this a bit difficult.

The iron gates at the border close behind us and we are now in Iran. We immediately feel isolated. We are apprehensive, but soon realise there is really no need. We don't find suspicion or aggression, just friendly, helpful officials. But the same can't be said for some of the locals. I encounter my first case of 'invisibility' at the passport-control counter, when several Turkish and Iranian truck drivers push in front of me and show their documents to the official. The fact I was there first means nothing to them. I am foreign and I am a woman. The official makes my day when he waves the men aside and takes my passport. I feel like giving the truckies the finger, but I subdue the urge just as I subdue the desire to gush a huge 'thank you' to the official. I simply give him a smile instead.

The 'can't do enough for the foreigners' attitude continues. A young Iranian official takes us through the back door, past 20 or 30 truckies, to the customs hall where two officials rouse themselves from their slumber and check out our paperwork before directing us to another room. Inside, an official has a tray piled high with carnets – this doesn't look good. It seems we will be here forever, but he stops what he is doing and processes our paperwork. Within a couple of minutes the carnet is stamped and we and the bike are in.

We try exchanging our money at the bank to the side of the customs hall. Here, only US dollars are exchanged and, after giving us the correct exchange rate with no commission, the teller points Brian (not me, because I don't exist in the eyes of men in this country) towards an eager-looking money-changer standing outside the glass doors.

The exchange goes something like this:

Brian: 'How much for 60 million lira to rial?'

Money-changer: 'Two-hundred and seventy thousand.'

Brian: 'No – 300,000.'

Money-changer: 'Two-hundred and seventy thousand and I keep the rest for business.'

Brian: 'No – 300,000.'

Money-changer: 'Two-hundred and eighty thousand and I keep the rest for business.'

Brian: 'No – 300,000.'

Money-changer: 'Two-hundred and ninety thousand?'

Brian: 'No – 300,000 or no deal.'

Money-changer: 'But this way I make no money. It is not possible.'

Brian: 'No – 300,000.'

As he counts out the 300,000, the money-changer grumbles something under his breath in what we presume is Farsi. At this point a huge smile breaks out on his face. 'Welcome to Iran,' he says.

Well, I'll be buggered. It is all a game. He knows he made money on the exchange and we know he has made money on the exchange.

The paperwork is in order and we have loads of cash, but before we ride off there is a final warning from a very young, handsome Iranian official: 'You don't have any alcohol with you, do you? Alcohol is illegal in Iran.'

Brian: Riding through the Iranian countryside, we notice the air is thick with diesel. You can smell it, you can see brown-black smog hanging in the air, and you can taste it. This will be with us for months to come. There don't appear to be any rules about pollution or a high level of vehicle maintenance. We soon learn that at the end of the day, it doesn't matter how many times you wash your face, you will still wipe grey scum onto the towel.

On the open road we discover the trucks that are spewing out this putrid black smoke have a particular fascination with our side of the road. It seems to be preferable to their own. The trucks travel downhill at one speed: flat out. You'd think they'd be able to service their vehicles when you realise how cheap petrol is. For 15 L of fuel, we pay 9700 rial – about 7c a litre, which is less than $2 to fill the tank!

Shirley: Now we ride to Tabriz to meet Alec Simpson, an Aussie biker we've met over the Internet. It is an incredibly small world. Alec lives about a 15-minute drive from our home in Melbourne and his bike is serviced by Phil Marshall, our mechanic. We'd never met in Melbourne and we are planning to meet him in Iran. Alec's staying at the Morvarid Hotel at just 100,000 rial a night (a bit less than $20). Our guidebook says it's one star, has a Western toilet but no toilet paper, black-and-white television with two local channels, and we can keep the bike in the foyer. We take it.

We then take our lives in our hands and cross the major road outside the hotel to head to the bazaar. We don't expect the amount of traffic, but we shouldn't be surprised. Tabriz is a major city with a population of about two million. Women swathed in black from head to toe hitch up their chadors and straddle the pillion seats of scooters. There is no such thing as two-up here. We see families with two and three kids on these tiny scooters. Mum and Dad on the seat with a toddler standing in front of, or on, the tank and another small child in between the parents. And Mum might have a babe in her arms. No helmets, no protective clothing. We are gobsmacked. The locals seem oblivious to any dangers.

Tabriz is a thoroughly modern city with shops selling all the modern consumables – videos, televisions, fridges and the like. The clothing shops seem to specialise in the long, flowing coat and chador required by hijab law. There must be places for women to buy Western clothes to wear under their black garb, but we don't see them.

There are huge signs promoting Mecca Cola, a Muslim drink to keep the infidel's drink of choice out of the country.

Everyone stares. Foreigners are obviously a rarity these days. They stare at Brian because he has no hair (men here don't seem to lose their hair) and they stare at me because I have some hair showing and I'm not wearing black. And sometimes I am showing far too much hair. I am having a constant battle with the scarf and it is winning. You really need a Muslim mother to teach you how to deal with the head gear successfully! By the time we get back to the hotel I am heartily sick of being stared at. Brian is trying to be comforting and considerate, but I can see it is annoying him too.

In Australia, when we meet a new friend we adjourn to a pub or cafe. Not in Tabriz. When we catch up with Alec we sit in the hotel foyer sipping cups of tea. He is more than a little disappointed that we didn't meet in Turkey where we could have been drinking cold beers and reasonable local wines rather than tea. He has had an amazing journey. He shipped his bike to Amsterdam and then rode through the old Soviet Union to Iran. He is off to Turkey tomorrow.

Soon we will have to get used to Ramadan, the month of Muslim fasting, but the mullahs (the Muslim clerics who interpret the laws) haven't announced the exact starting time, so we can eat breakfast out at Alec's favourite restaurant. Spicy meat kebab with pickles and tomato on a roll about the size of half a loaf of bread with a bottle of Mecca Cola is not our usual breakfast, but there is no denying it is extremely tasty. Brian shouts breakfast, and it's about $2.50 for the three of us!

Back at the hotel Alec hands over a traveller's favourite gift: a roll of toilet paper. He is heading into Turkey, the land of Western toilets and toilet paper. We are heading east into the lands of squat toilets and no toilet paper. We appreciate this generosity.

When it's time to push the bikes out of the hotel foyer, a small crowd gathers outside. A farewell kiss and hug with Alec elicits a noticeable intake of breath from the crowd. I'm going to have to get used to the lack of public displays of affection in this part of the world.

We head out of town with Alec, wave him farewell and promptly get lost. We are heading to the Caspian Sea, but there are no signs and we need to fuel up. There is not a petrol station in sight as the suburbs give way to desert. The wind has picked up and there are a few spots of rain turning the swirling dust to mud in the air. Our solution is to head back into town for fuel and start the journey all over again. And once more we head out of town in the wrong direction, towards Turkey (wishful thinking!). When we stop on the side of the road a truckie offers to help. Yep, we are heading in the wrong direction. Back in Tabriz we are still bushed. Sitting on a plantation in the middle of a roundabout, a family is having a picnic lunch. (It seems a very Iranian thing to do – the locals take advantage of any green space they can find.) The woman is reluctant to help us, but her sons come over to the bike. While we are talking to them a group of men come to see what we are discussing. Brian squeezes my leg as we listen without understanding to the boys and men discuss where we are heading. They are pointing in different directions and seem to be arguing the point among themselves. When they finally decide on which way we should go, their directions see us heading back the way we came. To cut a very long story short, over the next hour or so we stop to get directions from at least five or six groups of people, all of whom are very helpful. Each time we seem to move further away from the centre of the city without finding the road we need. Brian's temper is getting frayed. We didn't leave Tabriz until nearly lunchtime, the afternoon is passing and we are still on the outskirts of Tabriz. I don't have to see his face to know he is angry; I can feel it through his back. Four people come up to offer help. It seems we are just around the corner from the road we need. Brian cuts through a pedestrian crossing and we head off, finally seeing a road sign for the first time!

Brian: The road is pretty bad and the Iranian drivers are even worse than those in Turkey. We ride through more dust storms and I have to wipe the grime off my visor so I can see. We ride over rutted and potholed roads, but worst of all are the kamikaze drivers. The reality of just how bloody awful these drivers are comes to us on a reasonably straight stretch of road at the bottom of a hill: car into truck, head on. The car is wedged under the truck and it is hard to imagine the people getting out of the car alive. If they did they would have had horrendous leg injuries. From the tyre marks, it is clear they were on the wrong side of the road. Apparently, 20,000 Iranians die on the roads each year. The drivers are often on the wrong side of the road and think nothing of forcing us to the very edge as they cruise along taking the whole road as their own. In the towns and cities, they just pull out in front of you without even looking. I have to have my wits about me every step of the way. The roads and the drivers are lethal. Alec's words come to mind: 'The drivers are so bad they stop me from enjoying the good roads. You never go into a corner without wondering what will be in front of you.'

And just when we begin to think things can't get any worse, the rain starts and night falls. This adds another interesting dimension to the traffic – Iranian drivers don't bother with lights! If they use them at all, it is just as parking lights. The only time they flash their lights is when they are on our side of the road and want to warn us to get out of their way! It is hard to believe that truckies would drive on the open road without lights.

Shirley: Ramadan has begun. At breakfast the curtains are drawn across the windows in the restaurant, so devout Muslims can't see those of us who have chosen to eat breakfast at the usual time rather than getting up before dawn.

The storm has blown over, so we stick to our plan and head to the sea. Not far out of town we come to the top of a mountain range. It is bright sunshine up there and we can see clouds below. The road is twisty, slippery and shrouded in fog. We creep along, making our way down the mountains. Luckily, the kamikaze drivers must be having a sleep in, because we don't encounter anyone coming the other way through the fog. Then a car drives up alongside us to pass. Its occupants give us a toot and a thumbs up. A few kilometres down the road we pass them and then they drive alongside us again. This time the front-seat passenger videos us! This sign of friendship is a fillip to our flagging spirits.

Ghazvin is famous for the Emămzădé-yé Hussein mausoleum, covered in polychrome tiles, so we ride out to see it on our way from town.

I've never seen anything like it. Its coloured and mirrored tiles make it seem surreal. Even though I am absorbed by the sight of the mausoleum, a group of about 20 women catches my eye. Nearby, men are milling around the back of a van. They pull out a green box – a quick double-take shows that it is a coffin. Some of the men hoist the coffin onto their shoulders and walk towards the mausoleum. They chant prayers while the women walk silently behind. I follow them through the gate trying my best to be discreet, but it is very difficult, as I stand out in my bike gear and scarf. I keep my distance and continue to stand in awe before this incredible building. Aside from the front being covered in the tiles that shine like mirrors, chandeliers hang from the ceiling. I have to walk past the funeral to get to the doors so I err on the side of caution, and take some photos and leave under the watchful eye of a Muslim cleric and his friend.

Brian: I don't share Shirl's fascination with funerals, and I'm not that keen on leaving the bike. The crowd grows, men and boys interested in looking at me and my vehicle.

The local police turn up and push their way through the crowd to see what is so interesting. They ask for my passport and then ask the strangest question: 'Are you a Muslim?' I've been told that the Iranians don't expect everyone to be Muslim but like it if you say you believe in God. Rather than give offence, I tell them I am not a Muslim but I do believe in God.

I also tell them I am a policeman and show them my badge. They are intrigued. They want to know about the problems police face in Australia and ask the all-important question: 'How much do you get paid?' When I give them a rough figure in US dollars they are awed. They tell me that many police in Iran are so poor they have to live in the police station and sleep on the floor.

Shirley: When I come out of the mausoleum I see the crowd and push my way through. I expect to find Brian there but I'm surprised to see the police. I hear this conversation between a senior policeman and Brian:

Brian: 'Police in Victoria went to their government and asked for better wages, more money to take home. The government gave police more money.'

Policeman: 'You asked your government for more money?'

Brian: 'Yes.'

Policeman: 'And they gave it to you?'

Brian: 'Yes.'

Policeman: 'They gave you more money?'

Brian: 'Yes.'

They are incredulous. The idea of governments giving people more money seems hard for them to believe. Obviously, the Iranian leaders don't work this way.

Everywhere we go people are keen to help us. On the outskirts of Kashan we need directions to a hotel. A young woman gets out of a taxi and I ask if she speaks English. She is so shy and seems uncomfortable speaking to foreigners, but she does know the hotel we are looking for and draws us a map. The entire time she avoids making eye contact with Brian and barely says a word to me other than describing her map. Her directions are perfect. Without a wrong turn, we find the hotel.

I am still waging a war with the scarf and the scarf is winning. At the end of the day I can't wait to rip it off. For anyone who has ridden a bike, helmet hair is a familiar concept (except for people like Brian who have no hair). You take your helmet off and your hair is flat and sticks to your scalp. It is a most unattractive look. Now, not only do I have to contend with helmet hair, I have to deal with scarf hair!

The next morning, we see the strangest thing at breakfast: a man putting a sugar cube between his teeth and drinking his tea through the sugar. Little wonder the Iranians have bad teeth!

Brian: Again the traffic is crazy and I narrowly avoid tailending a bus that has decided to do a U-turn across four lanes of traffic without an indicator or any other form of notification. Thank God for ABS and dual four-pot brakes. Some scooters can't brake as quickly, so they ride blindly around the front and back of the bus.

We head for Natanz and the wind picks up, pushing us around unmercifully. There is a constant dust cloud in the air as there is little or no vegetation holding the topsoil in place. We plug on and turn down towards the main road to Isfahan. We battle a strong headwind until I see the dual carriageway, but there is no turn onto it to take us towards Isfahan. I solve this by going cross-country over the dirt, timing my run for a gap in the traffic. Other than this it is an uneventful run into Isfahan, just the usual suicide jockeys trying to take us to paradise with them earlier than expected.

Shirley: When we finally get to Isfahan and find our hotel, we end up on the wrong side of a road divider. As we are about to do a presumably illegal turn, the police ride up – two-up on the one bike. I am sure we are going to get booked or the police will want money like so many others we have encountered along the way, but no. They wave and say 'Hello. Welcome to Iran.'

We wander the streets admiring the views and watching the locals go about their daily business. The main street is broad with grassed nature strips. There are very modern shops standing beside mosques covered in brilliantly coloured tile work depicting quotations from the Koran. Minarets, some under repair, tower above the streetscape. It is a bustling city. Here we see more women in short coats with jeans and designer shoes, rather than the chador. They have their scarves pulled as far back as legally possible and sometimes even more. Many have small plaster bandages across the bridges of their noses. We find out that they have had plastic surgery to remove the hook in their noses! This is seen as a status symbol.

As dusk settles, we head to the river. The distant call of the holy men that marks the end of the day's fast is heard right across the city. Couples sit on the grass beside the river with small boxes of exotic sweets and cakes. Men set up cauldrons of soup and casseroles. Families prepare picnic hampers. They are all waiting for the sun to set. Finally the holy men stop and it is time to eat. The food hampers open up and food is served.

Rather than a riverside picnic, Brian and I opt for Iranian pizza, and it's not bad. After dinner we stop at an ice-cream parlour, where Brian attracts a huge audience of giggling young women, who stop to watch him take the first bite out of the most enormous ice-cream. It is at least 15 cm high. The dollop of ice-cream on the end of his nose after his initial bite elicits smiles and more giggles. For once we don't mind being the focus of attention.

The centre point of Isfahan is an exquisite ancient square called Meidun-e Emam Khomeini. Many locals still refer to this part of their history by its traditional name, Meidun-e Naghsh-e Jahan. They seem reluctant to take on the name of the country's former religious leader and founder, Khomeini, but there is no getting away from him. Enormous framed photos of Khomeini and Ali Khamenei, Khomeini's successors, are everywhere – on the facade of the palace, in parks and on the highways. Other highways are named in honour of martyrs killed during the war between Iran and Iraq in the 1980s. The square was the site of polo matches in the seventeenth century; the shah would watch from the balcony of his palace. The square is lined with magnificent tiled mosques, the local bazaar and many souvenir shops.

We can't help but feel for the shop owners. Since the abolition of credit cards and access to international funds through local banks in 2001, their businesses have been going downhill. There are few visitors and of those who do come, not many bring enough US cash to buy a Persian carpet or traditional inlaid boxes. To combat this situation, the carpet sellers will give you the carpet to take home, asking you to put the money into their bank account when you get home. They have never been ripped off, which is amazing. Another way the traders get around the currency problems is to offer credit-card facilities in Dubai. They ring a carpet shop there and put through the customer's credit-card details and the amount required. When the money comes through, the carpet seller transfers the money to the trader in Iran. It is a slow process, but it is the only way they can sell some of the more expensive items in their shops.

At a magnificent fountain at the centre of the square, Brian and I are enjoying the sunshine and absorbing the beauty and serenity of the area when two young Iranian girls come up and ask where we are from. They are studying English at high school and want to talk about all manner of things – our home, our work, our family. These girls are happy to have their photo taken with me.

Only a few minutes pass and another group of older girls comes up to us. They are university students who have been told to practise their English by talking to tourists. These older girls want to know about Australia. They seem a little surprised when I explain to them that women in Australia don't wear the scarf, but Muslim women living in our country can wear it if they choose to. They can't really grasp the concept of going to the beach and enjoying the outdoor life, and are disbelieving when I tell them about kangaroos. I have to admit I am surprised that they don't know more about Australia.

One of the girls keeps glancing over at Brian, who is talking to the high-school students. Giggling, she whispers to me, 'He is very beautiful. Do you have any children?'

I show her a picture of Gavan and Stephen, Brian's sons; my stepsons. I think they are handsome, but then I am biased. The young Iranian woman looks for a long time, draws a deep breath, and says, 'They are beautiful – like their father. Are they married?'

'No, they are not married. Are you married?' I ask her. 'Do you want to have children?'

There is no hesitation. 'I want to be an English professor. This means I won't marry and have children.'

'But you can have both. In Australia, many women work and they have children.'

'No. If I want to be an English professor, there will be no time to stay at home and have children. My mother stayed at home to look after us. Women should stay at home with their children. I want to teach English.'

'Will you have your photo taken with me?' I ask her. I would like to have a picture to remember this day. She becomes very nervous. Her teachers told her to talk to visitors to practise her English, but her bravado in conversation doesn't extend to posing for pictures.

'No. No photographs. My teachers might not like it.'

Our small audience grows when a man joins us. He has a souvenir shop on the square and is keen to show us the Shah Mosque, or Masjed-é Emām. His presence seems to make the girls uncomfortable. They move off and I am sorry we haven't spent more time talking. I am surprised that they came to talk to us at all, and maybe with time we could have learned more about them rather than talking about ourselves.

The Shah Mosque, as locals refer to it, is said to be one of the most stunning mosques in Iran. The photos we have seen haven't prepared us for the beauty of the intricate tile work, the soaring domes, vaulted prayer halls and courtyards. The brilliant blues of the seventeenth-century tile work feature traditional Islamic designs with quotations from the Koran.

It is prayer time. Inside, worshippers sit and put their foreheads on a small piece of stone on the floor as they bend forward to pray. We are intrigued and our guide explains that with the stone, the worshippers avoid contact with the dirty floors. Now we know the purpose of the small stones wrapped in mats that have been in some of our hotel rooms. They are prayer mats, folded up and ready for use. Our guide explains that the arrows on the walls of our hotel rooms, which puzzled us, point to Mecca.

Our guide takes us to his shop to meet his business partner. Here we sit and drink tea and cola, chewing on the wonderful local delicacy, nougat with pistachio nuts. They show us miniatures painted on camel bone (the camel wasn't killed specifically for the artwork) using cat-hair brushes (the cats aren't killed for their fur), and boxes made from wood, metal, gold and bone. Here we can use our credit card through the carpet shop in Dubai (well, you have to trust someone). And while we do trust them, we still email my brother in Melbourne to make sure there is only one transaction put through on our card.

Just spending time with these men gives us another insight into the lives of young Iranians. The shop-owner's wife is a lawyer. She was able to study law in Iran, but she can't appear in court because she is a woman. Women can study anything in this country but not put their skills to full use. This young woman, according to her husband, tears off her scarf when she comes home. One day she hopes to have more freedom.

Isfahan is famous for the Rose Garden of Martyrs – Golestan-e Shohada, the final resting place for the men and boys killed during the eight-year war between Iran and Iraq. It is hard to know how many men are buried here, but it is a massive place. Each grave has a mounted photograph for a headstone. This brings home the tragic waste of life. Some of the dead were just boys. Brothers lie with brothers, fathers lie with sons. One photo is of a baby, presumably killed during the bombing of the city. Another photo is of a soldier's dead body, his bandoleer across his chest, taken on the battlefield.

It is a moving experience to walk through this sacred place. According to the official literature, hundreds of ground-to-ground missiles and bombs rained down on Isfahan, destroying and damaging many of the city's monuments, but these have all been repaired.

After we leave Isfahan, the road takes us through a desert. Along the way we pass small mud-brick towns enclosed behind mud-brick walls. It is hard to tell if they are still inhabited. There are no signs of life, no signs of water to grow crops – nothing to entice you to live out here.

On the outskirts of Yazd, an ancient mud-brick city, a truck crosses over onto the wrong side of the freeway and drives off using the on-ramp. This behaviour is now so normal to us Brian doesn't even bother to give the driver a blast on the horn as he cuts across our path. But this time, as the driver passes us, Brian starts blasting away on his horn. I crane my neck and look over Brian's shoulder into the rearview mirror and instantly see what is causing his reaction. Coming down the on-ramp are two boys on a small motor scooter. They have no helmets and no protective clothing. The boys laugh and smile, watching us as we ride past. They are not looking ahead, but then, they aren't expecting to see a massive truck coming up the ramp.

It happens as if in slow motion and there is nothing we can do to stop it: the boys career headlong into the front of the truck. The rider is wearing a bright yellow jumper, and I see the flash of colour pirouette through the air and land with a sickening abruptness. His passenger slides and then stumbles to his feet.

We stop, but what can we do? We don't speak the language. We don't have medical knowledge or a major first-aid kit. We are helpless. Police from the checkpoint run over and the truck driver leaps down from his cabin. Without a word, we ride off comforted by the knowledge that there are many people there who can help and that there is no way the truck driver can claim he was in the right. He was exiting via an on-ramp on the wrong side of a road. But that won't help the injured boys. We hope and pray they are okay.

A whole new world is before us when we wander the streets of Yazd. It is a city made from mud and perched on the roofs are *bādgirs*, the wind towers. They direct every whisper of breeze into the houses to cool them. In the local water museum, we go into a room with a *bādgir*. The drop in temperature is incredible. You can imagine these rooms becoming the centre of family life.

In the Yazd Internet cafe we meet Yusef and Hussein. Brian tells them about our journey and they are keen to learn more. Brian shows them our website. I can't believe it when he opens up one of the chapters from Turkey. There, as the centrepiece photo, is a colour image of Brian and me in our bathers covered in mud! This is probably Western porn for these young men from a country where the sight of a woman's hair is something only to be shared by husband and wife. The boys grow silent. Brian realises what he is showing them and switches pages quickly. It's a real pity the counter on the web page isn't running at the moment. It would be a laugh to see how many hits we have over the next few days as Yusef shows his mates these half-naked Western people!

Brian and I have read about an ancient Roman bath-house converted into a restaurant in the heart of the Yazd Bazaar and Yusef and Hussein take us there. Hamam e Khane is a restaurant and teahouse. At one end of the main pool is the teahouse with huge, brightly coloured cushions spread over Persian carpets around low tables. On the tables are hookah pipes and the young people of Yazd puff away. It would be fascinating to know what they are discussing. It looks like the kind of place where revolutions are plotted and people dream of a very different life. The kebab dinner is good and we are getting used to drinking cola with our evening meal. I'm sure we'll quickly grow out of the habit when wine is available again.

Without our guides and armed only with a very dodgy map, we start to walk back to the hotel. Brian, who I have to admit has a much better sense of direction than me, suggests a short cut. It takes us through the narrow, dark lanes of the ancient bazaar. It is spooky. Our footsteps echo off the mud-brick walls and the shadows in the doorways of the closed shops take on an eerie form. My imagination is taking over and I try to quicken the pace but Brian is happy to stroll. The faster I walk, the slower he walks; at this point I could throttle him. As we see the lights of the main street ahead, I can't help but laugh. We have just walked down the kind of streets you read about where tourists disappear in far-off countries, the kind of streets we read about at home and tut-tut as we think, 'They shouldn't have been there at that time of night'.

Yusef and Hussein arrive at the hotel armed with their Farsi–English phrasebook. They are keen to learn about the West – from Brian, of course. I am a mere woman, but they are fascinated by the freedom women have in our country and wonder aloud why it can't be the same in their country. They firmly believe that the people from the West are selfish and seem surprised when Brian explains our pension and welfare systems.

We talk to them about their country and tell them that we have been to the Rose Garden of Martyrs. Their spin on the Iran–Iraq war is interesting in light of current events. They tell us that after the Shah of Iran was deposed by the revolution, the Americans sided with Iraq and equipped them for war. It was the Americans who told the Iraqis that Iranian Muslims were not true to their faith.

Both boys are studying and they have great hopes for the future, but tell us it will be limited in Iran. Yusef would dearly love to come to Australia to study, but in the current climate that is probably impossible. If these two boys are an example of Iran's future, there is great hope for the country – as long as their will prevails.

Yazd was once the home of the Zoroastrians in the ancient world. Many moved to India in the tenth century, but about 30,000 are said still to live in this area. The basis of Zoroastrianism is good overcoming evil. To attain purity believers avoid contamination with dead things. To this end followers used to prepare their dead and leave the corpses to be picked clean by vultures in towers on hills high above the town and away from the living. Today the Towers of Silence, as they are known, are no longer used but they stand as a stark reminder of the past. At the base of the towers are ruins of the buildings used to prepare the dead, and a present-day cemetery where it is said Zoroastrians bury their dead in cement-lined graves to avoid them being contaminated by the earth.

The ruins of the mud-and-straw buildings create a maze of nooks and crannies. It is eerie being here alone. I don't see another living soul, so I throw caution to the wind and rip off my scarf. It feels bloody marvellous.

It is time to move on and I feel a sickening dread in the pit of my stomach, particularly after yesterday's horrendous crash. Brian does a great job but I fear for our lives when we take to the highways of this country. We climb through barren hills that are so high we feel the change in temperature.

For the first time in many weeks we are chilly and wish we had a little more clothing. After days of desert riding Brian is thrilled to see the winding road down the hills but before long we are back in the desert and the long roads stretch out ahead of us. There is no-one about, so we pull over to stretch our legs and take photos.

A bright yellow ute loaded with pomegranates hurtles past and then we hear a screech of brakes and spinning rubber. The ute pulls up beside us and two men with huge smiles leap out. They don't speak English and we don't speak Farsi, so charades kicks in. One drags out a water container from the front seat and washes his hands. He then makes us a cup of tea. This is amazing. They can't drink because it is Ramadan but they insist we share their tea. They want the usual questions answered: how much is the bike worth and how fast does it go? They are very impressed that I can write the answers in the dirt using Farsi numerals – after all, I am only a woman!

As a parting gesture, they give us half a dozen pomegranates, even though it is quite clear we don't have any room on the bike. They point to my jacket. There you go, how silly of us not to realise that I can, of course, carry six pomegranates down the front of my jacket! Brian loads me up and we mount the bike as I try to hold the pomegranates in place. The big smiles return when we ride off and they continue to wave as we ride off into the distance.

These men are probably as poor as church mice (or mosque mice), yet they are keen to share what they have with complete strangers – and infidels at that! We are constantly overwhelmed by the warmth and friendliness of these people.

Our next fuel stop is a bit tricky. I have to get off without dropping the pomegranates out of my jacket. It's a struggle, but I manage it and then good old Brian gives them away to motorists who have surrounded us to get a closer look at the foreigners and their bike. When we ride out we are led by the now-usual procession of motor scooters as an unofficial escort. There is much horn-beeping and waving when we get to the highway.

At the car park of the ancient city of Persepolis, we cover the bike with its invisibility cloak (Harry Potter, eat your heart out) – the grotty old bike cover we've had for years.

Persepolis was the heart of this part of the world from 559 to 330 BC. Then Alexander the Great visited and the city burned to the ground; historians don't know if the fire was accidental or arson. From the entrance gate only a few columns are visible; the true beauty of this city is hidden behind the massive city wall. The fact that much of it was covered with sand until the 1930s, when the sand was excavated, has helped with the preservation.

Persepolis is an incredibly impressive site. Carved friezes depict people bringing offerings to the king or the king himself single-handedly slaying ferocious beasts and his army bearing arms to protect him. If only he'd known how to handle Alexander the Great.

I am delighted with the design of the Grand Stairway inside the city wall. The steps are shallow so the dignitaries who arrived to trumpet fanfare could walk in their finery and talk without getting short of breath or messing up their clothing. It's a magnificent idea and I recommend it to all modern builders.

There are parts of the city that weren't submerged in sand. Beyond the magnificent Gate of All Nations, there is proof of this. The gate is festooned with graffiti from the nineteenth and twentieth centuries. Majors and captains from the British regiments carved their monikers into the stone. A high commissioner and his wife joined them.

Inside Persepolis we meet a group of young Iranians – Amirh, his wife and two friends. Amirh has just graduated as a doctor and wants to go to the US to study neurosurgery. His wife has a US passport; her grandmother lives there. They hope this family connection might make the move possible. One of their Iranian friends, a photographer, applied to emigrate to Canada, but the bombing of the Twin Towers put an end to any plans he had for a new life. They are yet another example of the dissatisfaction of the people with their government. Amirh gives us his mobile phone number 'just in case' we need help from someone who speaks Farsi.

Back in the carpark we meet Bicycle Bevan, an Adelaidian who had been travelling around Iran on a push-bike (insane!) until he was held up at knifepoint and saved by a passing motorist. Bevan is now travelling by bus and he's looking for a lift back to Shiraz. Brian tells him we are on the bike and he does point out that in Iran three-up is quite the norm. Sorry, Bevan, not on our bike.

The regime in Iran is extremely anti the West and this is clear when we spot a 'Down with America' demonstration by schoolchildren outside our hotel window one morning. When I look out the curtained windows there are hundreds of schoolboys and girls marching down the street carrying banners and chanting. We are told it is 'Education Day', when the children celebrate their education, but it is actually 'Down with America' day. The students are chanting 'Down with America! Down with Israel!' and waving their fists. At the centre of the group is a flat-bed truck mounted with an antiquated sound system. The mullahs are trying to whip the youngsters into a frenzy. It isn't working. As we walk past, the stragglers at the back of the demonstration welcome us and ask the usual question: 'Where are you from?' I am glad we aren't American, but they certainly don't seem threatening. They wave and wish us well, and then turn back to the front and resume their chanting. (Demonstrations like this are held throughout Iran today – the local news showed many similar demonstrations in various locations.)

A cab driver is keen to tell us his views of the current regime: 'I miss the shah – they were good days.'

'But how do you remember the shah? You seem too young,' I reply.

'I remember they were good days. The people were happy. In the days of the shah we had one thief running the country. Now we have many thieves. The mullahs are greedy and have taken much money for themselves.'

His is yet another voice of discontentment.

Brian: From Shiraz we are faced with an 800 km ride to Bam and the border with Pakistan. Through the desert we make very good time and when we get to the outskirts of Kerman we begin to climb the winding road across a small mountain range. The road twists and turns, which is great for us, but not so good for the old trucks and cars that struggle up the steep gradient. Down the other side, in the distance, is a long downhill slope to Kerman. It's two-lane and the rust buckets go flat out down the hill with little regard for safety as they buck and weave on balding tyres and worn-out suspension. If it wasn't so dangerous, it would be funny.

The sun is fading fast and the air temperature drops considerably. As dusk settles, we seem to be the only vehicle on the road with lights on. Every other vehicle drives in the dark. A truck cuts onto the road from the right, darts across two lanes and begins to turn left in front of us without even looking let alone indicating. There is no time to hit the brakes and dive for the inside. I gun the bike and get around the truck just in time. I can feel Shirl grip me with her thighs and arms. With hearts racing, we continue on our way – counting our lucky stars. We must have a guardian angel.

Shirley: We have been tossing up whether we should stay at Akhbar's Tourist Guest House, which has been recommended to us, or the Bam Inn, the mid-range option in the guidebook. We spy three bikes and a four-wheel drive in the yard of the Bam Inn and our decision is made. We know that the first stretch of road we will cross into Pakistan is dangerous and there is a definite safety-in-numbers principle in force. If this group is travelling east we can travel together. If they are travelling west they will probably have some good information on what lies ahead.

One of the group, Ingo, is on a Triumph Tiger and spending a few months travelling from Germany to India and Nepal. He must be home in May next year to resume his studies in forestry. Bernd and Heidi are also from Germany and are riding KTMs, heading all the way to Australia. South Africans Dagmar and Peter are taking their Land Rover around the world. We sit in the dark, Dagmar and I complaining bitterly about the scarves and coats we have to wear, and Peter and Brian talking travel. Peter and Dagmar are particularly keen to have company crossing the badlands of Pakistan, so we arrange to meet them in Taftan, across the border, in a couple of days. Bernd and Heidi aren't sure if they can make the journey in one day, so we all contemplate a night in Dalbandin, the only town safe enough to spend the night in on that part of the highway. This area is very close to Afghanistan and a popular spot for the Taliban.

The conditions at the Bam Inn are really poor, so we move to Akhbar's Tourist Guest House, a palace by comparison. Akhbar, a former English teacher, is friendly and welcoming. His rooms are clean, comfortable and fitted out with Western toilets and a double bed, and it's a third of the price we paid the previous night.

Around lunchtime we head to Arg-e-Bam, an ancient adobe city dating back to 224 AD, to meet Peter and Dagmar. Most of what remains of the town of old Bam dates back to between 1502 and 1722, when up to 13,000 people lived in the city. It was abandoned in 1722 after an invasion by the Afghanis. The site is impressive. The old city is six square kilometres, and its massive walls tower over date palms. We spend about four hours walking around the streets and laneways, taking in the remains of houses, the bazaar, the mosque, the caravanserai, the garrison and the governor's palace. Some of the buildings have been restored so well they still convey the majesty this city once had.

We climb high up into the citadel wall at the back of the ancient city, to a teahouse that is open today even though it is Ramadan. In deference to the Muslims, foreigners are asked to eat inside, but we sit by a window with views of the ancient city. It is breathtaking. The speciality of the house is date biscuits, made from a secret recipe that the woman who runs the teahouse is unwilling to share. They are delicious.

It is time to say farewell to Iran and head into Pakistan. As we approach the border with Pakistan we encounter a sea of vehicles and men. Utes packed with plastic containers of fuel and food jostle for a place in the queue. The Iranian soldiers push us to the top of the queue and check our passports before pointing us in the direction of the true border 10 km away.

We pass into the Iranian Truck Terminal for passport and customs checks. These go off without a hitch once we find the offices and officials. Our final check is by a man in a nondescript uniform who works in a concrete shed. Along the wall in front of the shed is the slogan 'Down with USA' signed by the Islamic Revolution Committee of Mirjaveh. On the other side of the concrete shed is what remains of another slogan: '. . . ept the Islamic law across the world'. I can only presume this originally had something to do with sweeping the Islamic faith far and wide.

We pass through a gate and are confronted by a run-down collection of buildings – Pakistan.

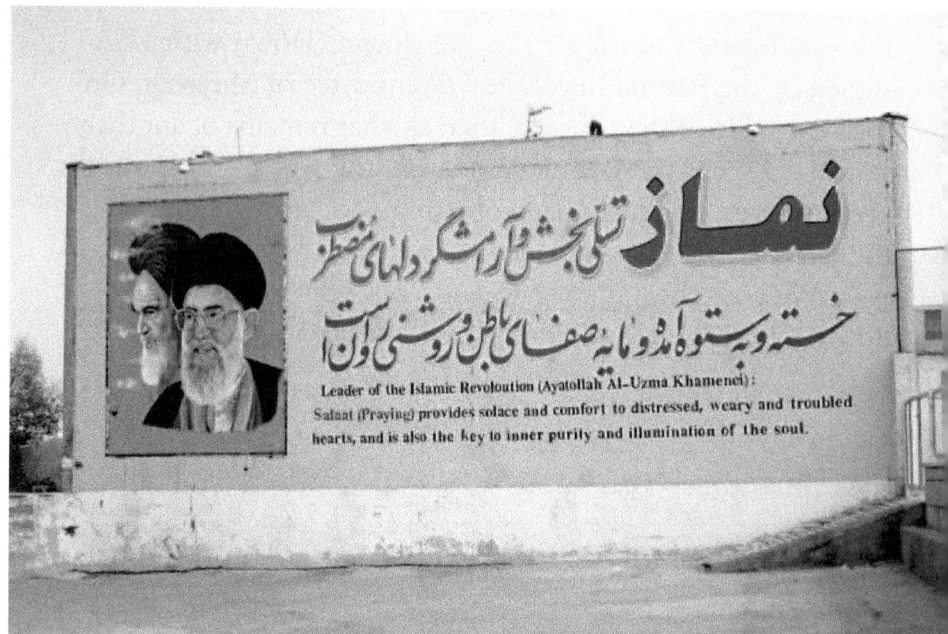
نماز تسلی بخش و آرامشگر دلهای مضطر
خسته و به ستوه آمده و مایه صفای باطن و روشنی روان است
Leader of the Islamic Revoloution (Ayatollah Al-Uzma Khamenei):
Salaat (Praying) provides solace and comfort to distressed, weary and troubled
hearts, and is also the key to inner purity and illumination of the soul.

A message from the Ayatollah in Esfahan

Rose Garden of the Martyrs, Esfahan
commemorating the victims of the Iran/Iraq w

jed-e Imam Khomeini, Esfahan

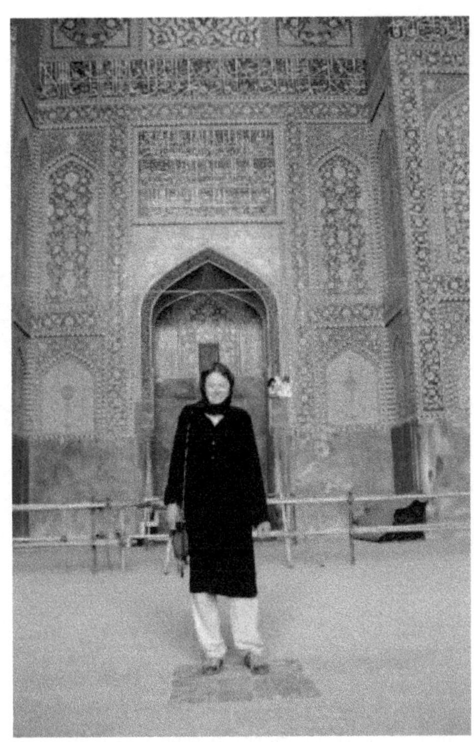

The local girls were keen to speak to Shirley about life in the West

Tabriz — with Melburnian Alec Simpson

Towers of Silence, Y

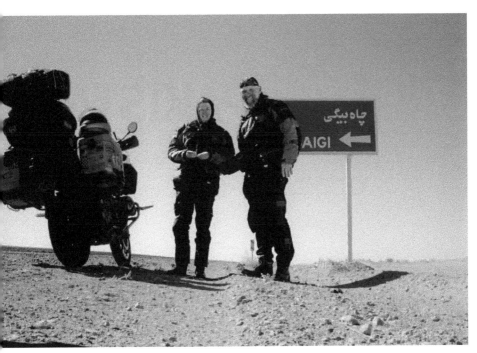

our own on the road — but not for long.

Pomegranate farmers stopped for a chat

ELEVEN

PAKISTAN

7 November – 3 December 2003

Shirley: In Pakistan, the immigration process is cumbersome. All our details are entered into enormous ledgers by bureaucrats sitting behind ancient wooden desks in rooms filled with blue smoke. The men are relaxed and friendly, sitting on their rickety chairs. They all wear the traditional Pakistani shalwar qamiz – loose pants under long, flowing shirts. Permeating the smoke is the mouth-watering aroma of curry. It is Ramadan and the men are preparing their evening meal.

'Welcome to Pakistan. Do you have any problems?' Before Brian can answer, the customs officer says, 'Of course you have no problems. You are in Pakistan now, not Iran. No problems.'

The conversation moves to Australia's ties with England, which leads us to a favourite topic in Pakistan: cricket. When you mention Australia to a cricket fan in Pakistan, their reply is just two words: 'Ricky Ponting'. They love him. The bond of sport breaks down barriers. The officials offer us tea, even though they are fasting.

We have organised to meet Ingo, Bernd, Heidi, Dagmar and Peter at the government-run motel in Taftan. The manager greets us at the door and tells us Ingo is already out the back, setting up his tent. Although it is Ramadan and daylight, we are offered cold drinks and samousa – fried pastry parcels filled with spicy meat and vegetables – which are a taste sensation after the bland kebabs we've had in Iran. At last I can shed the scarf and coat of Iran – no hijab laws here. This immediately gives me a feeling of freedom. From the motel's dusty yard, we can see the customs house. We are waiting for Peter and Dagmar to cross. Finally, at about 6.30 p.m., they drive in with three other vans. It is rush hour!

Alcohol is banned in Pakistan but can be purchased under licence at major tourist hotels in the main cities. At our motel, discreet questions reveal that it does sell local whisky. It's not cheap at 500 rupee (around $12) for a half bottle. And it is rough – 25% underproof, distilled in Pakistan – but it is whisky. There are a lot of laughs as we play the card game Uno with Ingo, Peter and Dagmar, and Ube and Bettina, a young German couple travelling in a four-wheel drive camper van.

Soon it's time for our ride across the badlands of Pakistan. If Bernd and Heidi don't arrive tomorrow we will head off without them, but that is not our preference. We don't want to leave them to travel to Quetta on their own. We've been warned that it is a dangerous stretch of road and far better travelled in a group.

Dagmar and I head into town to buy some supplies. It is an unnerving experience – the roads are dusty tracks and the buildings ramshackle. We find a shop and walk in only to interrupt a man praying to Allah at the back of the store – right near the biscuits. The other man in the shop signals that we shouldn't bother about this and just look through his produce. It is a very uncomfortable feeling stepping over the praying man to get a good look at the massive selection of sweet biscuits. We don't linger over our shopping.

The motel manager tells us that there are 'service stations' everywhere in town. He is right. What he doesn't tell us is that in this part of Pakistan a 'service station' is just a collection of steel drums on the side of the dirt road. A tin shed seems to be home to the young men who work there. Most of the servos are very shabby-looking affairs, but there is one that stands out from the rest. Instead of plastic drums and hoses, this tin shed provides jugs to dispense fuel and a muslin cloth to filter the fuel as it is poured into the tank.

After buying petrol at under 10c a litre in Iran, we are horrified when the young man, using a calculator, tells us the fuel here will be the equivalent of $4 a litre. When we work out that the decimal point is in the wrong spot it turns out to be a much more realistic 21.5 rupee (about 50c) a litre.

Bernd and Heidi finally make it over the border and we head off on the road to Quetta – the only road out of town. We travel just 16 km before coming to our first police checkpoint, a tin shed in the middle of nowhere. There are more dusty ledgers to fill in with our passport details. The police are incredibly friendly. The whole setup seems stuck in a time warp. On a rickety old stool outside the shed is a windup Bakelite phone that's probably been in use since World War II. Wooden and rope beds with coarse blankets and wooden chairs and tables seem to be the only 'comforts' for the men placed here in the middle of nowhere. These checkpoints are not here to keep local officials busy. If we disappear, the authorities will be able to pinpoint when and where we were last seen alive. I am not comforted by this thought.

The road takes us through a desert landscape so barren nothing will grow out here. Yet there are people in small communities along the railway to Quetta. As our convoy passes, children run out of the settlements, waving madly. We must be quite a sight – Dagmar and Peter in their Land Rover followed by Brian and me, Bernd, Heidi and Ingo on bikes.

The first major settlement we come to is Dalbandin. On its outskirts are about 30 shanties selling petrol from containers. It is getting dark and we are warned not to press on from here. This is an area where foreigners need to be tucked up inside before night falls. We must find accommodation and, as towns go, Dalbandin doesn't seem very promising. Peter and Dagmar head to a hotel with a camping area to park their truck. We opt for a hotel the local police tell us is the best in town.

If this is the best place in town, I'd hate to see the worst. The power doesn't come on until 6 p.m. There is no hot water, no shower facilities and only a squat toilet without running water. You have to fill a bucket to flush. The bathroom, such as it is, looks as though it hasn't been cleaned for weeks and the bed sheets are putrid. The only thing dirtier is the clothing worn by the assortment of men working here (including a dwarf named Commando, who sleeps on a shelf under the reception desk!). The only advantage is a restaurant of sorts that doubles as the overnight motorcycle parking area.

Our room has a window without glass, which looks out onto the internal stairwell. As I change out of my bike gear, I see the curtain move and half a dozen sets of eyes watching me. I am completely taken aback and shout at them. Without flinching they wander off. This is the breaking point for me.I am too old to bother with dirty hotel rooms, stinking toilets and dirty sheets. Brian is trying to be supportive and attempts a positive spin on things. This only makes me feel worse, knowing he now has to contend with a weeping woman.

While lying awake in our shabby room something occurs to me. We have been in Pakistan for three days and we haven't seen any women – not even young girls. Taftan and Dalbandin seem to be towns inhabited by men only. Where are the women in this country that boasts of freedom in comparison with its fundamentalist neighbour?

The next stretch of the road to Quetta is said to be the most dangerous. Close to the Afghan border, we pass through an area where foreigners are not welcome. We've been told not to stop on this road for any reason. Max Ng, the Singaporean biker we met in Turkey, had a nasty spill on this stretch of road when he was chased by locals on bikes.

The road conditions worsen the further we travel. The desert winds raise up sand across the roadway. On occasion, we slip and slide our way through drifting sand up to 20 cm deep. There seems to be no life on the road apart from camels, but occasionally we see a man just sitting on the rocks looking down or wandering along the side.

There are the occasional small settlements by the road and it is here we see our first Pakistani women. They are wearing the most magnificently coloured saris – magenta, aquamarine, brilliant yellows and bright greens – as they toil in the barren fields. Groups of them wander along the side of the road carrying enormous bundles on their heads.

One hundred and thirty kilometres from Dalbandin we are stopped at yet another police checkpoint. This time they won't let us move on until we have an armed escort. They want to put the armed guard into the Land Rover, but there is no room. We sit in the heat and wait while the police use their windup phone to find a vehicle to escort us. When they can't find anyone we are told to move on without a guard. The checkpoints are there solely for the safety of travellers, who are at risk from Taliban insurgents.

A further 50 km down the highway, we pull into the town of Nushki. Here we are ordered into the police compound and berated for not waiting for a guard at the previous checkpoint: 'You don't realise how dangerous it is for tourists in this part of Pakistan. You are just 50 km from the border with Afghanistan. Where is your guard?'

Everyone looks to Brian for an answer. He seems to be the unofficial leader of our little group. 'We waited at the checkpoint but they couldn't find a vehicle,' he replies. 'There is no room in the Land Rover and no room on the bikes. We were told to move on.'

'Not only is it dangerous, but if you go missing it causes trouble between your government and our government. While you are in this area you are my responsibility and you will not go on without an escort. And you cannot travel on these roads at night. They are far too dangerous and we cannot guarantee your safety at night.'

The haranguing goes on. This official is furious. Someone from the other checkpoint is going to cop it when we leave, that's for sure. As a way of stressing his point, the official tells us about a group of foreigners who were forced to camp in the compound last night because they were travelling after dark. 'They were lucky we let them stay here.'

On that note, he gets his gun and jumps into the passenger seat of a small van, signalling that we are to follow. He might be the officer in charge, but he is our escort. With a spin of the wheels in the dirt, the police car heads off at a frenetic pace with the convoy of foreigners following in its dust. For the next 50 km we speed through the desert. We are the only vehicles on the road. When we hit the foothills the policeman pulls over and signals Brian to move alongside.

'You should be safe from here,' he says. 'There is an army presence in the hills. They will watch over you. Be careful and make sure you are off the road by nightfall.'

It doesn't take us long to find the 'army presence', but at first glance it is frightening. Brian spots it first: 'Shit!' I feel his body stiffen against my chest.

'What? What?'

Brian tells me to look into the hills, and before long I see something glinting in the sunlight – a rifle. Before I have time to have a complete panic attack, I feel Brian's body relax. 'It's an army sharpshooter,' he says, pointing to another man hiding in the rocks.

Well, he and his mates aren't hiding too well. About every 500 m we see sunlight glinting off firearms or the hat of a soldier partially hidden behind rocks high above the road. These are the sharpshooters protecting us as we make our way into Quetta.

The closer we get to the centre of Quetta, the busier the roads become. Donkey-drawn carts, push-bikes, motorbikes and cars vie for the restricted road space. We try to follow Peter and Dagmar, but it doesn't take long for us to get separated. Our saviour takes the form of a foreigner on a BMW GS Adventure, who leads us through the city to our hotel. We learn he is Andrew Fisher, a prison officer from Alice Springs.

In Quetta, we notice an unpleasant smell in the air, and then we notice the open drains. There are women here but they are covered from head to toe – even their eyes are covered by a thin veil in their burqas. They seem far more demure than their Iranian sisters. They travel in segregated buses; the women are separated from the men by an internal wall. Men standing guard make sure women get into the right section of the bus. The women's clothing might be brightly coloured, but to us they seem very repressed.

The Sajji houses of Quetta serve the popular local cuisine: legs of lamb cooked on a stick over an open fire. We head out to dinner with Peter, Dagmar, Andrew, Bettina and Ube, taking one of the motor rickshaws, the popular local transport. We try chicken and lamb Sajji and it is delicious. Over dinner Andrew regales us with stories of his travels and the corruption he has encountered on the road. Ube and Bettina are having trouble understanding him, even though they speak very good English. Little wonder why. Andrew uses some rather colourful language. 'I was getting sick and tired of being ripped off by the coppers. Every time they see foreigners as an easy way to get cash. I vowed I wasn't going to hand over any more cash,' he says in an Aussie drawl that makes us homesick. 'A copper pulls me up and asks for money. No way! I give him fuck-all and tell him to piss off!'

It's a hilarious story but poor Bettina and Ube couldn't get the joke. Brian explains: 'He didn't give the policeman any money and told him to go away.'

Oh, right. Now they get it. But it is a lesson to learn. Australian is a completely different language from English!

It is late when we leave the restaurant and there are no motor rickshaws on the streets. We begin the walk back to our hotel, breaking all the rules. Rohan Pike, an Australian Federal policeman working at the embassy in Islamabad, warned us not to walk the streets of Quetta at night. There are armed men on every street corner. They aren't police and they aren't soldiers. They are tribal men. We can hear the distant sound of gunshots. Quetta is a wild town.

Quickening our pace, we notice the only other unarmed person on the street is an urchin, probably about four or five years old. He sees us as we come out of the restaurant and follows close behind, holding out his tiny, dirty hand. It is very cold, and he is wearing only light clothing. I have some coins in my pocket and give them to him. I can't bear to think of him walking the streets along with these gunmen. Glancing at the coins, he beams, showing perfect white teeth, and then charges off into the night. It is a heartbreaking encounter.

Some of the roads from Quetta are closed to foreigners even with an armed guard. We decide to take the road to Loralai and DG Khan and then on to Multan with Peter and Dagmar. Finding the road to Loralai proves a bit of a problem. We ride into a bustling market town called Sumuni. We know there should be a turn here, but we can't find a road sign. A fairly new-looking car drives up alongside us. Its occupants wave madly. 'Where are you going?' the driver asks.

'Loralai.'

The driver becomes very agitated. 'No. Turn back. This is the road to Afghanistan. You are just 30 km from the border. Turn back. The road to Loralai is behind you.'

We are in real Taliban country. There were so many people in Sumuni we didn't even see the road let alone the sign to Loralai. If we hadn't turned back we could have ended up in Afghanistan or on one of the roads out of bounds to foreigners.

We find the road to Loralai. It's potholed but not too bad. It is early afternoon and we are sure we can push on to DG Khan before nightfall. About 20 km further along the road, the asphalt disappears and is replaced by roadworks.

Brian: I think I can push through the roadworks for a few kilometres, but it just goes on and on. The clay and dirt has been ground into a fine powder by the ever-present trucks. In places it is more than 30 cm deep. The bike ploughs through it, and I feel the dust billowing up over my feet like a fine spray of water. Following trucks through this, all visibility is lost and I follow my instincts.

In places they have watered this mess, turning it to a slippery mass. It is like glass and treacherous for motorcycles. Even some of the trucks are slipping sideways. We slip and slide our way along, and I'm sweating with concentration and adrenaline. I turn on my lights and ignore the oncoming trucks flashing theirs at me. Lights on means 'I am overtaking' in this part of the world.

Shirley: The last 55 km from the service station has taken us an hour and a half and the road is getting worse and worse. We wind our way across sand traps and over potholes so big you could park a small car in them. My head is throbbing from the constant bumping and the sand and dust. I can only imagine Brian is feeling even worse. Light is failing fast and we need to find a place to stop for the night.

We drive up alongside Dagmar and Peter and they suggest we camp. They propose we stay the night in their van. It is an offer too good to refuse and we will forever be indebted to them for this display of friendship and hospitality.

The first camping spot we try is near a camp for road workers. Before Peter can ask if we can stay near their camp they chase him away. A little further down the road we see what looks like a deserted settlement on a flat section of land. We go off the road and follow the track only to find a small truck, donkey, dog, man, wife and three children in an adobe building. The man, who seems very young, comes out to talk to us. His wife stands at the door nursing a baby and two small children peer out of the door. I wave at the children and the wife begins to walk towards us. Peter is still talking to the husband and I get off the bike and say hello to the woman. She is quite weather-beaten and the hand she offers me is like sandpaper. Her baby has the most exquisite eyes, which are made up with kohl. The woman is very friendly. She seems intrigued by the foreigners but her young husband is nervous. He won't let us camp.

Dark is falling quickly and we are all more than a little nervous. We must find somewhere away from the road and the workers' camps dotted along it. There is barely any light when we find a suitable spot and park a long way off the road. We are all tired and hungry, and Brian and I are filthy. We try to clean up as best we can, but water is scarce and we would all rather have a cup of tea than a clean face.

What would we do without Peter and Dagmar? They clean out the back of the Land Rover and make a space for us to sleep. Then they open their food boxes and, on their kerosene burner, they prepare a meal fit for a king – pasta with a curry, tuna and vegetable sauce.

Dressed in thermal long johns, socks, jumpers, scarves and woolly hats, we climb into the back of the vehicle. We might not be the picture of sartorial elegance but we are warm. And although we can hear the trucks, they are a long way away and are not venturing off the road. During the night I wake a few times. My knees throb because I can't stretch out and my feet get cold occasionally. When Brian turns over I turn over. Grateful to Dagmar and Peter, we make the best of our situation.

When day breaks I have a closer look at the collection of rocks near our camp. It is a cemetery! No wonder the locals gave us a wide berth. Our first visitor is a worker wandering across to the village, and he barely gives us a second glance.

We hit the road, knowing it will be a long, slow day. The sandy tracks lead us through more roadworks, where the sand is even deeper than yesterday. This is, without doubt, the worst ride we have done on any bike. Occasionally, as if to lift our spirits, we get back on the asphalt road, which is still potholed and littered with boulders, but preferable to the sandy track. We can't believe they are actually repairing about 167 km of road all at once and without any warning signs or diversions.

A bridge is down and the track takes us across a river. Now the thick layer of dust on us and the bike turns into mud. And to make things even more interesting, there are animals on the road – dogs and goats running this way and that.

The roadworkers watch us pass. Some smile and others just stare. Everything is done manually here. Groups of men sit on the side of the road with piles of big rocks, breaking them down by banging them against smaller rocks. Other men take these medium-sized rocks and bash them into smaller rocks, and so on.

When the roadworks finally end we find ourselves on a very steep and twisty road that's just one lane wide. The trucks move over to let us pass and always make enough room for the Land Rover to get through.

It's been a long and difficult couple of days. We are looking forward to spending time in Multan in order to get cleaned up, wash the dirt out of the bike and our clothes and get some rest.

Brian: The bike is idling very slowly – 600 to 800 rpm – so I pull out the air cleaner and find it choked with dust, after just four days of desert riding. I use Peter's air-filter cleaner spray and let the bike dry in the sun. The bike then needs three washes. Next, I belt the dust out of the sheepskin seat covers and replace the black spark plugs with my only spare pair. Surprisingly, the bike has held together well. I fire her up and adjust the idle by ear. First one side, then the other, and our faithful companion sounds like she's raring to go again. The noise of the engine attracts spectators and I spend the next half hour explaining the bike and our journey to eager listeners.

Shirley: Since Persian times Multan has been known for its heat, dust, beggars and burials. Being Ramadan, beggars have converged on the town and are lying around outside its religious monuments. At the Mausoleum of Sheikh Rukn-i-Alam (a scholar who died in 1334 and is widely revered as the patron saint of Multan) children in rags and old men with horribly deformed legs wait for handouts from worshippers. A man with no legs crabs his way up the hill in a small box on wheels. He uses his hands wrapped in rags to pull himself along the rough streets. It is a depressing sight but fascinating to see how the more affluent Muslims give generously to this underclass during the religious festival. Without this generosity, the beggars would surely die of starvation.

Outside, a young man approaches and asks if he can be our guide. He takes us through the Multan bazaar. Stalls selling golden bangles shimmer under bright lights. Women fuss over the magnificently embroidered shalwar qamiz that, by Australian standards, are incredibly cheap – about $10 for pants, long top and shawl-cum-scarf. Dagmar and I can't resist these one-size-fits-all outfits. There is much hilarity back at the hotel when I realise the outfit is so big, Brian and I and a small refugee family could all fit into the pants at once!

We are never alone on the open road. While in places the roads are modern, the traffic is something from the past – horse-, bullock- and donkey-drawn carts, bicycles with impossible loads, colourful trucks and buses. And the most important instrument on a vehicle here is the horn. Every time you pass or are passed by another, you are expected to sound your horn. The cacophony is overpowering and this safety device loses its impact after a while.

We are in Lahore, a large city with a population of eight million and diabolical pollution. Brian has taken to wearing a scarf over his mouth to filter out the acrid taste of the fumes. It takes us an hour of negotiating our way through bumper-to-bumper traffic to find the hotel recommended in the guidebooks. Every time we stop it takes just 30 seconds to pull a crowd of about 100. They spill onto the streets and stop the traffic, then the impatient drivers behind us lean on their horns continuously for several minutes.

We decide to take a taxi to the old city rather than deal with the traffic again. This proves to be even more terrifying, as the car zigzags its way around bicycles, motorcycles, rickshaws, buses, trucks, horses and donkeys pulling carts, and even camels hauling large loads.

The Lahore Fort is a knockout. Construction began in 1566, but it has been ransacked by the Sikhs and the British. It doesn't take much imagination to see how regal this place was when it was home to the Mogul emperors. Unfortunately, as is so often the case in the Middle East, there has been little maintenance to retain the beauty and majesty of this monument.

Across from the fort is the massive, seventeenth-century Badshahi Mosque. It can accommodate 60,000 worshippers in the central courtyard alone. In front of the mosque is a pretty park with green lawns and a small pavilion. We see many people sleeping here, and our guide assures us they are not homeless, but tired after long journeys. This is interesting, considering the local paper says there is a problem with the number of beggars who come into Lahore during Ramadan to get easy money for food.

Walking through the old city, we find the Pakistan we can live without: the crowds, which push and shove their way past us, and shouting and horns. But the stench overrides everything else. It is stomach-turning. There are small open sewers along the laneways and rotting garbage lies about.

Men urinate wherever and whenever they feel like it. They crouch down and hitch their long shirts up and pee to their heart's content. In small alcoves, water runs into open gully traps. Men sit in these – bathing! It is an assault on the senses. The old city is dirty and run-down.

In the modern area of Lahore are shops catering to the more affluent residents, but you can't get away from the reality of the Third World. While out for a walk we see a naked man sitting in a gully trap, washing. A woman and several children sit on the pathway, just watching the world go by, their clothes drying on a tree. The family must live on this part of the footpath. We can't get used to seeing this kind of poverty.

The problem with trips like ours is the constant farewells. We have thoroughly enjoyed our time with Dagmar and Peter; a chance meeting in the yard of a scungy hotel in Iran has developed into a real friendship. We've shared experiences on the road that only travellers can understand. It is with enormous sadness that we say goodbye. Dagmar and Peter have had enough of Pakistan and are heading to India. We are heading up the Grand Trunk Road to Islamabad. But we promise to meet again.

There is a magnificent tollway connecting Lahore and Islamabad. It avoids all the towns and the dangerous drivers, but we can't use it. For some reason motorcycles are prohibited. This is ridiculous when you consider our bike is bigger and faster than so many of the cars in this country. We have to take the historic Grand Trunk Road. The towns we ride through seem more modern than those in the country's west. There are still bustling marketplaces and masses of demonic traffic, but the towns seem relatively affluent. The shops are more modern and the cars outnumber the horse-drawn carts. As we get closer to Islamabad, the weather gets colder and we hit some rain. The further we go the worse the weather gets, and soon the rain is pelting down amid thunder and lightning.

On the outskirts of Islamabad all is very different. Gone are the narrow streets. In their place are wide, paved boulevards with the traffic keeping to designated lanes. Police man the intersections and the drivers seem to take notice of their directions. Islamabad is quite easy to get around. The city is divided into sectors, and with a minimum amount of stress and fuss we find Rohan Pike's home. Rohan is a friend of Brian's cousin, Tim, as well as a Federal policeman working at the Australian embassy, and has offered us a bed for a few days. We have been more than grateful for his advice along the way and are looking forward to meeting him and spending time with an Aussie.

Islamabad is a modern capital city, very un-Pakistani. There are obvious security issues for foreigners living here. Rohan, like most foreigners, has 24-hour security on his house. There is a house boy, Faisal, and an exuberant puppy named Harry to greet us. Rohan has been working in India for a few days and will be home later.

Faisal shows us our room, which has its own bathroom and a huge, comfortable double bed. As an Australian High Commission house, it is wired for Australian appliances and you can drink water out of the taps! We find our way to Rohan's beer fridge and discover cold Hahn beer and some good white wine. It's time for a drink. We have arrived in heaven!

Faisal wanders around in his socks and regularly frightens the living daylights out of me when he appears, silently, behind me. I am on my way to the laundry when I hear him: 'Memsahib. You cannot wash. I will do it for you.'

After peeling myself off the kitchen ceiling and collecting my pile of clothing from the floor, I agree that it is Faisal's job and leave him to it.

My hair continues to be a bother. It is lank and scraggly and, worst of all, the grey is showing through. I can't bear to look at myself in the mirror. Brian thinks I spend far too much time worrying about my hair: 'Most people would be worried about getting killed on a trip like this, not whether they have grey roots showing!'

I doubt finding a good hairdresser is easy anywhere in Pakistan except Islamabad. In rural Pakistan, we have seen people getting haircuts and shaves under a tree on the side of the road.

Rohan's assistant at the embassy gives me the name of her hairdresser. She works from home on the edge of the city and Jan assures me she is very good. 'Working from home' conjures up an image of a chair and mirror set up in a kitchen. In actual fact, the 'salon' is in the basement of a very swish house in a wealthy area of the city. Security men guard the house and downstairs a staff of about six young Pakistani women fuss over expat women who are there for manicures, pedicures or to have their hair done.

For the next hour I am pampered and preened with a head massage, treatment and a colour that makes me look years younger. When I am done and have passed over 2500 rupees – just over AUD$60 – I ask about getting a taxi back to Rohan's. There are no taxis but the 'driver' will take me to the taxi rank in the salon car. I sit back and relax in the limousine – this is the life! When we get to the taxi rank, the driver gets out and speaks to a taxi driver, then turns to me with a huge smile: 'Madam, the driver will take you home and you must pay him no more than 100 rupees.'

What a service. Not only do I get a limo ride, I don't even have to barter the cab fare.

Brian likes my hair, but I don't have the heart to tell him how much I paid. 'It was cheaper than in Melbourne,' is all I say. He seems happy with this.

One of the highlights of Pakistan is the Karakoram Highway that links the country with China. With winding roads that follow the course of the Indus River through the mountains, it is a motorcyclist's dream. It is here that the Himalaya, Hindu Kush and Karakoram mountains meet. The scenery is said to be spectacular and it is the main thing we have been looking forward to seeing in Pakistan.

We head to Murree and the beginning of the Karakoram Highway and are bitterly disappointed. There is snow and ice on the road, which makes it extremely dangerous on the bike. We slip around a corner and pull over to the side to have a bit of a think. We know it is time to turn back when a small van carrying about 20 people passes us. It skids around the next corner and then slides backwards down the hill, completely out of control. Two army officers, who opted to walk down the hill rather than take their chances in the bus, walk past us. 'The road is closed,' one of them says to Brian.

Rather than heading back to Islamabad, we decide to go on to Peshawar. After six hours on the bike – and only 280 km, we head to a hotel that, according to our guidebook, has a bar (a rarity in Pakistan). The Pearl Continental is quite a place, but at 11,000 rupees (AUD$275) plus 20 per cent tax for a double, it is way out of our price range. We opt for another hotel recommended in the guidebook. This one is only 400 rupees (about AUD$10). It is fairly clean and has undercover off-street parking for the bike, so it will have to do.

There are two reasons to come to Peshawar – the Khyber Pass, the road connecting Pakistan and Afghanistan, and Darra, the town where illegal firearms are manufactured under the blind eye of officialdom. To travel up the Khyber Pass you need a permit, an official guide and an armed guard from the Tribal Police. We organise all this through the hotel. Before we leave, our guide, Sohail, tempts us to take a trip to Darra. There is no permit required here, as it is strictly off-limits to foreigners. That gives us something to think about.

Sohail arrives with a tiny car. The driver and the guard sit in the front, and the guard carries his Kalashnikov rifle across his knees. Sohail isn't a small man, so it is very tight in the back with him sitting between Brian and me.

The Khyber Pass is part of the North-West Frontier Province, which doesn't actually come under Pakistani rule. They have their own police and there is a general feeling of lawlessness in the area. There are also some areas that are dangerous for foreigners. We can't get out of the car in certain places. We can in others, but our guard sticks to us like glue to make sure we are safe. And we are warned not to photograph the women. There was a 'problem' when foreigners did this on another tour. Sohail won't elaborate, but we heed his advice.

There are many armed Tribal Police patrolling the road. On the side of the road are the usual yellow traffic advisory signs. In Australia they warn of koalas or kangaroos crossing the road or of sharp curves. Here they warn of armed men. I make the guide stop the car when I see two armed men sitting underneath one of these signs, as if trying to prove a point. It was too good a photo opportunity to pass up.

Along the road we pass an enormous fortress and mansion. It is the home of Aube Khan Afridi, a local hero and counterfeiter. It is with great pride that we are told he has served time in prison in the US and Pakistan for currency forgery. Our guard asks the Afridi security men if we can come inside the fortress walls and see the garden, but they don't think it is such a good idea.

At the top of the Khyber Pass are numerous trucks

waiting to cross into Afghanistan with all sorts of things – food, cars and consumer goods.

The last stop for us is Michni checkpost, an old Khyber Rifles fort that offers a good vantage point into Afghanistan. It looks much like the landscape we have just driven through – dry, desolate and uninteresting. A boy comes up selling souvenirs of Afghan money for 200 rupees a set. We don't buy until Sohail tells us the lad's income is drastically reduced because of the decrease in tourist numbers since September 11. I buy one set for 100 rupees – its only $2.50 to us but will mean a lot to the kid.

We opt for a tour of Darra. Our guide drills us on what to say if we are stopped by the local police and insists that we don't tell the people at the hotel where we have been. Darra is a tiny village with just one industry, the manufacture of illegal firearms. It was once the heart of Pakistani heroin manufacturing and sales but the government closed that down due to foreign pressure. I wonder how long it will be before the trade in illegal firearms also becomes an embarrassment to the officials.

In the dusty town, a policeman gestures at us to pull over. I am sure this means the end of our tour until I work out that the policeman is actually taking us to the gun shops. He runs the tour. He takes the money – or the bribe.

After discussions with the driver and the guide, the policeman finally gets into the back seat of the car with us and says hello. He seems very friendly. He directs the driver down a dirt laneway and we come across a large vacant block – a makeshift cricket pitch. We drive right through the two games being played with the same earnestness as a test match. The players seem about to complain until they see the policeman in the back seat.

Over the shouts of the cricketers we hear the sound of gunfire coming from a single laneway on the edge of the town. There are a number of small, dilapidated tin shacks lining the dirt lane. We are told each one of these houses an integral part of the firearm industry.

We wander down the street with the policeman as our guide. He shows us where they make the barrels, the handpieces, where they colour the metal, where they polish it and where they make all the bits and pieces that go into handguns and rifles of all shapes and calibre. He is proud that the gunsmiths can produce an exact replica of any firearm in about four days.

No-one worries when Brian and I come in with our camera. The workers are delighted when I show them their photos on the camera's screen. They don't see too many digital cameras in this part of Pakistan. One man we photograph asks if the photo will come out of the camera!

No-one worries when Brian handles the guns and no-one even flinches when they learn he is a policeman from Australia. Our guide actually has a grand idea (well, he thinks so). He suggests a career swap. He and his wife and nine kids will move to Melbourne, and Brian and I can come and live in Darra. Oh, crikey!

As part of our tour, we are taken to a valley at the back of the town to test-fire some of the merchandise. I find firearms abhorrent and refuse, but Brian is interested in the quality of the firearms. He is sure this is where some of the illegal guns found in Australia originate. We walk down the street to a very dirty, litter-filled creek bed. We are followed by about 10 boys. These urchins are filthy and smell. We get to a clearing and Brian is told to shoot up and aim for a break in the rocks. As he fires the Kalashnikov machine gun, the kids scramble for the discarded casings. Now I know why they were so keen to follow us. They get the empty casings and sell them back to the gun manufacturers for 10 rupees per 10 pieces. What an awful way to make a living.

Brian is appalled by the fact this industry is flourishing

under the watchful eye of the local police. The policeman has no compunction in taking money to support his family. The attitude is that the illegal gun trade and the endemic corruption are okay.

The prices for replica handguns are ridiculously cheap. The tradesmen of Darra pride themselves on the fact that they can copy firearms from Italy, Germany, Russia and China in a few days. They may not be as good as the originals, but they are just as deadly.

'Since the end of the Afghan war, business is not too good,' explains the policeman. 'But there is still a reasonable market for pistols with the Russian mafia and other criminals from the West. Making guns keeps the town alive and the money I get helps me support my wife and nine children. My wife is worn out.' (Little wonder – after raising nine children in this area!)

Even more staggering is the shop where you can buy handguns for 1000 or 1500 rupees and a replica Kalashnikov for just 5000 rupees. Pen pistols are just 500 rupees and they charge 1500 rupees to fire off 30 rounds from a Kalashnikov. It is incredible to think I paid 2500 rupees for a hair colour in Islamabad. I could have bought two handguns and a pen pistol for the same price!

We are glad to leave this area of Pakistan. Sitting in the hotel, having breakfast, we look down onto an intersection where horses, just skin and bone, go by. Their skin bleeds where they are whipped to keep hauling their heavy loads. The hustle and bustle is relentless and even though it is only 8.30 in the morning, dirt hangs in the air. The only sound you hear other than the honking of horns is the constant one of men hacking their lungs up. It is stomach-churning, something we can't get used to and won't miss.

We are determined to head into the mountains, so we try another road, this time avoiding Murree. Once we hit the Karakoram Highway we are riding through lush agricultural land with eucalyptus trees lining both sides of the road. Apart from the run-down villages, the scenery gets better and the air is cleaner as we climb into the hills. But the drivers are still crazy. Brian overtakes a small bus with at least 20 people hanging off it. As he pulls out, the driver veers across in front of us without indicating. My heart stops and I stiffen, getting ready for the collision, but Brian rides alongside the bus. In a split second, however, another bus heads towards us. We squeeze between the two. There is a huge joint intake of breath as we breathe in to make ourselves thinner. It is a close call, with just centimetres to spare. We seem to have a guardian angel travelling with us.

We have been warned that some of the towns in the North-West Frontier Province are home to fundamentalists who have no love for foreigners and are not afraid to show it. We are advised to stop only in the major towns and not venture off the main highway. We can feel the animosity. In some towns small kids pick up stones to throw at us, but they frighten easily when Brian rides straight at them. It is the teenagers who are menacing. When they appear, Brian guns the engine and scoots past.

The highway now follows the Indus River. It is a most striking turquoise colour. At times we are about a kilometre above the Indus as it winds its way through the craggy mountains. A couple of kilometres down the road and we are right alongside it. Coming out of the corners, we look ahead and glimpse the magnificent snow-capped peaks of the mountains standing guard over barren, brown and dusty hills. We pass goats, sheep, cows and donkeys grazing on the side of the highway. Boys and men sit on rocky outcrops and watch with suspicious eyes as we go past.

Even though the sun is out and the sky is a brilliant blue it gets very cold as we climb high above the river. I commit the cardinal sin of motorcycling and ask Brian to stop so I can put on my winter gloves and polar-fleece jumper. I get the irate reaction I expect. It's okay for him, he's got the heated hand grips! A little way on, he stops to change the battery in the Minidisc. There is something about areas like this that really creates the need for music.

Along the way, we are surprised to meet another motorcycling couple – Richard and Lisa from New Zealand. While we share a meal and our travel tales on the side of the road, a man in a small truck pulls over. He has business on his mind. He would like to swap some whisky for hash. Well, he's out of luck. We don't have any whisky and we don't want any hash. He is obviously disappointed.

Heading into Gilgit we cover some pretty lousy roads with huge sections washed away by landslides. Truckies have left markers to warn other drivers – a small circle of rocks indicates a potentially lethal drop to the river below. Above the washouts, rock ledges hang precariously above the road. Brian loves every twist and turn. He is truly in his element.

Brian: I am fulfilling a dream. Riding the Karakoram Highway is exciting, dangerous, difficult, and breathtaking all at the same moment. There are signs that proudly extol the virtues of the road builders, and fair enough, too. They have cut a route out of vertical cliff-faces.

It's nothing to see one or more huge rocks scattered across the road. There are numerous stream crossings, most of which have a concrete bottom, making the going easy as long as the water isn't too high. In full flow, the stream would wash a motorcycle over the edge to the river about a kilometre below. No wonder they close the road from the end of November through to May.

Shirley: The Hunza Valley, high in the Karakoram Mountains, is the most beautiful part of the highway. Mt Rakaposhi, at 7788 metres, towers over the area. It is breathtaking and our camera can't capture the height of the jagged peaks that soar above us. It is the most impressive scenery we've seen on this trip, even when we take into account the Pyrenees, the Dolomites and Mont Blanc.

But there is a drawback – it is getting colder and colder. After a night in Gilgit, it is time to crack out the thermals before heading further into the mountains. I am in the bathroom when I hear some extremely colourful language coming from the bedroom. I can't help but laugh when I see what is causing Brian such consternation. He is sitting on the end of the bed with his thermal long johns around his calf muscles. There is absolutely no way they will budge any further. 'Look at this,' he says, 'the bloody things have shrunk. I told you not to let Faisal do the washing.'

I can't stop laughing. His thermals would now fit a small child; the top is too small even for me to wear! Just as well Brian doesn't feel the cold as much as I do.

The closer we get to Karimabad the colder it gets. We push on. Brian is keen to get to the Chinese border. We are now only a couple of feet from the fast-flowing Indus River and the water is beginning to freeze over. I don't think I've ever been this cold. I am quietly cursing Brian. When I ask about the temperature, he happily tells me it is probably a couple of degrees below zero!

When we turn a bend and head into Pasu, the first thing we see is the most incredible glacier down the mountainside. It is like a river frozen in time. The sun glistens on the surface as if the water is set with diamonds. It is truly beautiful! We press on even though by now my hands and feet are aching with the cold. I can't even think of taking photos, as this would mean undoing my jacket to get the camera and taking one glove off.

On the outskirts of Sost, the last town before the border, a water crossing is frozen solid. Hotels are already closed, as there aren't too many visitors up here at this time of the year. The road to China is open but icy. Richard and Lisa, the New Zealand couple, told us they dropped their bike a couple of times trying to make the border.

We turn and head back to Karimabad and the wonderful Ismailis. These Muslims believe their spiritual leader, the Aga Khan, is a direct descendant of Mohammed. He is the 49th hereditary Imam. He's also a British citizen and well-known racehorse owner. He believes in educating women. The owner of our hotel is proud of his daughter, who has a Masters degree and is hoping to do her PhD overseas. 'The Aga Khan says if you have two children and you can only afford to educate one, educate the girl, because she will educate the family,' he says.

Across the valley, the people are Shia. They don't agree with their less-regimented neighbours. We are sad to learn, a couple of months after visiting Karimabad, that men from across the valley stole into the town in the middle of the night and blew up the schools so they couldn't continue educating their children, the boys as well as the girls.

The people of the Hunza Valley are renowned for their longevity. The oldest man so far was 118 when he died. We ask the locals the reason for this. They say there is no stress, no competition (everyone has about the same amount of land, animals, etc.), good food and 'Hunza Water'. We think this means the mountain waters, but they explain it is home-made wine. The mulberry wine is 45 per cent alcohol! The apple, apricot and grape wine is like 'French' wine, about 13 or 14 per cent. (When we asked about alcohol at the hotel, the owner did mention he could get us a mineral-water bottle filled with mulberry wine, but we declined. Knowing what we know now I am glad we did. It would have ironed us out!)

Ramadan is over and Eid, the celebrations marking the end of the month of fasting, has begun. As we ride through the mountain villages, we see men outside, celebrating. They are wearing flowers under their hat bands, feasting in the fields and playing cricket on makeshift pitches. But along with their cricket bats they carry guns over their shoulders and periodically we can hear gunfire from the hills. I just can't believe we don't see any women. They don't even take part in these important celebrations.

Murphy's Law takes effect on the highway 38 km outside of Besham. It is our first flat tyre after 38,000 km on the road. Brian makes some running repairs and they hold for more than 300 km until we are on the outskirts of Islamabad. Of course, we can't get tyres for our bike in Pakistan. So we have to repair the damage and keep our fingers crossed. For just 50 rupees (about AUD$1.25) and two bottles of Coke, a local tyre repairman fixes the tyre. Only in Pakistan.

Pakistan has been an interesting experience. In some areas, women aren't integrated into society. They are revered as mothers, but kept isolated in their homes. In some areas, honour killings are still condoned when a woman shames her family. We read of one case where a young woman 'committed suicide' after running off and marrying a young man she loved rather than the family's choice for her. Her family buried her in a shallow grave in the cemetery in the early hours of the morning, without a service. It was only when the boy's family went to the authorities that anything was done, but whether the family will be punished is another thing. Women working in some of the embassies tell us many stories of 'suicides', gas explosions and acid-throwing incidents that all point to honour killings.

Our last vision of Pakistan is a bleak one. We travel on the highway to India and it takes us through impoverished villages with cows and goats and urchin children rummaging through the rubbish on the sides of the road. Our last conversation is with the customs officer. We talk about cricket and he indicates that Ricky Ponting is his pin-up boy.

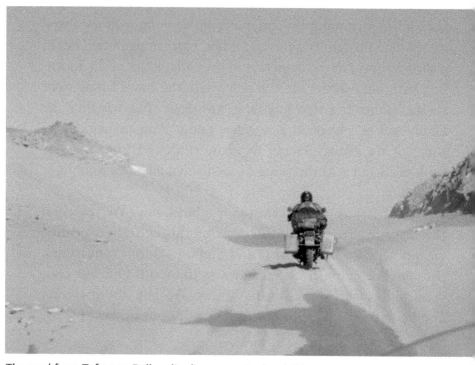

The road from Taftan to Dalbandin disappears in the shifting sands

Not much can live out here in the des

ra gun market

Our hotel's security guard in Multan

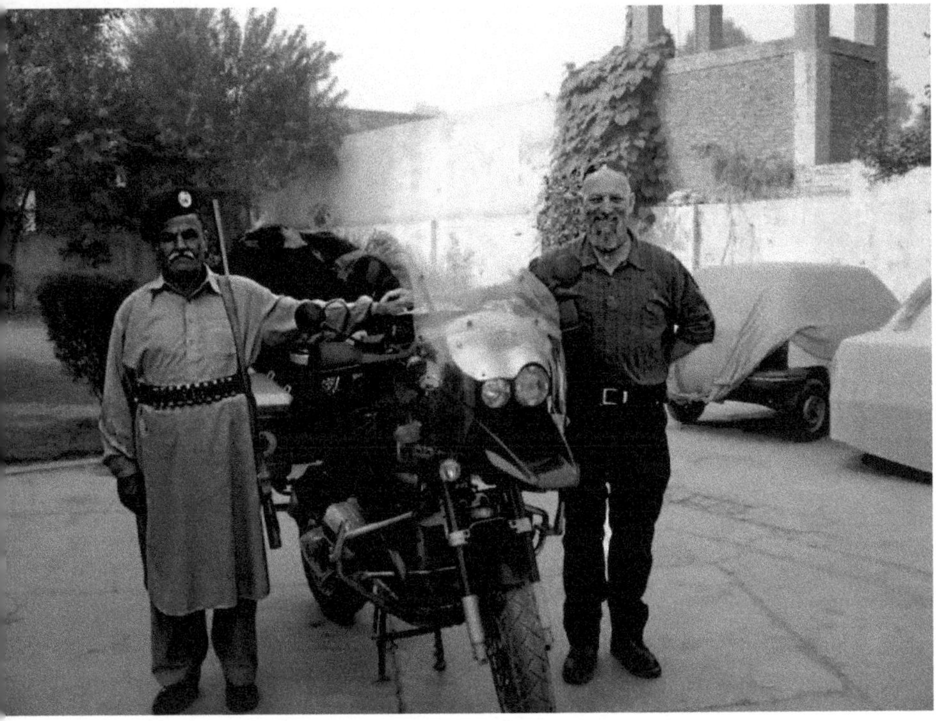

With our security guard

Heavy traffic through the Khyber Pass

Snow on the Karakoram Highw

nza Valley on the Karakoram Highway

Spectacular scenery on the Karakoram Highway between Gilgit and Sost

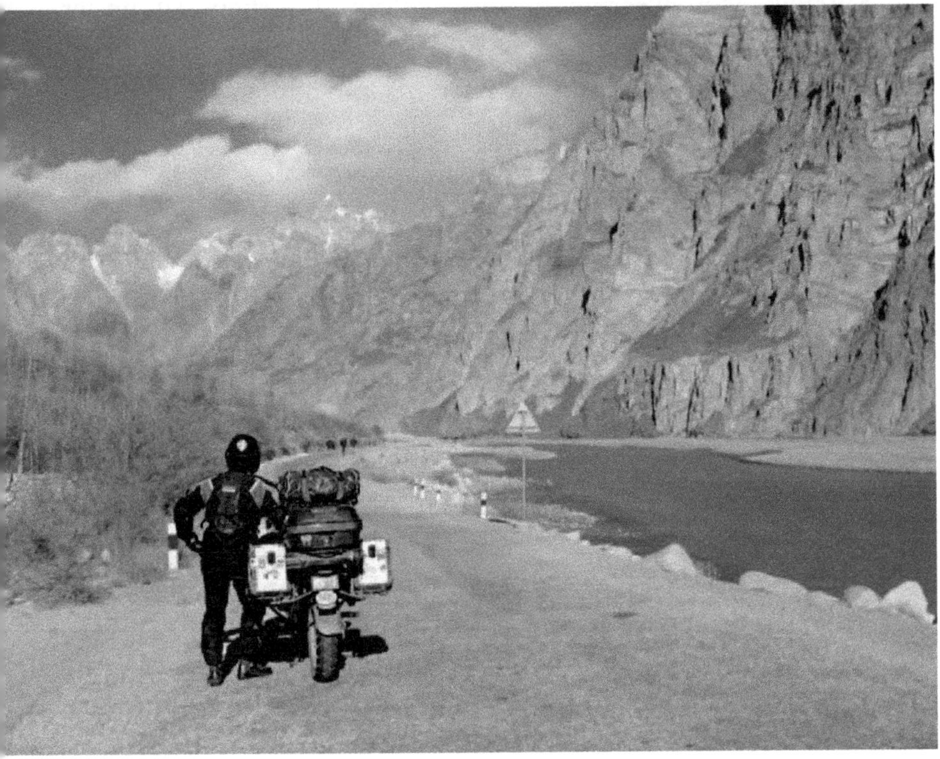

TWELVE

INDIA

3 December 2003 – 23 January 2004

Shirley: Men wearing brightly coloured turbans sit under the sign declaring India is the world's largest democracy. They jostle around the travellers, hoping to get the job of carrying their luggage across the no-man's-land between the two border gates. They are disappointed when we tell them we don't need their help.

The Inspector of Police writes down all our details and then directs us to the health officer, who doesn't want to see our vaccination cards. Now, for the first time, our details are entered into a computer rather than an ancient ledger.

We know we have crossed the border when we move through the glass doors into the customs hall. The two people working in here are women! Apart from the women at the Islamabad post office and a couple of hotel workers in the Hunza Valley, we haven't seen working women for weeks.

The men working in the area check out the bike and for the first time, we've been asked to open the panniers. I'm not sure if it is just done to embarrass me or is a genuine question, but one of the men produces my tampons and asks what they are. I try not to be rude as I snatch them back from him.

Everything must be okay, because back in the customs hall we are invited to tea. The two men and two women all pull up chairs around one table and we join them. Just as well we are not in a hurry. They want to talk about Australia and Australians. The women are big fans of Australian television. I am hoping they will be fans of some of the great dramas made in Australia, but no, the show they never miss is *Who Dares Wins*. I think I would rather they said *Neighbours* or *Home and Away*, as at least these shows give work to actors and writers. Still, there is no accounting for taste. They are also intrigued by Brian's profession and want to know if he has his badge, is working and carrying his gun.

The border staff is very proud of the new tourist toy they have and go to the trouble of waking up the local tourism representative to show us. It is a touch-screen computer that tells you everything you want to know about Punjab, the region in northern India and east Pakistan where we are heading. The highlight seems to be the Sikhs' Golden Temple in Amritsar.

Everyone, including our friend Rohan in Pakistan, Dagmar and Peter, and the customs officials, has told us about Mrs Bhandari's guesthouse in Amritsar. The guidebook also recommends it. So we have no choice but to head straight there. We have literally only travelled 100 m into India when we notice some startling differences between this country and its neighbour. First, women ride motorcycles and not just as pillion passengers. And there are pigs snorting their way through piles of rubbish on the sides of the roads. We haven't seen pigs for ages. While the sights might be different, the smells are familiar. The canal is virtually an open sewer, and the odour is even more of an assault to the senses than the streets of Quetta. When we stop and ask for directions we also notice not so many people speak English, whereas in Pakistan all the police and military speak English. Here they look at us blankly.

The city of Amritsar bustles with activity. Men in rickshaw bicycles call out as we pass. Children are jammed into motorised rickshaws on their way home from school. Their bags are hanging off the mirrors to make room for more kids inside. Horses pull carts loaded with country produce. And the pigs continue to eat the rubbish, oblivious to the commotion.

Mrs Bhandari's is an oasis amid the noise and smells of the city. Hidden behind a high wall, the garden is a haven from the hustle and bustle. The house itself is plain in its design but impressive in size. The guestrooms are dotted around the grounds, and ours looks out over the lawns and rose garden. There is something distinctly Indian about the gardens. Water buffalo spend their days in the courtyard just inside the gate. The houseboys take the animals out of their shed at the back of the property every morning and take them back again every night.

Mrs Bhandari is now a very old woman and restricted to spending her days in her home, looking out onto the gardens. The guesthouse is run by her granddaughter Shirin. She welcomes us to her home and introduces us to Sam and Whisky, the guesthouse dogs. Travellers are welcome here and everyone makes us feel at home.

Late in the afternoon we head back to the border, not to cross back into Pakistan but to witness the famous closing ceremony. Every night the border gates are slammed shut, symbolically showing the differences between the two countries. There are hundreds of Indians, including busloads of schoolchildren waving Indian flags, queued up waiting to be let into the seating area of 'no-man's-land'.

The border guards are resplendent in their uniforms and ceremonial hats festooned with red, black and gold fans, white spats and polished boots. They are very tall and the fans add to the impression of height. Their moustaches are waxed and twirled. They paint a striking picture of authority and control – and that is what the ceremony is all about.

When the guards open the gates, we are swept along with the crowd and herded to concrete seats on either side of no-man's-land. Through the gates we peer into Pakistan, where another crowd is gathering. Finally, it is show time – the border between Pakistan and India is about to close. It's theatre at its best.

The Pakistani soldiers march backwards and forwards, menacing their Indian counterparts on our side of the border. The Indian soldiers march at what seems to be triple time. Their high kicks put the can-can dancers at the Moulin Rouge to shame. One by one each set of soldiers marches up to the border and faces the 'enemy'. The flags of the two countries are lowered simultaneously with enormous pomp and ceremony. The soldiers fold the flags with style and march them back to the border offices for the night.

The crowds on both sides of the divide yell, cheer, jeer, shake their fists, stamp their feet and sing. Their chants are probably the equivalent of 'Aussie, Aussie, Aussie, oi, oi, oi!' The schoolchildren sing and wave their flags with gusto. The border guards blow whistles, trying to get the enthusiastic patriots to sit down. It is an impossible task and eventually they give up on it. We are swept up by the emotion of it all. It is exhilarating.

A young entrepreneur, about 8 years old, comes up to us as we are leaving and offers for sale photos of the ceremony.

I take a couple to look at and an enormous soldier appears at my shoulder. As he leans over and takes them from me, the children run in all directions. Clearly they are not meant to sell the photos. The soldier smiles at us and then tears the photos in half.

In Turkey we saw people drying cow dung into pats for the fire. Here, we burn them on the small open fire in our room. They throw out incredible warmth without an unpleasant odour – perfect recycling.

Nights here are cold enough for an open fire, but the days are warm enough for breakfast in the garden. The serenity of the morning is shattered when a pig comes through the gate of the guesthouse. Pandemonium breaks out when Sam starts to bark and chase the terrified pig. It tries to get out, but keeps running into shrubs and bushes in the garden. The houseboys appear with brooms and sticks and join in the chase. Then Shirin comes out of the house and we really have a three-ringed circus. There are dogs barking, people yelling and the pig squealing. Whisky is a sheepdog well past her prime. She watches this performance from a shady spot in the garden until it all becomes too much for her. She stands up and waits. As the pig comes around the corner again, she is off, forgetting that she has arthritis. In minutes she has herded the pig out of the gate and the drama's over. With a shake of her head, Whisky remembers her arthritis and limps over to our table. She deserves the toast that is waiting for her.

One of the first things we notice in India is how people of different religions seem to live side by side in peace. In Amritsar, the Hindu Mata Temple and the Sikhs' sacred Golden Temple are both on the tourist agenda. Their differences are dramatic.

Mata Temple is filled with brightly coloured statues of deities. It honours Lal Devi, a female saint, and many women come to pray here. Our rickshaw driver takes us into the temple. We climb stairs in our bare feet, crawl through tunnels only a couple of feet high and clamber through holes into pools of water and past an incredible collection of statues of Hindu deities. Many people are praying and singing in this holy shrine, but we find it a little hard to take seriously. To us the deities seem fantastic rather than religious. There are women with many arms, men with the head of an elephant – nothing like the statues we are used to in Christian society.

The Golden Temple has the consumer side of religion sewn up. Before you reach the temple you must walk past numerous shops selling scarves, T-shirts, spoons, CDs – you name it and you can get it here with the Golden Temple motif.

As in the mosques of Pakistan, we must cover our heads here and leave our shoes outside. Inside the white-marble entrance is the sacred pool – the pool of nectar. In the middle of it is the Golden Temple, the holiest of the Sikh shrines. They say there are 100 kg of gold in the temple and indeed it glistens in the sunshine. We walk along the marble walkway that skirts the pool. Pilgrims rest under awnings, Sikhs pray, some washing their faces and hands in the pool. Others just kneel before it. There are petitioned-off areas where devotees can immerse themselves in the water several times. It doesn't seem very clean, but it is home to enormous carp, so it can't be too dirty.

The Sikh holy book is kept inside the temple. Holy men read from the book, preachers sing and followers pray. The men wear turbans and ceremonial daggers tucked into their belts. It is a beautiful, peaceful place in the centre of the madness that is Amritsar.

At the guesthouse, we are honoured to be invited to

visit Mrs Bhandari. Shirin takes us into the main house where her grandmother spends her days. She is 97 and very frail. This doesn't stop her firmly grasping Brian's hand when she is introduced. She then places her head on his hand. It is amazing to think that this little old lady was such a progressive woman in her youth. Raised a Parsi (a Zoroastrian sect), she married a Hindu (Mr Bhandari), which was certainly not the thing to do. In the house there is a photo of Mrs Bhandari in a sari. She was beautiful. An independent businesswoman, she continued to run the guesthouse after the death of her husband, who was the love of her life. The house is filled with beautiful china and furniture that were gifts from Britons who fled India after independence.

In the heart of Amritsar there is a poignant reminder of the struggle for independence – Jallianwala Bagh. In this park, in 1919, 2000 Indians were massacred by the British during a peaceful demonstration against an act that allowed the Brits to imprison Indians without a trial for suspected sedition. The Indians were in the park when the British arrived, sealed off the only entrance to the park and ordered the Indians to disperse. When they didn't, the British opened fire. Two hundred bodies were found at the bottom of the park's well. Today an eternal flame commemorates the dead.

When Richard and Lisa, the two Kiwi bikers we met in Pakistan, arrive at Mrs Bhandari's it is the perfect excuse to stay another day. It is also an excuse for me to do some shopping with Shirin. Shirin takes me to a small shop in town to buy some traditional Punjabi slippers. The salesmen are very patient and don't get the slightest bit annoyed when I try on at least 50 pairs of slippers – some very simple, some incredibly ornate and some just garish. I try some on two or three times and then once more, just to ensure I make the right selection. That's the easy part. Now I have to pay for them. The starting price is 700 rupees a pair (about AUD$20). With Shirin's help and determination and numerous threats to walk out and not buy any shoes, I get the price down to 500 rupees (about AUD$15).

The Golden Temple is even more beautiful at night, with the lights accentuating the gold detailing. Brian and I are here to watch the ceremony in which the holy book is taken back to its place in the Sikh Parliament building for the night. It is a privilege for the Sikhs to be able to be a part of this ceremony and it is a privilege for us to witness it at close hand. The book is ceremoniously wrapped and placed on an ornate sedan chair decorated in gold, brocade and velvet. The sedan chair is then carried out of the temple. A trumpet sounds and men (not women) jostle for an opportunity to be a part of the procession. They push and shove, but without anger or animosity. Everyone has a turn and at the end of the night they all leave happier for the experience.

On the road to the Buddhist enclave of McLeod Ganj, the home of the Dalai Lama and the Tibetan government in exile, we discover another impediment on the roads: cows. These sacred beasts have right of way and wander out onto the roadway at will. They are a motorcyclist's nightmare. Add to this the warning signs of 'Bridge Damaged – Drive Slowly' and 'Road Damaged – Drive Slow', and it is a lengthy ride to our destination.

We stay in Cloud's End guesthouse, which was once the home of the local maharaja. Perched on a hillside under the town, it has sweeping views across the Kangra Valley. In the mornings the mist in the valley is crowned by sunshine reflecting off the bases of clouds, giving rise to the name Cloud's End.

The majority of the population here are Tibetan refugees. Even though the town is busy, there is an undercurrent of serenity. Monks in flowing robes walk the streets and are always quick with enormous smiles. Shopkeepers sell the traditional prayer flags, prayer wheels and the traditional Tibetan Buddhist paintings known as Thangkas, as well as kitsch items. The food is good too. At the Tibetan restaurants, noodle and won ton soups ward off the cold and the *mo mo* (steamed dumplings filled with fried vegetables) are a taste sensation.

Tsuglagkhang is the Dalai Lama's home in McLeod Ganj. Here, the ever-smiling monks and their religious leader work towards a free Tibet. Golden Buddhas and statues of Avalokitesvara, the Tibetan deity of compassion (the Dalai Lama is said to be an incarnation of this deity), and Padmasambhava, the Indian scholar who introduced Buddhism to Tibet, are housed in the temples. Smiling portraits of the Dalai Lama look down from the walls. Again, there is a feeling of serenity here, something we find wherever we meet Buddhists.

Another monastery, Tse Chok Ling Gompa, nestled in the valley, is home to many young monks, some of them only children. In the prayer hall we sit and listen to the monks chanting; it is hypnotic. But our presence is clearly distracting one of the younger monks who is more interested in us than in his devotions. We ponder the fact we have never read or heard of Buddhist monks or devotees causing trouble or injury to others, even in the name of freedom for Tibet. It's a pity the same can't be said for other religions.

Before it became home to Tibetan refugees, McLeod Ganj was a favourite with the British. They came to this hilly haven to escape the blistering summer heat in other parts of India.

The 1852 St John in the Wilderness church, just outside the town, is a reminder of the days when Christianity was the area's dominant religion. Inside a plaque commemorates a man who was killed by a bear in 1883. Many children are buried here as well as several of the church rectors. The church and its graveyard are set in a garden of pine trees. It is peaceful and we feel very distant from the tourist hub that is McLeod Ganj.

Riding in India is slow and tedious. In every town we need to ask directions. Signs just don't seem to play an important part in Indian life. When the going is good we average about 50 km/h. And the roads are tough on the bike. The constant jolting has cracked the mount supporting the top box in four places. Everyone says the Indians can fix anything, and that is probably true. The problem we have is the rack is in aluminium and there aren't too many people who can weld aluminium. We strap the top box in place and go in search of a repairer. We find plenty of welders, but none who can help us until we get to Chandigarh, 140 km down the road.

Chandigarh is a modern, planned city; not as glamorous as Islamabad but built on the same principle with sectors rather than suburbs. We seem to end up in the suburbs when we hit town and ask for directions to the hotel suggested in our guidebook. We ride back and forth, being sent in different directions by different people. A favourite instruction is to tell us to 'go straight', which is fine until you come to a deviation or intersection. Even the police give us complicated and confusing directions. Eventually we find a hotel – not the one we are looking for, but a hotel. And it is fortuitous that we do. The manager not only knows an aluminium welder, he has a houseboy who would love to go on the bike with Brian to show him the way and act as interpreter while the repairs are done.

Brian: One of the hands at the hotel is press-ganged into going with me to the welding shop. He is even given a helmet to use while on the back of my bike. His workmates give him the Bronx cheer as we ride off. My guide takes me through a maze of streets, a drab-looking housing estate and an even worse-looking industrial estate. The whole area is devoted to mechanical repairs for cars and scooters. It is typically Indian: each 'shop' has a frontage no wider than 3.5 m and with a concrete apron where all the work is done. Consequently, as soon as we pull up, we gather a crowd of about 100.

The welder takes one look at the bike and says he can repair it. We agree on a price of 450 rupees (about AUD$13). I wonder if you could get a welder to get off his chair in Australia for that!

As we start to pull the back of the bike apart, the crowd swells to around 300, blocking the small street! More than once I stand on toes and hear a yelp. They all push in and it is very claustrophobic. Two boys from the shop are helping. Stray fingers from the crowd are touching everything on the bike and I'm trying to lay pieces out so I will know where they should go back. That's impossible. The crowd pushes closer until I yell for some space.

As the welder does his best to turn two pieces back into one, I try to take stock of where all the bits and pieces are. It's almost impossible with fingers from the crowd picking them up. They all seem to want to inspect everything and then put it back.

The welding takes ages and the people around me ask

the inevitable questions: 'Where are you from?' 'How much does the bike cost?' 'How fast does it go?' 'How big is it?' 'What is the brake horsepower?' 'How much petrol does it use?' This goes on and on and on. I see a very tall black man in the crowd. He comes up to me and speaks perfect English with an American accent. He is Kenyan and is in Chandigarh studying at university. He asks the same questions.

After three hours the welding is complete. The final result is not pretty, but hopefully it will work. The once-polished aluminium supplied by BMW is now blackened and rough. It takes a further hour to sort out where every nut, washer and spacer came from as the two boys and I put it all back together. They insist on doing most of the work. I think they just want to handle the bits and pieces, and often I have to rearrange different-length screws they are trying to put in the wrong place.

It has been a hard day and I'm knackered. After a quick shower back at the hotel, Shirl and I head to a bar next door. Three beers don't even touch the sides.

Shirley: An attempt to get cash from an ATM creates a real 'blonde' moment for me. I put my card into the machine and try to withdraw 15,000 rupees, but the machine refuses to give me the money. Then it won't give me the card back. I can't believe it.

Brian checks the machine for one of the false-card rorts and says everything seems okay. By now I am sobbing. Brian moves into control mode and uses the mobile given to us by Rohan in Pakistan to ring the emergency-assistance number on the machine. I am getting hysterical, telling the man on the other end that the machine not only has my card, it wouldn't give me any money. He assures me that is not possible.

'We are visitors in your country.' I am starting to sound shrill. 'This isn't good enough. It is going to ruin our holiday.'

Twenty minutes later, a nice young man from the bank arrives to sort out the problem. He opens the machine and there is no card inside. He starts to pull the card reader apart and demonstrates with his card how this machine works. The card doesn't go all the way into the machine. It couldn't possibly take the card. 'Are you sure you don't have your card?'

I check my wallet and, sure enough, there is the card, safely tucked away in its normal spot. I burst into tears again. We apologise and make our escape, leaving a grinning technician who is sure to tell the story of the idiot tourists.

Brian: The road to Delhi isn't too bad, but the traffic is thick with wandering cows, pedestrians, bicycles, motorised rickshaws, trucks and, worst of all, crazy bus drivers. They overtake no matter what is coming and pull up to let passengers on or off without pulling over to the side of the road. Few have brake lights. Plus, there is no such thing here as leaving a safety gap between vehicles – gaps just get filled with impatient drivers cutting in front of you. The only way to ride is like the locals, to use the speed and manoeuvrability of the bike to make headway, and stay as far left as possible.

After around 250 km, we see the aftermath of two accidents, which look like head-on collisions. Both involve trucks. One is on its side, blocking half the road, with both cabins crushed beyond recognition. I would be very surprised if these accidents were not fatal. They say there are six or more fatal accidents each day in Delhi. I don't doubt it.

Shirley: Nine million people live in Delhi and it seems like most of them are on the roads when we arrive in the city. After getting hopelessly lost, we pay a rickshaw driver to take us to our guesthouse. Unfortunately, it's booked out, but our rickshaw man knows another hotel he can take us to. He admits he gets 50 rupees for taking us there. What the heck, it's business.

The Hotel City Castle in Karol Bagh is okay. The sheets are clean, the water is hot and the staff seem friendly. In Delhi everything is in designated areas. If you want air tickets, you go to Connaught Place and if you want car parts you go to Karol Bagh. So while we can get anything for a car – from a sticker to a stereo system that will be heard in other countries – you can't get food. There are no restaurants or street food stalls, just auto shops. We end up ordering room service and now we know why the staff are so friendly. They see us as cash cows and just hang around waiting for tips.

At breakfast the next morning, the tipping fiasco is on again. At one stage, the porters bring a man we haven't seen before to our room and demand we give him money because he works behind the scenes. What a lurk!

While New Delhi is like any other major city, the old town is fascinating. The Qutab Minar, a massive carved tower that marks an Islamic victory over Delhi's last Hindu kingdom, dates back to the twelfth century, Islamic times in India. It has been struck by lightning and shaken by earthquakes, but has stood the test of time. A fifth-century iron pillar bearing inscriptions in Sanskrit has archaeologists puzzled. It has stood in the elements for around 1500 years, yet it hasn't rusted.

The Gandhis are idolised in India. The Delhi home of the late Indira Gandhi, prime minister of India from the 1960s to the mid-1980s before she was assassinated by her Sikh bodyguards in 1984, is now a memorial to her. The displays are fascinating and macabre. The sari Mrs Gandhi was wearing when she was shot is on display, bloodstains and all. Her son Rajiv was also assassinated, and charred remains of the clothing and shoes he was wearing when hit by an extremist's bomb are in a nearby glass cabinet. Her other son,

Sanjay, was killed in a plane crash. In the garden, the path of Indira's final steps is now covered in glass. One end of the glass marks the spot where she fell. The blood stains are still on the grass beneath.

On the banks of the Yamuna River is a black-marble memorial that marks the place where Mahatma Gandhi was cremated (not far from the site of Indira, Rajiv and Sanjay's cremations). Yet another victim of an extremist assassin, Mahatma is still revered and people come here to pay tribute to him. Mahatma led his country to independence and today an eternal flame burns in his honour.

With some effort, we leave the hotel without giving any more tips and take the road to Agra and the Taj Mahal. The highway is smooth and wide, a prime ministerial project that's almost completed. But good roads don't necessarily mean incident-free driving. We come across the aftermath of a horrendous accident: a donkey lies in the middle of the road, struggling to get to its feet. It's been hit by a vehicle and has two broken legs. We see another donkey, closer to town, who was hit days ago and has a terrible maggoty wound on its back. Both these animals are in incredible pain, yet no-one seems to care. We are getting used to seeing mangy, scrawny dogs, but the sight of these two unfortunate animals is incredibly distressing.

The road from the highway to Agra is not so good and we hear a loud crack when we bounce into a major pothole. Yep, the welding has broken on both sides.

At Agra, the incredibly helpful hotel staff send a houseboy with Brian to find the local welder. This time he takes the bike apart at the hotel rather than risking the probing fingers of all and sundry at the welder's. I just have to make sure the monkeys that play in the hotel garden don't knock off some bits and pieces. For 200 rupees, we are back in action in a couple of hours. Hopefully the mount will last.

The Taj Mahal is the ultimate monument to love. We have seen hundreds of photos of it, yet nothing prepares us for its beauty in the early morning light. When we walk through the gate, the sight takes our breath away. The entrance price of 750 rupees (about AUD$23) is worth it.

You can't look at the Taj and not think about that poignant shot of Princess Diana sitting here on her own. We can't resist. We get our photo taken on the same spot; it is perfect. The morning sun glistens on the semiprecious stones inlaid into the white marble. It is an unforgettable sight. We sit for a while and take in the splendour.

The only downside to Agra is the appalling pollution. The Yamuna River runs behind the Taj Mahal and it is so polluted that nothing can live in its murky waters. People excrete in the river, wash in it and do their washing in it; cows swim in it. The air pollution is slowly destroying the Taj itself and there is now a monitor at the back of the monument recording pollution levels. To try to reduce it, there is a 'no go' area close to the monument for rickshaws, cars and buses.

I have been hit by a lurgy and need something to stop my incessant coughing. Brian, ever compassionate, is complaining because I sound terrible and am keeping him awake at night! A rickshaw cyclist outside our hotel hears my cough and knows we need a chemist. He shows us the way after we promise we will let him take us to dinner tonight. At dinner time, he is waiting for us. We negotiate a price, but when we get to the restaurant it is closed. The driver has another in mind and will take us there for no extra money, and it is miles away. He must certainly be fit to cart us around! On the way back from dinner, he asks if we will go to a marble shop. 'I have three daughters and dowries are very expensive. I get paid 50 rupees if you go and look around,' he says.

Brian tries to explain to him that I am sick and we need to go home, but he is insistent. In the end we agree, just for some peace and quiet. When we walk into the shop, the owner greets us with open arms and then I get a coughing fit. People in the shop stare and move away. I sound incredibly contagious.

The shopkeeper can't get rid of us quickly enough. We are very bad for business. Not only does he push us out the door without us having to look at his stuff, he gives us the names of some good drugs that will clear up my cough. And the rickshaw driver still gets his tip. Everyone is happy!

We've hardly been on the road 30 minutes when we hit a huge pothole and the bloody welding breaks clean through again. A man stops to help and tells us about an aluminium welder in the next town. He is having trouble describing the way when a policeman wanders over from a nearby shop. He offers to direct us, waving down two men on a small bike. He orders them to take him to the town, with us following close behind. Three up on a bike is quite the norm here. They turn off the highway and lead us through markets crowded with livestock, carts, cars and people. We begin to doubt we are being led the right way but the policeman keeps signalling us to follow. After about 15 minutes he pulls up at a workshop and, yes, the aluminium welder can do the job.

Brian unloads the bike and unscrews everything, leaving it all on the roadside for me to guard. He then disappears with the welder and the broken frame. The bike only attracts a small crowd here – about 20 to 30 young men who just want to look and ask questions. The men cruise around the bike, but they don't touch anything. A young Sikh begins to talk to me, proudly telling me about the One Day International between Australia and India played in this town. The entire town closed for the day. They love their cricket.

When the bike is back in once piece we head to Jhansi with some very convoluted directions. Some young boys on bikes say they are going there and offer to lead us. It seems odd, because they aren't carrying any luggage. Still, we follow them. They take us through the back streets and don't seem to know where they are going. We pass the same cricket ground three times and we are now sure we are going to be robbed. Then, just as we are about to leave, the boys pull over and tell us we are at Jhansi – the Hotel Jhansi!

Some more discussion and the boys realise we actually want to go to the town of Jhansi – not the hotel. Another group of boys three up on a bike say they can lead us to the road to Jhansi and within five minutes we are finally heading out of town. Nothing is easy in India – even when people are trying to help you.

It has taken us a couple of long days on the road to get to Khajuraho, where we find a hotel with a bath – and a mongoose in the garden! This is a very good sign. It means there are no cobras here.

About 1000 years ago, people chose the remote location of Khajuraho to build remarkable temples decorated with erotic carvings. Why they did this remains a mystery. The carvings depict men and women having sex in all manner of positions and groupings, men having sex with horses, women having sex with monkeys and voluptuous bare-breasted women of all ages, shapes and sizes. The area's remoteness has saved the carvings from destruction by

Muslims, who cut a prudish swathe through India a couple of hundred years later, destroying many of the Hindu temples in their wake.

From Khajuraho, we want to head to Bandhavgarh National Park, and we are told it is only 250 km away. That sounds all right until the locals add that the road is pretty bad and it will take us at least 10 hours. We decide instead to cut through central India and stop at Kanha National Park on our way to Goa for Christmas.

Brian: We expect the road, being on the way to a tourist attraction, will be okay. Wrong. What little asphalt remains is rough and potholed beyond belief. Some holes are a metre deep. I am very conscious of the weakened aluminium top-box bracket and take it especially easy, looking for the smoothest option, which often sees us bouncing along on the dirt verge mixing it with the pedestrians and bicycles.

We are averaging less than 40 km/h and that's really pushing it. After four hours, we stop in a rural area for a rest and some peace and quiet. Not for long. People appear from nowhere and within five minutes we have half a dozen of them staring at us. Road signs are few and far between and we are at a crossroads. By using my compass, I think I know the right road but ask a man for directions anyway: 'Which way to Maihai?'

I can't understand the reply and his arms going in all directions give no clue, so I follow my instincts.

The road continues to deteriorate until it is nothing more than a goat track winding through remote villages without power lines and with little naked kids running around. Men sit around in groups by the road. They don't seem to have any work to do. It's a pity they don't develop some community spirit and fix up the potholes in their one and only street!

We dodge cows, dogs and pigs before finally ending up on National Highway Number 7. The surface is good for a kilometre, but then there's 5 km of terrible, metre-deep potholes and anything faster than walking pace is a challenge. I hit one bump a bit too fast and we are airborne for a couple of seconds, hoping that the bike holds together as the suspension bottoms out with a jarring thud.

In the major town of Murwara we end up in gridlock. We have no choice but to sit among all sorts of vehicles spewing out noxious fumes. An impatient rickshaw driver pushes forward and bangs into us. Luckily, the highway pegs protect us and scrape his paintwork.

Finally, a traffic cop, looking a bit like a British Army captain complete with handlebar moustache, eye glass and baton under the left armpit, decides to do something and starts directing traffic down a side road. I have no idea where we are going, but we follow a heap of motorcycles down lanes too narrow for a car until we finally come out past the traffic snarl. From here, the road improves and we cruise into Jabalpur.

Shirley: It is bitterly cold when we arrive at the gates of the tiger sanctuary just before dawn. Our guide rolls up in thongs! He is sporting an impressive gash in his ankle from a motorbike accident the day before.

It's not cheap to visit a tiger sanctuary, but where else do you get to see these creatures in their natural habitat? It seems like we have to pay for everything – admission to the park, the guide, the 'gypsy' (an open-topped car), petrol and even to use our camera. Once inside the park, we pay another 300 rupees (about AUD$10) for the tiger show. If you are lucky, the park rangers will find tigers and take you to see them on the back of an elephant.

The undergrowth is so high after the monsoonal rains, a dozen tigers could be a metre off the road and we wouldn't be able to see them. We see deer and monkeys, but our main target for the day is the tiger. There are 180 in the park with eight cubs – but the park is 900 square kilometres. Our guide tells us that many people spend days in the park and never see a tiger. We think he is just softening us up for disappointment. We love the sights, sounds and smells of the jungle, ever hopeful we will be lucky.

And we are – there is a tiger show today. We don't mind handing over 600 rupees (about AUD$20) and head into the jungle. Our guide advises us to take the smallest elephant and pay the mahout a minor amount of cash. We use the gypsy to clamber up onto the elephant and lumber into the jungle.

The mahout leads the elephant into a small clump of trees at the side of the meadow, where there are two larger elephants with park guides. They must be keeping an eye on the tiger. We go into the clump of trees and, sure enough, lying under the trees is a tigress dozing on her side with a small sapling near her middle. She is beautiful. As the elephant walks closer, she opens her eyes, but shows little interest in the elephant or its passengers. She is the most magnificent creature we have ever seen. She is lean and long, with a smooth, lustrous coat. I feel like climbing off the elephant and giving her a big cuddle or perhaps a tummy tickle. As we move alongside the clump of trees and undergrowth, the tigress shifts her head and looks at us again before going back to sleep. She knows that this elephant and the human visitors are no threat. The tigress no longer seems so cute when we see a bloodied deer's head, complete with antlers, under the trees.

Now our little elephant comes into his own. Because of his size, we can move further into the dense bush and to the back of the tigress's lair. Here, hidden in the undergrowth, are two of her cubs. One is lying down with her paws stretched out sphinx-style, the other is walking in circles like a domestic cat, trying to get into a comfortable position. We then circle back around the sleeping female. The advantage of having a smaller elephant is the access to the babies. Visitors on large elephants only see the mother.

The visit has been money well spent. Even if it was a little orchestrated, with the park guides tracking the tigers, we feel blessed that we have seen these majestic animals in their natural habitat. It is so important that tiger sanctuaries continue to exist to ensure the future of tigers and other Indian jungle creatures.

Brian: We are under the hammer now to get to Goa for Christmas. Adding to the usual obstacles of goats, cows, dogs and kids on Indian roads, we now come across monkeys sitting on the warm road. The villages look poor in this part of India but the children on their way to school are impeccably turned out – there isn't a spot of dirt on their starched school tunics and shirts.

We are starting to get paranoid about a loathing Indian truck drivers seem to have for foreigners on motorbikes. They have no regard for our safety, moving out onto our side of the road whenever they feel like it. We are forced into the gravel several times and at others have to come to a complete stop to avoid a head-on collision. It is little wonder we see two head-ons today as well as at least three overturned trucks. One vehicle is crushed and torn apart. Whoever was in that vehicle had little or no chance of survival. To add to our woes, the bike is starting to give in to the bad roads and a heavy load. The welded top-box rack is tilted backwards, but seems to be holding, and oil is leaking out of the oil filler's key lock.

Shirley: We have booked into the Hotel River Sal in Mobor, Goa. We've been told it is opposite the Leela Palace, Goa's best-known hotel. What they fail to mention is that there is a river between Hotel River Sal and Leela Palace. It is dark when we arrive at the hotel, after ending up on the wrong side of the river. Oil is leaking out of the bike, the fuel is getting lower and Brian's stress levels are sky high. Just to top off the day, the hotel is not what we'd hoped for. It's run-down and shabby, and we have paid for 10 days' accommodation!

The next morning, after a good night's sleep, we don't feel so bad. The room is clean, the bed is comfortable and the water's hot. The hotel has a boat to take us across the river, where we can walk to the shops and beach.

The beach 'shacks', which are small, open-air restaurants, offer sunbeds and umbrellas on the water's edge for free. The waiters meander down every hour or so to see if you need a drink or something to eat. There are lots of touts selling fruit, jewellery and massages, but they take it well when we tell them we aren't shopping.

On Christmas Day, Brian and I feel more than a little homesick. We go to the public phone in town, which is set up in a small shop, and the owner pushes us to the top of the queue to make our calls home. The phone is metered and the locals watch, fascinated by the amount of money we are spending on a phone call!

Brian: I'm close to tears talking to my boys. I feel a deep disappointment that I am not with them on Christmas Day. When Mum gets on the phone, she bursts into tears, but composes herself. She is missing us terribly and it's great to hear her voice. Dad gets on the line and sounds really good.

He had triple by-pass heart surgery last year but his

health seems to have picked up and he is enjoying life to the max. He's back on the bowling green and picking fruit every day. We have got a lot closer since his illness and hearing his voice brings a lump to my throat.

A few hundred rupees later and we are alone again. Poor Shirl can't even contact her brother and his wife because they have gone away and we can't call a mobile phone from here.

Shirley: Something good comes out of everything and the Hotel River Sal is no different. We meet Phil and Sheila, an English couple who have been coming to Goa for years. They know all the good places to eat and the best bars in town, suggesting Betty's Bar for our Christmas dinner. Chilli crab and local fish make a delectable meal.

One thing we don't miss out on is the Boxing Day cricket test – India versus Australia – which is live on cable TV in the hotel bar. While we're watching the cricket, some visitors arrive and ask if we've heard about the earthquake in Iran. We turn over to BBC World and are shocked to hear that Bam, the beautiful mud city, has been severely damaged and tens of thousands of its people are dead or injured. The citadel in the ancient city is no more. We can't believe the news. It has only been a couple of months since we were there, wandering the streets with Peter and Dagmar and enjoying the beauty of this ancient wonder. We wonder if Akhbar, the guesthouse owner, has survived and if any travellers are in the town.

Brian: The bike needs some TLC and I've found a local mechanic, Rudi, who is happy to work on it with me. We change the oil, clean the oil filter and refit it. He pulls apart the key lock on the oil filler and completely rebuilds it with new seals. He is patient and thorough. Mid-afternoon, Rudi produces cold beers, spicy Goan sausages and noodles. We sit in his lovely indoor–outdoor sitting room and discuss everything from religion and relationships between India and Pakistan, to Rudi's business interests. We get back to work and change the oil in the engine, gearbox and differential. We fit the plug repaired by Rudi and find it won't lock. He patiently pulls it apart and reworks it again until it fits. I sit down with Rudi to pay him, but he refuses to accept anything more than the cost of the engine and gearbox oils. That's 500 rupees (AUD$15) for a day's work!

When I return to the hotel, Peter and Dagmar are there. It is fantastic to catch up with them and share our respective adventures.

Shirley: Bam is still the top story on the international news. Akhbar is alive! He is interviewed, saying that his guesthouse has been destroyed. Everyone in the street is dead. An English tourist was killed in Akhbar's – the only foreigner to die. It is distressing to see this wonderful man so upset, yet it's good to know that he has survived.

'All my friends are dead. Everyone on this street is dead,' says Akhbar. When the reporter asks if he has hope, Akhbar replies. 'I am alive. Where there is life, there is hope.'

It's New Year's Eve. We've travelled 40,000 km across half the world, endured difficult times and enjoyed marvellous experiences. Phil and Sheila have been into Margao and bought the most incredible collection of fireworks. As the clock strikes midnight we let them off, lighting up the night sky.

Bernd, Heidi and Ingo, our companions across the badlands of Pakistan, are at Agonda, about 30 km further south, so we leave the Hotel River Sal and head to the Dunhill Beach Resort right on the beach. There are coco huts on the sand, but they are too rustic for us. Made from woven fronds and built on stilts, they seem a bit rickety and I prefer something more substantial. At least our room at the guesthouse has solid walls, a cold shower and toilet. You don't need hot water here, but you can get a bucket of the stuff if you want it.

Agonda is the Christmas meeting place for many overlanders. German travellers are parked in their vans under the trees on the water's edge. We get together for dinner at one of the local restaurants. The fish is to die for and the whisky is cheap. We have a few drinks and lots of laughs. Age and nationality are no barriers socially – we are all travellers, a long way from home.

The waters of the Arabian Sea are warm and therapeutic, and the beach at Agonda is almost deserted. There is nothing to do here but swim, eat and read; this is the life. Goa, and Agonda in particular, are not like India. And if you ask the locals, they say they are not Indians. They are Goans.

There are more farewells. Bernd, Heidi and Ingo are moving on. We will meet up with them again in Nepal. Bernd and Heidi will eventually make their way to Australia.

Bettina and Ube arrive after making the long 11-day journey from Nepal. They have good advice about where to stay and what to see in Nepal, and how to avoid the mozzies. Bettina got a dose of malaria and was feverish for nearly two weeks.

Tonight we have some uninvited guests in our room: frogs. They have taken up residence in the toilet and sink. Brian uses half a water bottle to scoop a frog out of the toilet. I use the toilet and when I flush I turn around and see another frog on the wall. Brian takes this one outside and washes his hands, then finds yet another frog on the bathroom wall. An entire frog family has moved into our loo!

We delay leaving Agonda as long as possible before heading to Saligao to meet Peter Baird, the Kiwi we met at the Horizons Unlimited meeting in England. It is hard to leave this paradise and our three days turn into five. Peter is staying in a 450-year-old Portuguese mansion with his bosses, the Poms running motorcycle tours around India. They have 16 Royal Enfields parked in their lounge room and bats living in the roof. There is no running hot water or flushing toilets, but there's lots of atmosphere.

Saligao is in northern Goa, and it is very different from Agonda and Mobor in the south. The restaurants are modern and expensive by Indian standards but the bars are trapped in a time warp. It is full moon and Peter takes us in search of the full-moon party. We don't find it, but then maybe it is too early as it is only 11 p.m.! Instead, we head to a bar where we appear to have walked back into the 1960s. The whole place is enveloped in a haze of blue smoke. The patrons wear tie-dyed pants and tops with dreadlocks cascading half way down their backs – and that's the men! It's as if they have been here for the last 40 years. Brian and I don't feel old very often, but tonight we do. We seem so conservative in comparison with these ageing hippies.

It is so long since we've been on good roads in India, we have forgotten what they are like. The highway to Mumbai is terrific and we can even travel at 100 km/h.

When we are pulled up by the police, we're sure there will be another attempt to extort money from us. In actual fact, the policeman is just keen to get a closer look at the bike. He touches everything, including the engine, which is red-hot! He flinches briefly, but doesn't show any other sign of pain. He waves us on and probably heads off to find some cold water.

The Taj Mahal Hotel in Mumbai is one of the best in India. It is way beyond our budget, but we deserve a Christmas treat after the dump in Mobor and rooms with frogs and bats. While we talk about the pros and cons of our expensive room, the Sikh security guards become agitated. They want to know if we are staying or going and for us to move the bike. We can't work out why, until a chauffeur-driven car pulls up outside the main doors. Salman Rushdie gets out with an extremely attractive Indian woman. We can't believe it. I grab the camera and push through the media throng to get a photo. The hotel manager tells us Salman is on a private visit to Mumbai with his girlfriend, a local Bollywood star. Now the guards' irritation is understandable. Imagine what we must have looked like, hanging around outside the hotel when Salman Rushdie is about to arrive.

The receptionist offers us an upgrade with no reason given. I wonder why, as after a day on the road we look pretty terrible. If I were her, I'd tell us they were booked out! Our Executive Room just oozes luxury. There are silk robes, a deep bath, the biggest, softest towels we've ever seen, a complimentary bottle of local red wine and chocolates. It is a dream and I am afraid I will wake up in the hotel in Dalbandin.

The dichotomy that is India is visible outside our hotel. While we have been enjoying the luxury of the Taj Mahal Hotel and Salman Rushdie has been enjoying the company of his 'muse', as the local papers describe his companion, people are begging on the streets. The beggars make a beeline for us, seeing foreigners as cash cows. The Indians staying at the Taj are bound to have much more than us, but they are invisible to the beggars.

As we ride out of the city, I watch a young woman in a sari walk out onto the roadway. She hitches up the edge of her sari and squats over a drain in the road. I can't imagine living on the street and I am struck by the deprivation of some Indians. We both find it amazing that the Indians pride themselves on being the world's largest democracy and potentially the most populated nation in a couple of decades, overtaking China. This is despite the fact that the government can't feed and educate the masses now. You often see children who should be at school just hanging around tiny rural communities. Tens of thousands of people, and possibly more than this, live in shantytowns consisting of dwellings made from plastic sheeting over wooden frames and situated on the outskirts of cities. We see women working on the roads, carrying baskets of stones from the trenches. Initially, I thought women working was a good thing, but then I realised that they are the lowest caste and will never be able to do anything but work on the roads.

Some friends in Australia told us that no matter what we thought of most places in India we would love Rajasthan. They were right. The local maharana and his family have turned their guesthouses and palaces into hotels. Some are not very expensive, but each offers a different accommodation experience.

The first accommodation we stay in is the Rang Niwas Palace Hotel in Udaipur. The hotel is set behind a high wall in peaceful gardens with a pool and our room has a balcony with a sofa. Brian settles into the sofa before I even get through the door. He has found his resting spot.

The maharana has left many legacies in Udaipur, such as a palace that is now an incredible museum and the family crystal collection on display at a hotel that was also once a palace. Maharana Sajjan Singh bought the crystal in 1877 and never got to enjoy it. By the time the crystal arrived from England the maharana was dying and the boxes were left unopened until after his death. At the museum, we view crystal chairs, tables, beds, chandeliers, hanging fans operated by the hands of servants, a throne, lamps, table settings and more. There is enough dinnerware and glassware to have everyone we know to dinner every night for a year and never have to do the washing up!

There is a commotion outside our hotel window and the hotel dog is barking madly. As I walk out to see what is going on, a huge monkey, about a metre tall, runs past the window and jumps into a tree. For the next 15 minutes or so, a family of about five monkeys climbs past our window into the trees in the hotel garden or onto the roof. The dog is still barking and one of the guests (a Swiss woman who enjoys a tipple) chases the monkeys with a big stick, trying to get them out of the garden. One monkey sits just outside our window, watching the entire proceedings. He looks across at me and then back at the goings on as if to say, 'Can you believe this hullabaloo?'

Another of the maharana's homes, his principal palace, is now the Lake Palace Hotel and it's set on an island in the middle of a lake. We can't afford a night here, but we can splurge on dinner in the restaurant. The band strikes up when we arrive at the boat ramp. We make our way down the carpeted walkway to the boat and everyone greets us with great deference. When we get to the hotel girls shower flower petals onto the ground in front of us and men wave small hand fans. It is so over the top!

Over dinner, we get chatting to Merrill and Joe, a couple from Sydney. I have the most amazing feeling I have met them before but can't put my finger on it until well into the night. While Brian and I were staying at our time-share in Port Macquarie a year before, they arrived, wanting to look around. The managers were away, so Brian gave them a tour. Fancy meeting them again, in Udaipur.

Brian: The maharana has the most incredible collection of cars, which are on display at the royal garages. There are the first diesel-powered mass-produced Mercedes Benz and other Mercedes models from the early 1960s, as well as Cadillacs, Chevrolet trucks and even two Morris Minors. Then there are two Rolls-Royces, one converted into a ute for hunting trips and the other converted into a bus with three rows of seats for the local cricket team. Now, there is a sign of someone who has far too much money!

We must be losing our adventurous spirit. We eat at the same restaurant overlooking the lake, but the food is good and the view is to die for. Our rickshaw ride home is reminiscent of *Octopussy*, the James Bond movie shot here in Udaipur. Our maniac driver has equipped the rickshaw with the biggest, loudest ghettoblaster I've ever heard. Cat Stevens blasts out as we career, almost out of control, all the way down the hill.

Shirley: The maharana's cousin, who runs the Rang Niwas Palace Hotel, suggests we stay at a luxury tent camp, Chhatra Sagar, run by another of his cousins. The camp is on the shore of a large dam that was once the maharana's hunting ground but is now a bird sanctuary. Normally it is 7500 rupees a night, all inclusive, which is way beyond our budget, but as the season is slow and they have space we can have full board for 2500 rupees. How can we say no?

The tent accommodation is very luxurious and every room has a private sitting area with a view and en suite with running hot and cold water. It is only a few kilometres out of the way. The spoiling just keeps going on. We make our decision to stay. What a guy my husband is!

It is about 1.30 p.m. and we are just in time for lunch. The food is all locally grown and delicious. There is rice, peas with coriander, a corn-pasta dish, salad, dhal and a yoghurt sauce with berries, fruit and nuts. We try a mouth-watering dessert, about the consistency of rice pudding but made from lotus seeds.

The dining area looks out over the dam. It is peaceful. Waterbirds fly overhead and an owlet that should be sleeping watches us from the hollow of a tree. There is no traffic noise, only the sounds of birds, and the air is clean. Can this really be India?

After lunch we are shown to our tent, which looks out over the dam and has its own sitting area under a canvas awning, with two deck-type chairs and table. Inside is a massive bed and two bedside tables complete with lamps with bases shaped like camels. There is a dressing room area behind curtains and a pristine bathroom with shower, toilet and vanity. We have our own hot-water system and a powerpoint.

We relax outside and read in peace. The only harsh sounds are the yells of farmers trying to keep birds away from their crops. As the day comes to an end, we hear the calls as the birds settle for the night.

In the outdoor communal area, we relax in comfortable cane chairs that surround a roaring fire with some other guests, Robert and Carmen Ashforth, a Canadian doctor and his wife; Peter and Heidi, a couple from Switzerland; and a French couple who don't speak much English. Our host tells us about the conservation work done by the family in what was once their hunting area. They didn't hunt for pleasure in the old days (it is against their religion), but took it up as a sport to impress and entertain the British. Now they have begun replanting trees for the birds and animals, and grow a 'weed' tree to use as firewood. They are making quite a difference here.

We are called to the dining tables at 8 p.m. Dinner is another sumptuous Rajasthani feast. And just in case we are feeling the chill of the night air, the staff bring in braziers filled with coals from the fire and put one next to each table.

When it is time to go to bed we are given large torches. Once the guests stop reading, the generator is turned off so we are not disturbed by its low hum. Our bed has been turned down. I can't find the T-shirt I left on the bed, then find it wrapped around the hotwater bottle that is in the bed to take the chill off the sheets. Luxury . . .

We are advised to leave our blinds up to enjoy the dawn. About 6.15 the sky is light, but there is no sunrise to speak of. We are a little disappointed and turn over to snooze again. At about 7.15 the sun has risen – a huge red ball catches my eye. It is a wonderful sunrise over the distant hills beyond the lake. What a way to begin the day. At 8 o'clock our morning tea arrives. It is a joy that we have another day of such comfort ahead of us.

After lunch, we visit the local village. We are asked not to give the villagers money or gifts, as they are paid well to work at the resort and for their produce. They still make their own butter and sesame oil and spin goat's wool into yarn. The silversmith makes exquisite jewellery and determines the price by weighing the silver on an ancient set of hand-held scales. It is a journey back in time.

Over the centuries these people have had to deal with invaders. The Mogul invaders came to Rajasthan and took the best-looking women. Today the village women still cover their faces when strangers visit!

Back on the road, we are back into the madness. We have travelled only a little more than 200 km and have passed seven truck accidents – rollovers and collisions. Brian does some trick riding to avoid a couple of head-ons of our own, as trucks bear down on us without any intention of moving over.

The Hotel Madhuban in Jaipur is another former royal residence run by a member of the maharana's family. There are photos of the royal family in the halls and sitting rooms. We feel as though we are visiting the family rather than staying in a hotel.

Mr Singh, a tour guide, takes us on a tour of Jaipur and its spectacular Amber Fort, the sixteenth-century palace of the Maharajah Singh (no relation to our guide!). The fort is a maze of corridors and stairways, marble columns and graffiti. Many of the small rooms have been used on more than one occasion as a toilet. The Indians' lack of respect for their historical sites never ceases to amaze me. All that is forgotten when we get to Sukh Niwas or the Hall of Pleasure, pleasant gardens in the central courtyard with fountains and waterfalls. One pond runs through a room inside the fort to keep it cool during the sweltering summer heat.

The entrance to the maharana's private apartments is decorated with incredible inlaid panels, mirrored tiles and exquisite stained-glass panels with delicate flower etchings in vibrant colours. Most of the semiprecious stones have been looted over the years, but restoration work is under way. One of the maharanas had a passion for astronomy. The paraphernalia he used to study the stars and planets look like massive sculptures or rides from a way-out theme park.

On our way out of town we stop at Jal Mahal, a water palace set in the middle of a lake. It is quite beautiful, even though the water is so polluted you could probably walk across it to get to the palace.

We make good time on the road to Delhi until Brian notices the back tyre isn't holding the road as well as it should. Sure enough, we have a flat tyre. We can't really complain, considering this is the tyre we had repaired in Islamabad. It won't take another patch so we will have to find a tyre in Delhi.

We have a contact, Arun Maddan, and he assures Brian he can get a tyre. He offers to send someone to us to take the wheel, but Brian doesn't like that idea, so we remove the rear wheel ourselves and take a rickshaw to Arun's workshop. It is in the heart of the motorbike area of town, around the corner from the tip-driven Hotel City Castle. Arun isn't there, so while we wait we talk to his father, Sohan, who tells us about the family's main business – the restoration of 30-year-old Royal Enfield motorcycles. I roll my eyes. I know what is coming. Brian is fascinated by the idea of the ultimate Indian souvenir: a Royal Enfield of his very own.

Brian: I'm interested, all right! I've been fascinated by the old Enfields for years as they have a magical appeal. One problem, though, is that they are so unreliable. Sohan shows me a 350cc that is ready to be shipped to a client in England and a near-complete 500cc. I am impressed with the workmanship.

Arun arrives, has a look at the tyre and tells me they will be able to find one. He comes up with a 130/70 17-inch Metzeler. I'm sure it is old stock, but it will have to do.

Arun says that they do the 'Egli' conversion on vintage bikes to improve performance and reliability. Franz Egli is a great modifier of motorcycles from Europe and offers modifications to frames and engines to get the most out of machines. His company recently turned its attention to the Indian-manufactured Royal Enfields and I have read good reports about these in English motorcycle magazines.

Arun tells me that their most successful bike is the 350cc. They rebore the cylinder to make it 535cc. Next, they install a more powerful oil pump and re-route the external oil lines to the head to ensure the exhaust valve gets first use of the cooler oil. The modified bike puts out around 28 bhp (the BMW puts out 70) through the standard four-speed gearbox (of course, the lever is mounted on the right-hand side and has a one-down three-up pattern). They convert the electrics to 12 volts and have a disc-brake front-end conversion if you want it. They are experimenting with an aluminium cylinder to solve the overheating problems of running an air-cooled iron barrel.

Arun takes us to his warehouse, where he has about 100 bikes in various states of repair. Some old Piaggio scooters from the 1950s and '60s will be shipped to Brisbane. There is a Grey 535 conversion ready to go to the USA and the workers take it out onto the street for me to test-ride. I am surprised at the lowdown grunt this little bike puts out. The clutch action is easy, and the engine is responsive and feels like it will rev to its 5750 red line easily. The gearbox is slow but this is a 35-year-old bike. The sound out of the traditional exhaust is lovely to the ear. When I return to the workshop, I find the workers standing outside – they were wondering if I was going to come back! Truth is, I got lost (that's easy in Delhi) and I stopped the bike to see if I could start it, which took me a while.

Shirley: I have no problem with Brian getting an Enfield. It will make any further purchases of mine pale into insignificance. Now I can shop till I drop in Nepal with an entirely clear conscience!

Arun promises to have the wheel to us by lunchtime. In typical Indian form, he arrives at four in the afternoon. Over tea in the garden, we do the deal and buy a 1966, 535 Enfield

Bullet. It will be racing green with black seats and matching black saddle bags.

When we finally get to the Nepali border it is closed, but only for an hour and just to motor traffic. Nepalis and Indians are walking across at will. We stand with the local border patrol, discussing the usual topics: the cost of the bike and the cricket scores. When the border opens, one of the soldiers whispers some advice: 'Don't pay anyone anything.' It's good advice. We've heard many stories of the Indians' love of baksheesh but haven't been asked for any bribes yet.

A slippery mud track leads to the Indian immigration office, where we fill in our forms and have our names checked in huge ledgers that seem to be the backbone of officialdom in this part of the world. At customs Brian makes a grand entrance by breaking one of the chairs. It gets a big laugh from all the officials and probably gives them something to talk about for days to come.

The muddy track takes us through a shantytown selling snack foods and music cassettes, of all things. After passing through a final checkpoint, where our names are written in one more ledger, we head into Nepal.

created a crowd everywhere we stopped — even if it was only to fuel up.

The crazy Indian traffic

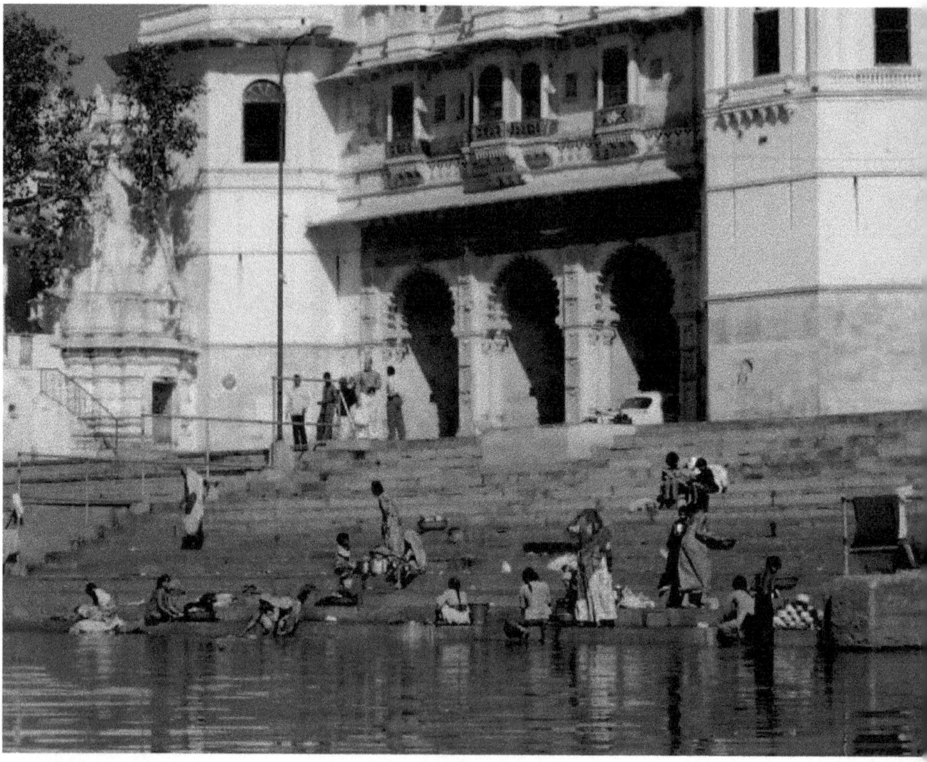

Lake Pichola, Udaipur

Udaipur tra

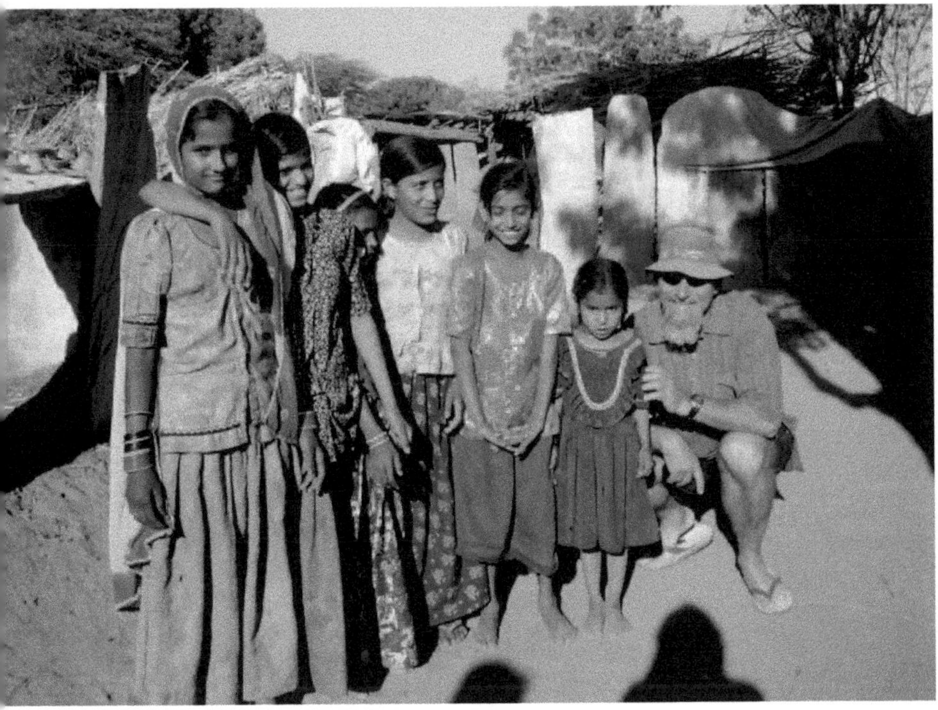

an with the local children at Chhatra Sagar

Tsuglagkhang, McLeod Ganj

The Monsoon Palace at sunset, Udaipur

Taj Mahal, Agra

The security guards at the Taj Mahal Hotel, Mumb

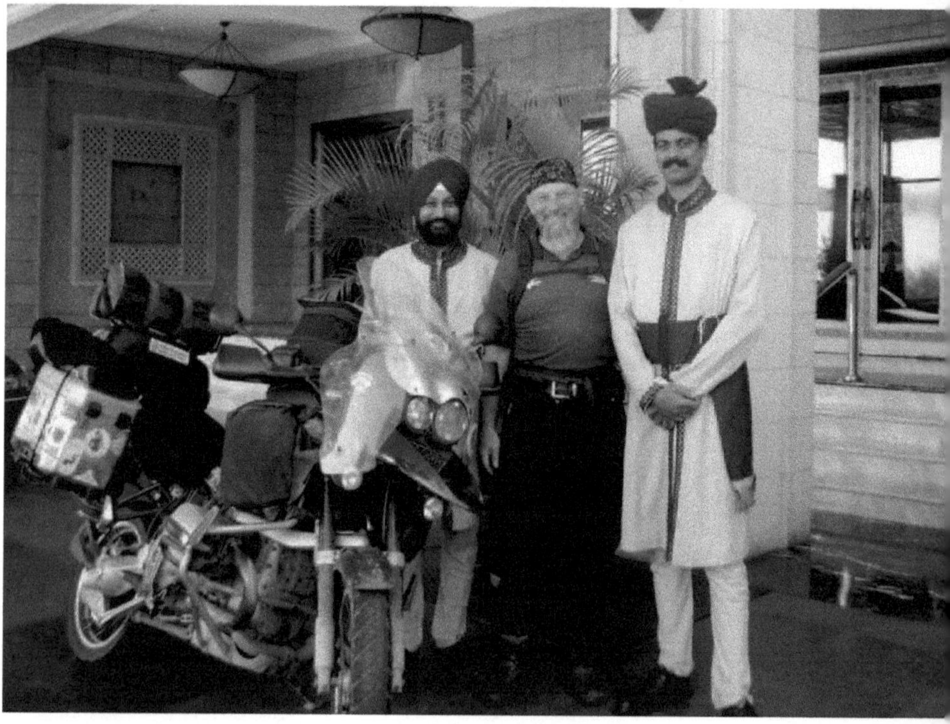

THIRTEEN

NEPAL

23 January – 16 February 2004

Shirley: Keen to avoid the horrendous Indian roads, we cross into Nepal in the far west of the country at Mahendranagar. Around 20 young soldiers watch us ride past without interest. We are warned that this part of Nepal is Maoist territory. Nepal is in the grips of a civil war, with Maoists fighting against the monarchy and the army. A ceasefire collapsed a few months ago and the death toll continues to grow. From all reports, the Maoists don't bother the tourists but do encourage donations to their fighting fund if they meet you on the track. They even hand out receipts to show that you have donated to the cause. If you meet more of these freedom fighters, you just show them your receipt and then don't need to give another donation. We are not at all concerned by these reports. We are not trekking and shouldn't have any problems, but the same can't be said for people travelling through Nepal by public transport.

While we are having breakfast at the hotel in

Mahendranagar, we are intrigued to see the army pull a public bus over. All the passengers get off and walk through a checkpoint with their luggage. Some of the soldiers check paperwork and search luggage while their comrades in arms search the bus. It is a long process.

When Brian and I come up to similar checks on the highway, we are waved through. The authorities are keen not to disrupt the tourist industry. Because of safety fears, some people have stopped visiting and that can only harm the locals.

The difference between India and Nepal is striking. Roads in Nepal are better. There is very little traffic and the countryside is lush and green. The villages are neat and tidy and there isn't the sea of empty plastic bottles that India seems to be drowning under. The road east is surprisingly good, apart from the odd pothole large enough to consume the bike. Luckily, Brian is on his mettle this morning.

We head to Royal Bardia National Park. We've been told the road deteriorates a bit when you leave the highway. That is a real understatement once we have crossed the Chisopani suspension bridge. This is a modern monument to international aid that was built by the Japanese with funding from the World Bank, and seems incredibly out of place. With its towering suspension it looks like it should have been built on a modern freeway.

The road is very muddy and bumpy. We are only on it for a couple of kilometres when we come to a river crossing, and it is a beauty. The river is about 25 m wide where the road disappears into it. It comes out at the other side. It is really hard to tell just how deep the water is. Brian has the perfect solution to gauging the water level: he gets me to walk across the river! The water is pretty deep. It comes over the top of my boots and runs inside. Brian mounts up and goes for it, and gets across with no trouble at all. Now we just have to pray that there won't be any rain. If the river rises and the track gets muddier, getting out of the national park could be a problem.

The roads go from hard-packed gravel to mud and slush and back again. As we ride through small villages, children run out of houses yelling 'Bye, bye!' They seem to think this is a greeting. There are naked children being washed in the creek and women are doing their laundry, smashing their clothes on rocks. It is a lovely scene.

The Bardia Jungle Cottages are rustic, to say the least. The floor in ours is hard-packed dirt. There is no glass in the windows and no running hot water. We can get a bucket of hot water if we give the staff an hour's notice. But the rooms are clean, as is the bedding, and the beds have enormous doonas. For less than $10 a night, we can't complain. The accommodation staff double as park guides. Prem and Indra will take us for a day-long walk through the jungle park tomorrow.

Before we settle for the night they tell us to shift the bike because they wouldn't like to see it damaged when the local rhinoceros visits the camp. They are not sure if the rhino would actually try to mate with the bike, but it's not worth the risk. We think this is fanciful. As if a rhinoceros would come into the camp. Brian shifts the bike just to humour our hosts.

While we are having dinner, the dogs start barking. We have a visitor. Sure enough, an enormous female rhino wanders through the camp. Indra grabs a torch and we follow the unwanted guest as she wanders around the cottages. They reckon she weighs 300 kg. She ignores us and ignores the barking dog. She even ignores the wall at the back of the cottages, pushing it over to get into a field. It is amazing. We don't need to go to the national park – it comes to us.

The sun is warm, but once it sets the temperature

plummets. After dinner I am determined to have a shower with a bucket of hot water in our ice-cold bathroom. When the hot water runs over my body, it's lovely. While I fill the jug again, I freeze. The Bardia Jungle Cottages are definitely a location for summer and not set up for the cold Nepali nights.

Early morning is the best time to visit the national park. Our guidebook and commonsense say that walking into a jungle that is known to have rhinos, tigers and wild elephants is a rather foolhardy venture, but it sounds like a wonderful experience. This morning, the area is shrouded in fog. It's cold and misty in the dining room! Breakfast is a little late because the cook has slept in, but he throws together some terrific banana pancakes and sandwiches for our picnic in the jungle.

Prem and Indra arrive armed with long bamboo poles and present us with one each. I can't help thinking that a gun would be a bit more useful than a stick against a wild animal. The safety briefing doesn't lessen our apprehension: 'Don't turn your back on the tigers. If you see tigers, just stare at them and make a lot of noise. If you see an elephant, run like crazy. If you see a rhino, climb a tree, if there is one nearby. If not, find something big to stand behind.'

I look across at Brian and wonder if he would be big enough to hide behind. I don't have to speak. He knows what I am thinking and doesn't seem to appreciate it. Prem assures us that there shouldn't be any problems unless we have a chance encounter with an animal that neither the animal nor we were expecting.

Armed with our sticks and a lot of hope, we start down a track that disappears into the heavy fog. Our first sighting is of a spotted deer. They proliferate here as they did in Kanha.

And, of course, we see monkeys – langur monkeys at first and then rhesus monkeys. We plod along a bit further without meeting any animals. It must be too cold for them. The birds are abundant – pied hornbills, eagles, forest tits, kingfishers, peacocks and, the most wonderful sight, woodpeckers. We hear them tapping away on trees before we see them.

As the sun breaks through, Prem thinks the animals will come out onto the riverbank to enjoy the sunshine after the cold night air. No such luck. The only large animals we see are domestic elephants out for a morning walk with their mahouts.

Prem starts tracking a female rhino and her baby. We walk through grasses one and a half metres high – I'm just about disappearing from view. Now I think it is ridiculous to be searching for an animal that won't be happy about being found, particularly when we are armed only with sticks. The rhino is elusive, as is the tigress and her four cubs. Everyone but the deer and monkeys are keeping a low profile today.

Just when we give up hope of seeing anything interesting, there is a noise on the other side of the river. To my untrained ears, it sounds like a gunshot, a loud crack. With trousers rolled up, we wade across the river and go in search of the culprit making all that noise – a wild elephant ripping branches off trees.

We follow the sound through the bushes and come onto a track. The elephant is on the other side of it and should cross in front of us. We wait and wait. The whole time we can hear the elephant having a lovely time grazing in the jungle. Prem becomes concerned that if the elephant crosses the track and sees us, he might charge, so he signals us to move back and around to the other side of the animal. We can still hear the cracking of more trees and branches and even see the leaves waving in the breeze from the force of the elephant's munching, but we can't see the elephant.

It is getting late, and we have a good hour's walk back to the park gate and have to leave before nightfall. Just as we are about to give up, he comes into view: a colossal bull elephant. From 20 m away, we can see his back, his head and ears. He continues to eat, oblivious to our presence – for a few minutes. Then he senses that we are nearby. He turns and runs. For such a big animal, he has incredible speed. Thank goodness he chose to run away from us and not towards us. The experience has been terrifying and wonderful.

There is no fog the following morning as we leave the park and the track is a bit dryer. The small wooden bridges over the creek are slippery, though, and our new back tyre isn't that good. As the bike mounts the bridge, the back tyre gives way and we do a very stylish 180-degree turn. We are lucky we didn't spin off into the stream. With the help of a bemused local, Brian manages to get the bike upright and off the bridge. We assess the damage: bike – check; Shirl – check; Brian – bruised shin and ego, but both will recover.

The lack of rain has seen the river level drop and we have no problem getting across. I still have to walk, just in case Brian drops the bike. This time the water doesn't seep over the top of my boots. Just as well, really. My socks have only just dried from the drenching on the way over.

We need cash and in Nepalganj in central southern Nepal there are no ATMs, so I have to go into the bank armed with credit card and passport. Brian waits across the road with the bike. It is a long and slow process. I have to meet the manager. He introduces me to his assistant, who takes my passport to photocopy it. The manager then gets me to fill in the form and sign it. Nothing is done in a rush.

When I finally get the cash I go outside and can't find Brian. There is no sign of him at all. Then he appears, riding up the street. He's not happy. The local police told him to move on because he was creating a traffic hazard – the crowd around the bike was spilling onto the roadway and no-one could get through.

Riding along the highway we pass a cyclist carting so much luggage he has to be a traveller. We pull over and wait for him to cycle up to us. Cornel is Romanian and he's been cycling around the world for six years. What a character. He looks like he hasn't had a shower for days and has a very laid-back attitude. I can't imagine travelling for six years by myself. While we talk about the joys of travel and the pros and cons of push-bike over motorbike, Cornel eats a lemon with sugar on it for energy. He's hoping to cycle through Myanmar. We wish him luck and head to Lumbini, the birthplace of Buddha.

In Lumbini, we encounter a crisis. After more than 5000 photos, our camera decides to stop working. There is only one solution: to travel straight to Kathmandu to see if we can get the camera fixed. If that fails, we will have to buy a new one.

Lumbini is shrouded in fog, which adds to the mystery of the place (pity about the camera). The local Buddhist temple is a very plain concrete building on the outside. Inside, it is a house of worship, with golden Buddhas and Thangkas telling the story of Buddha's life.

A monk introduces himself. He is the senior monk, and the oldest, he says with pride and a smile that lights up the room on this bleak morning. He is a joy. He shows us the story of Buddha's life and the stages of life fulfilled by all Buddhists.

A man from the visitor's centre takes us for a walk around the area – no fees, no tips, just free information. In the centre of the property is the sacred pool. It is now a concrete pool, but in 623 BC it was a pond and Buddha's mother, Maya Devi, bathed here before giving birth to her son under the shade of a nearby tree. The spot where this tree stood is now under the temple. This is a sacred site for Buddhist pilgrims.

A few people have told us that the road to Kathmandu is dreadful, with a 36 km stretch that is potholed and badly damaged by landslides. We hit the bad section and realise everything we have been told is an understatement. The road is corrugated and littered with large rocks and the potholes are a metre deep. In some places it is wet, muddy and slippery. And being a major highway, there are lots of trucks and buses. They seem to travel faster here than in India, and for me this road brings back all the nightmares of life on a bike in Iran and Pakistan. It is up there with the worst. At one stage, a bus is right on our tail. If we slip off, it will be disastrous. However, just as soon as the poor road conditions start, they end, and it is a clear run through into Kathmandu.

On the outskirts of the city, the traffic is heavy and the air is thick with smoke. We have to constantly ask for directions, and after a stressful hour or so we find our hotel tucked away behind the tourist shops of Thamel.

Lyall Crawford, the consul at the Australian embassy, has an important parcel for me – my new credit card – so we get a taxi to avoid the traffic. Lyall looks an unlikely career diplomat. He has a beard nearly to his waist! While he might not look the part, he is certainly very professional. In the boardroom there is a certificate of appreciation from the Victoria Police to the embassy staff for their endeavours in bringing home Paul Carr, who perished on Tibet's Cho Oyu mountain. Without Lyall's expertise, contacts and determination, Paul's body might still be on the mountain. Today Lyall is being presented with his Australia Day Medal, an award he was nominated for by the three surviving climbers. Ambassador Keith Gardner invites us to stay for the ceremony. It is an honour. It is a simple ceremony in the ambassador's residence with just us and the Nepalese staff present. Keith asks Brian to speak, and he tells of Paul's love of mountain climbing and their friendship.

Over drinks after the ceremony Lyall tells us that the bad road we travelled yesterday wasn't damaged by landslides at all. The Maoists landmined the road a few weeks ago. They planted the very rudimentary landmines, waited for an army truck to pass by and then detonated the devices with maximum effect. More innocent lives were probably lost in this internal battle.

From Nepal, we plan to fly to Thailand, avoiding the road through Myanmar. We don't have the permits or the time to take the overland route and, anyway, we're not sure taking the bike through would be possible. We've been recommended a cargo agent and, as luck would have it, his office is just around the corner from our hotel. Many overlanders have used Eagle Eyes, as they know what has to be done and how to accomplish it. They even bring the carpenter to our hotel to measure up the bike for the crate. It's not cheap. All the following figures are in US dollars: we have to pay $1.37 a kilo for the crate and seven cents a kilo for insurance. Add to that local charges for making the box, handling fees, taxes and our air tickets to Bangkok, and the total comes to more than $1000.

It is frustrating being without the camera in a city like this. Kathmandu is living history. Walking to the camera repair shop, we pass a Buddhist temple and one for the worship of the sun god, with tiered roof and burning incense outside. And that's before we go to the normal tourist spots such as the Monkey Temple and Durbar Square.

But there is plenty to do – shopping (and, of course, Brian can't complain after the Enfield purchase) and eating. The food is brilliant. After the curries and rice of India, we are thriving on the international foods available. All the weight we lost travelling through Ramadan and avoiding meat in India and Pakistan is getting stacked back on here – plus some. We go from Mexican for lunch to Italian for dinner and have some delicious French pastries for afternoon tea. And then there are the delightful Tibetan *mo mo* (dumplings) made from buffalo.

Then we receive some bad news: the camera is dead. We were told that we won't find digital camera gear in Nepal, but that is wrong. We pick up a four-megapixel digital Canon for about AUD$535 – around a third of the price we paid for ours a year ago.

Brian: Armed with our new camera, we take to the skies to fly over Mount Everest with the appropriately named Buddha Air. I'm anxious to get there and I'm not too proud to admit that I'm also a bit emotional. I really want at least to see Cho Oyu, where Possum died. I know Mick Harvey, Nick Farr and Jack Carmody, who were with Paul when he died here, stuck by their mate and would not leave without him. That Aussie spirit is what makes us special. Now, meeting Lyall and learning what he did for them and the lengths he went to in order to bring Paul home, I can hardly wait. Possum, as the boss of the Special Operations Group, and I as ranking officer at different crime squads, did a lot together. We planned many successful arrests and early morning raids on crooks over the years. When we decided to take a stand against the reduction of police numbers and services in Victoria, we stood for election on the same ticket for the Police Association. We didn't agree on everything, but had the same ideals of improving the working coppers' lot.

I have felt Possum's loss even more than I thought I would; I think it is because he set out on his mountain expedition when we set off on our journey of a lifetime. His adventure was his last. Now, here we are about to take a flight over the area Possum loved so much.

Our takeoff is delayed due to fog, but eventually we board and taxi to the end of the runway. In the 18-seat plane there are about 12 Americans whose constant mindless chatter and gratingly loud voices start to get on my nerves. The hostess comes down the aisle to tell us the view is not good, with only three peaks visible, but all the Yanks want to go so we are going. Now I'm pissed off. I would prefer to wait a week if need be to get a good view.

We head off over Kathmandu and in less than 10 minutes we are over snowcapped mountains, which disappear into the clouds. Buddha Air allows passengers to go up to the cockpit one at a time and have a look out the front windows. When it's my turn, I tell the pilot and co-pilot about Possum and the efforts of Colonel Madan KC, the Nepalese Army helicopter pilot, to bring him back. They tell me that usually Cho Oyu is visible and they promise to try their best to get below the cloud to see it. Still, we do get to see Everest peeking through the clouds and Makalu, with its dramatic sheer face and snow whipping off the surface. I have to admit it is spectacular and I can see what attracts adventurers.

On our way back, the co-pilot beckons to me to come up to the flight deck. He points out the vicinity of Cho Oyu and the town from which everyone leaves to trek up there and to Everest base camp. On my way back to my seat, I look at Shirl and her eyes are misty.

The flight is only about 45 minutes, and before we

know it we are back over Kathmandu and landing. I'm a little disappointed we haven't seen Cho Oyu, but I'm glad we made the effort.

Shirley: It had to happen. Brian is crook and we must leave Kathmandu today. The Maoists have called a general strike, or *bandh*, so no-one can travel on the roads tomorrow. Well, that's not quite true. You can travel, but you are likely to have your vehicle set alight! Shops and businesses close whether they agree with the *bandh* or not. When the Maoists call a *bandh* to reinforce their position against the royal family, everyone obeys. Some restaurants in the tourist areas remain open – discreetly, behind shuttered windows.

I jump into a cab to drop a bag of souvenirs at the embassy. We can't fit it on the bike and Lyall will look after it until we return to Kathmandu. The roads are closed because of a student demonstration, so we take another route. The driver gives me a completely different slant on the Maoists. He tells me how corrupt all the politicians and public figures in Nepal are. By way of example, he explains why the fuel is so bad here – it's topped up with kerosene. The petrol-station owners get away with it by bribing the officials to say their petrol is clean.

When I return to the hotel, Brian is no better but insists we leave for Pokhara today. We ride through the countryside of central Nepal, which has wonderful terraced gardens and the first clean river we have seen in months flowing through green pastures. We get to Pokhara and the traffic is far less hectic than in Kathmandu. We only get one set of wrong directions and find our way to the lakeside. Our hotel is set in a lovely garden and would be in the shadow of the Annapurna Range in the Himalayas, if you could see the mountains, but they are hidden by cloud this afternoon.

As soon as we get to our room, Brian goes to bed and falls asleep. He is really very ill and running a fever. I organise another blanket, turn on the heater and decide to read the paper in the garden to give him some peace and quiet. Instead of doing that I throw myself down a step, landing heavily on my knees and shoulder and banging my chin on the concrete, jarring my jaw. Three English people having tea in the garden stop talking and look, but not one of them even asks if I am all right let alone gets up to see if I need help. I hear footsteps and one of the Nepali men having tea in the garden comes running up to make sure I am okay and offers to ring the doctor. No need for that. I think my pride has suffered the greatest injury. I am now sporting sore knees, an aching shoulder and a grazed chin.

We've arranged to meet Bernd and Heidi at the Lhasa Tibetan Restaurant. Between the three of us we devour a wonderful Tibetan feast of cheese balls, meat balls and fish and vegetables cooked in a soup with rice noodles. It is delicious and only surpassed by the good conversation.

The next morning, Brian is still not well, but the cloud has gone and the Annapurna glisten in the sun. While Brian rests, I wander around the lake spending some time with Bernd and Heidi. The Tibetan women are selling trinkets on the roadside and it is hard to refuse them.

T-shirts embroidered in any design are available everywhere in Nepal. I order a couple of custom-designed 'Aussies Overland' shirts in town and get talking to the embroiderer. When I tell him Brian's symptoms, he asks if Brian could have malaria. Oh shit. I hadn't thought of that. It dawns on me that Bettina picked up malaria in Bardia National Park and we have just come from there. He offers to act as interpreter and ambulance if Brian is no better in the morning. The friendliness of the Nepali people is heartwarming. This guy doesn't know us from Adam, but he is prepared to shut up shop and look after Brian. Luckily, we don't need to take up his kind offer, as Brian only has the flu.

Our spirits lift when the cloud that has descended again breaks. The setting sun sprays the most incredible pink light across the snowcapped peaks.

Sunrise over the Annapurna is said to be a sight to behold. Unfortunately, we don't get to see it. After dragging ourselves out of bed super early, we drive to the lookout and can't see anything but cloud. The locals try to convince us that the cloud will lift in time for sunrise so we sit and wait, freezing to the core. The cloud and fog just gets heavier, but some Japanese tourists have the right idea. They buy a poster of the Annapurna at dawn, hold it up to the sky and take photographs of it. I can't resist taking a photo of them taking a photo of the photo.

Bernd and Heidi have been here for days and have a favourite restaurant that Brian and I try for breakfast for the first time. It's owned by a family of nine, who live in two small rooms at the side. There is a woman, her two children, her sister and her four children and their mother. It is a hand to mouth existence. The only time the woman's husband turns up is when he needs money for drink. She is having so much trouble getting the money she needs to pay the electricity bill, she asks Bernd and Heidi if they would like to pay for their meals for the next couple of days in advance. Generous souls that they are, they agree.

Nepal is a wonderful place and the people are friendly – if only they could sort out their political problems, so more visitors would come and enjoy the scenery and the people. Every day we read more stories in the paper about Maoists killing and being killed, kidnappings and strikes. Amnesty International is here trying to get the warring parties together for discussions without much success.

The snake charmers not only charm the snakes out of their baskets, they charm the money out of your wallet by embarrassing you until you pay up. Decked out in brightly-coloured clothes and turbans, they sit for pictures, then they want 100 rupees per camera for their trouble. During the tourist season they must make a killing!

Bernd and Heidi have a surprise for us – Ingo has arrived. We didn't expect to see him again. As he is studying forestry, he plans one day to come to Australia to see our wonderful forests. He will spend a couple of months in Nepal before heading back through India and home to Germany to continue his studies.

The five of us take a paddle around the lake. I admit to being very uncoordinated and happily let Brian paddle our canoe, while Bernd and Ingo let Heidi chauffeur them across the lake. Our leaky little canoes aren't state-of-the-art but the new paint job seems to be keeping the water out. The same can't be said for the public water taxi that jams 15 on board to make the journey from the island temple back to the shore. The taxis are just above the water line, the driver and passengers oblivious to the catastrophe that could befall them.

Brian and I say goodbye to Ingo again and turn south to the Royal Chitwan National Park. Not keen to travel over the landmined road again, we arrange to meet Bernd and Heidi down there. We head across the hills past fields of green. Above us, eagles soar in the sunlight. It is the perfect day for a ride. We even pass a wonderful smiling seated Buddha, about 3 metres tall, to add to the pleasure of the scenery.

A modern bridge takes us over a creek; then we end up on a goat track again. Why they didn't pave from the bridge through to the roadway is a mystery. After more bumps, slips and slides, we end up at our hotel on the banks of the river running though the national park. There aren't too many guests. There is another *bandh* in Kathmandu and those who were expected can't get through. The troubles make it very difficult for the traders to survive.

We sit by the river and have a cocktail at sunset. Here one of the locals joins us – a one-year-old rhino. This young lady stands a metre tall and would make a mess of your foot if she trod on it. She was found wounded in the jungle and has been raised by the rangers. She has no fear of humans, but will be returned to the jungle before she gets too big to handle. Only yesterday a local woman was killed by a rhino on the edge of the jungle.

Brian: Being on holiday is hard work! Today is a tough one: we drag ourselves out of bed at 6.30 for breakfast at 7 to meet up with the others at 7.30 for our day in the jungle.

The river looks eerie in the early morning mist. Dugout canoes are lined up to take tourists for a paddle. Each dugout sits eight on very rudimentary homemade wooden seats with small back supports. The 'canoeist' stands up the back with a bamboo pole for propulsion. The waterline is, at best, 10 centimetres from the lip of the dugout and it is unstable. The river is flowing fast and filled with logs, rocks and debris. I plan how to keep the camera dry if and when we come to grief.

The canoe trip lasts about 45 minutes and, once we get used to the idea of impending disaster with every push of the bamboo pole, it's quite enjoyable. The mist is very thick and it is difficult to see the bank on the far side. We pass villages coming to life and fishermen going about their work. We hear men talking and see huge black shapes appear out of the mist – elephants coming back from the jungle laden with grass.

They walk straight towards us in the water, their white tusks standing out against their black bodies. Such a magnificent sight makes the early morning chill worth putting up with.

The Rapti River is wide but not very deep at this time of year; still, you can see the huge cuts it makes into the riverbank during the monsoon. Our guide explains that this river is a tributary to the Ganges. The fast-flowing water keeps this part of it fresh and clean.

Our river pilot heads towards the bank on the jungle side. I can't see where we will land, but I know it will be fast and hard. The dugout is pushed into the sand and the current quickly spins it around its full length. We all scramble out and clamber up the steep bank.

We have two guides, little Nepali men carrying bamboo sticks, to protect us during our walk through the jungle. Such wild beasts as tiger, rhino, wild elephant and sloth bear are all aggressive to humans. It is shades of Bardia all over again. The safety briefing goes along the lines of: if you see a tiger, stare him in the eye and back off slowly; if it's a rhino, run in a zigzag, not straight line, and climb the nearest tree; if you see an elephant, run like crazy; a sloth bear, crowd together and don't climb a tree – they are better climbers than us. With these words of wisdom at the forefront of our minds, we head off into the jungle.

We don't have any encounters with wild beasts, but we do encounter an army patrol. Four elephants lumber up the dry riverbed, each carrying two heavily armed soldiers and the mahout. They are on patrol looking for poachers.

Shirley: It's not all work for the elephants. Each day, at lunchtime, they come to the river for a bath. It is such an incredible sight to witness the bond between man and beast. The elephants loll about, thoroughly enjoying the attention and the scrubbing. They try to splash their mahouts and get shouted at for their trouble. It is all part of the theatre. One mahout takes a young Asian tourist into the river on the elephant's back. Before long the inevitable happens – the elephant dunks his passenger. He takes it very well and is still laughing when he emerges and lays all his money, his airline ticket and passport out to dry.

After lunch, we again pile into the dugout and cross over into the national park with our guide for a jeep safari. Our 'jeep' is a 1940 Russian open-top four-wheel drive. Ten of us cram in.

After our poor luck on foot in the jungle, we don't expect to see any animals of interest other than deer and monkeys. We couldn't be more wrong. We travel only a short distance when we spot our first rhino. By the end of the afternoon we have seen seven, a bit of a record for this time of year. We also see mugger crocodiles basking in the sun and kingfishers diving into the water with lightning speed. We are blessed. We spy holes dug by sloth bears looking for termites, but not the creatures themselves. On the way back to the river, our guide just about falls out of the jeep in excitement. He has spotted a bison. It is a rarity in these parts, so our guide takes off to get a close look, leaving us in the jeep wondering if he will ever come back. When the bison loses interest and wanders off into the jungle, our guide returns only to discover that one of the canvas things they call tyres is flat. In no time it is replaced with something similar, but this one has some air in it.

It's my birthday. I'm a long way from home and I'm homesick. For a special treat we take an elephant ride into the jungle. Our elephant is a 35-year-old female called Pon Colly. Colly is the family name for all female elephants and Pon is her pet name. Pon Colly pushes her way through the undergrowth to get us close to the animals. She pulls branches aside with her trunk and then moves closer to some deer. They just stand and stare, unfazed.

A rhino grazing in a clearing is also undisturbed by our presence. It is as if the animals see the elephant and don't sense our presence. Some monkeys and another rhino just go on with their lives, ignoring us and giving us a chance to see them at close range.

On the way back to town we pass a pair of sunglasses on the roadway. With one indecipherable command from the mahout, Pon Colly picks up the glasses with her trunk and gives them to him.

At dinner Bernd and Heidi produce two bottles of French red wine they have carried from Pokhara as a birthday present. I am very spoilt – and loving it.

At the elephant breeding centre the elephants are chained and this seems terribly cruel until we are told that every day from 10 to 3 they are taken into the jungle to walk about and graze. And when visitors come they get extra rations, because they feed them bananas.

The babies and the mothers love the treats and want more. One of the young elephants wraps its trunk around my hand, hoping it is a banana. I am surprised by its strength. It's a real photo opportunity and we get Bernd to take a shot of us with the baby, who wraps his trunk around my leg, dragging me closer. I have to hang on to Brian to stop myself from falling. It is an unusual photo.

Brian: The ride out of the village is interesting. Everyone waves at us as I take the lead with Bernd behind and Heidi tailend Charlie. When we get to the river we can see the brand-new bridge, but the road doesn't lead there. It takes us to a fragile-looking old wooden bridge about one and a half metres wide. It slopes precariously in places and it looks as though there is nothing to stop us from sliding into the water. Bernd and I stop and look at it closely before deciding to have a go. The planks are loose and rattle ominously under the weight of the bike, but we make it and scramble up the slope back onto firmer ground.

We take the scenic route back to Kathmandu. As we get above 2000 m, the road deteriorates to a gravel-and-rock track. With the not-so-good back tyre, we slip, slide and clutch-slip our way to the summit of this range, at 2480 m.

As we come down the other side, the views are spectacular, with the Himalayas laid out in front of us and not a cloud in the sky. I go quiet for a little while and think of Possum and how much he loved this place.

The closer we get to the Kathmandu valley, the more testing the roads become. They are very narrow, and the constant threat of trucks and buses careering around blind corners on our side of the road keeps us on our toes. Twice I come to a standstill and pull over towards the edge of the mountain to let trucks squeeze past.

The broken road stretches the suspension to the max. Finally, we bump and grind our way down to the main Kathmandu–Pokhara road. The traffic pollution is almost stifling. Trucks and buses spew black smoke all over us, but we make good time to the Kathmandu ring road.

We find we have to be aggressive to get through the traffic here. Heidi does a great job keeping up, and we find our way to the Courtyard Hotel. Pujan, our host, greets us like long-lost friends. He invites us all to a Nepali welcome feast with his friends from the US embassy and a local band.

Shirley: Before flying out of Kathmandu for Bangkok, we need to pack the bike for shipment. Putting the bike into a crate seems like an easy task, but ours is a big bike. To squeeze it into a small crate, we would need to take off the front wheel, nose cone and instrument panel. To leave it in one piece, we would have to have a huge crate, but when we do all the calculations with varying sizes and weights it will cost us only about $40 more to leave it together, so we opt for that. The size of the crate comes to 561 kg in volume – they make us pay for the actual weight or volume weight, whichever is larger. This means we pay $1.07 per kilo plus 7c per kilo for the insurance. Then we add all the extras – $2 for the airway bill, $20 for the dangerous-goods certificate, $55 to make the crate, $34 for the company's handling charges and $8 in government tax. Then it's another $225 for each of our one-way tickets to Thailand – it's a total of US$1205. Now we have weight to spare, so we load our gear into the bike to save carting it on the plane with us to Bangkok. With the bike safely lodged at the airport, we have a few days sightseeing before our flight to Thailand.

We bump into Cornel, the Romanian biker, again and catch up over dinner. He has some Irish backpackers with him. Cornel shares with us his experiences of fleeing Romania and his life on the road. The solitude and peace of cycling has a certain appeal, but not as much as life on two motorised wheels. Cornel lets us into his health secret: garlic. The restaurant serves up clove after clove, which he just munches on – raw! He says this is why he doesn't get sick, but adds that it is also why he doesn't have a girlfriend or boyfriend!

We get the usual directions to the Monkey Temple: go straight! Walking through Kathmandu, we realise just how poor these people are. And while the rivers in the country flow freely, the river in town is clogged with rubbish and filth. The stench is overpowering. People defecate in the river, because there is nowhere else for them to go. There is a makeshift plank bridge across this swill and we make the perilous journey over it, hoping we don't slip in.

Most of these homes in this area don't have even the most basic sanitation, yet the people are clean and they work hard to get their kids to school. Sadly, though, 48 per cent of Nepali children leave before they finish primary school.

The steps to the Buddhist Monkey Temple are guarded by stone elephants, lions, horses and peacocks – and live monkeys. These bad-tempered and mischievous creatures lord it over the temple. They steal the offerings that have been left, try to light-finger trinkets from the tourists and take the food from the restaurant and cafe tables. They swing off the prayer flags and generally put on quite a show.

The golden stupa dazzles in the sunshine. The Buddha's eyes watch over all that happens here. The sounds of Tibetan Buddhist chants emanate from all the souvenir stands and the pleasant aroma of incense permeates the smoggy air. It is crowded with people, monkeys are everywhere, and yet it has peace and serenity. It's that Buddhist thing again.

We meet up with Bernd, Heidi, Cornel, Linda and Michael (the Irish backpackers we met last night) to go to the New Orleans Cafe to hear Full Circle, Pujan's friends, play. It's a modern cafe where visitors and expats come to enjoy the music and the ambience. Here you can get Nepali food or burgers and fries. For us it was burgers. There is a big surprise waiting for us. Ingo has arrived. We are delighted – we thought we'd said our final farewell in Pokara.

The open-air bar is warmed by huge bins of fire scattered around the tables. While this form of heating clearly works, you get the feeling it would be banned in Australia because of the dangers. The band plays Nepali blues and jazz. The music is terrific – just flute, guitar (acoustic and bass are played at different times), African drums and, in the finale, a didgeridoo-type bamboo tube.

Today there is a *bandh* in Kathmandu. When we get up for breakfast, the gates are locked and outside the streets are unusually quiet. The narrow streets on the way to the Durbar Square would normally be choked with traffic. Today they are empty. The going is certainly a lot easier without having to dodge hundreds of rickshaws and cars.

The Durbar Square was once the royal palace and dates back to the seventeenth and eighteenth centuries. There are temples and shrines to Hindu gods. Some of the temples have towering golden spires, and many have magnificently carved windows, roof supports and doors. And there is the palace of the Kumari, Nepal's living goddess. This prepubescent girl is selected to be the living goddess and will live in the temple with her family until she reaches puberty, when she becomes a mere mortal again and she and her family will go back to their home. The temple pays the Kumari a dowry when she retires. Local legend has it that it is unlucky to marry a former Kumari. It is just another intriguing part of Nepali culture.

We spend a couple of hours looking at the temples. There is a small one built under a tree. The tree has now overtaken the temple, nearly obscuring it, and has grown around it – it must be more than 100 years old. Others have brightly coloured effigies of the gods and lions to guard the entrances. There are also areas where goats and buffalo are sacrificed during special festivals, even today. The constant badgering by touts selling everything from Tiger Balm to flutes is very wearying. It isn't long before we are all fed up with it.

Today is 'B' day, the day the bike begins its solo journey to Thailand. We meet Jaween, the cargo agent, at Eagle Eyes and follow him to their airport. This is a prize target for the Maoists, so we are all searched before we can ride into the freight terminal. We have learned to live with these inconveniences.

Brian: Inside the customs terminal, I find a quiet corner and start dismantling the bike. The screen and fairing comes off, and the top box. The customs official comes over to inspect what we are shipping. He empties out the top box and looks inside both panniers. He even checks out the inside of our bike boots.

The audience around the bike continues to grow. The people are intrigued when I take the tank off and drain the fuel. We disconnect the battery and let some air out of the tyres. Then it is time to build the crate. Here, every member of our audience becomes an expert. They have advice on how to get the bike in, how to tie it down, even where to anchor the tie-downs. Eventually it all fits in and the actual size of the crate is a bit smaller than we anticipated – 532 kilos, so the total bill is US$1178.

Life is simple in Nepal. In the customs hall they don't have forklifts, so our audience comes in very handy when we have to push the crate into the holding shed. Here's hoping it will arrive in Bangkok in one piece.

Shirley: The local cinema is showing the latest *Lord of the Rings* film in English. The tickets are cheap – only 135 rupees (AUD$2.50) for back stalls and you get an allocated seat. We are searched on the way in, but the staff member who does so is more concerned about us smuggling in food we haven't bought at the cinema than she is about us concealing a bomb.

While there are warnings to turn off mobile phones, they are not heeded. Throughout the movie, phones ring and people conduct lengthy conversations. There is even an old-fashioned interval. When the subtitles are on the screen, a hush falls over the audience. When the action begins without dialogue, the chatter starts and it gets louder and louder.

We have dinner at the restaurant Kilroys of Kathmandu, which is an institution in this town. The chef specialises in desserts and good old-fashioned Irish food. The liver and onion is wonderful, but it is the desserts we mainly came for. Brian's apple crumble is delicious and the lemon tart is to die for.

Brian: Another day without the bike means I have no excuse to stop Shirl vying for the 'Tourist of the Century' award. She maps out yet another day packed with the sights and sounds of Kathmandu. She has her heart set on visiting the cremation ghats near the temples on the riverbank at Pashupatinath, the holy place for the Hindus.

Like Varanasi on the Ganges, this is *the* place to be cremated. There is a brick structure with a veranda where the poor and infirm lie under blankets, waiting to die. I find this heartbreaking. It's as if they have nothing left to live for, so they come here and wait for death to take them.

We walk down to the river and the stench of acrid smoke hangs in the air. Fittingly, it has started to rain and the area is very grey. In front of the temples, there is a stone-terraced area that leads down to the river, where stone platforms are placed at intervals. As we cross over a bridge, we can see at least four funeral pyres burning remains. The ashes are then washed into the river.

Outside the main temple a body is being prepared. It is wrapped in white cloth and festooned with bright-orange floral leis. A crowd of hundreds is gathered here. The deceased man must have been important in the community, judging by his obviously distraught wife and family members. We watch as clods of grass are laid on the stone platform, then a large funeral pyre is built. Next, the men lift the body onto the top and rotate it three times, presumably to confuse the spirits. Then, everyone is invited to gather water from the river and sprinkle it over the corpse. The 'funeral director', for want of a better name, makes sure a linen screen is put up so the grieving family do not see him remove the bamboo supports holding the body over a litter. We are on the other side of the river and see it all. Then a young man stands next to the body and gives a speech before the fire is lit.

Meanwhile, the resident monkeys vie for position to steal the food offerings placed at the foot of the pyre. Interestingly, some men give the monkeys the food. Going by the number of cremations that take place, the monkeys don't have to venture too far to be fed.

I have seen enough – I see plenty of dead bodies in my job and don't really need to witness others' grief. I know the ceremony fascinates Shirley, but she also finds it disturbing. We are not used to these rituals and have coffins to hide the realities of death.

After this trauma it is pleasant to visit the Tibetan enclave of Boudah. The exiled Tibetans have built a gigantic stupa, which is painted a brilliant white and festooned with prayer flags. The Buddha's eyes seem to follow you around the temple.

The circular courtyard is a jumble of tourist shops selling everything Tibetan. The prices are high, but I am in the mood to barter. I know Shirl really wants a Tibetan singing bowl, a metal bowl that resonates with an impressive tone when rubbed with a wooden stick. We find a little shop selling properly engraved singing bowls rather than the painted ones. They are heavier and give a wonderful, deep tone when they sing. I do a deal and Shirl gets the woman to throw in a small string of prayer flags. Her bartering skills are getting better. God help the butcher and greengrocer at home – I can just hear her now: 'A leg of lamb thanks, Brendon . . . is that your best price? How about throwing in a couple of lamb chops?' Look out, fellas!

Shirley: It is our last night in Nepal. Pujan is putting on a dinner to farewell us and has invited our German friends. We feast on traditional Nuwari food of potatoes, beans laced with too much chilli and garlic and *mo mo* – and that's just the entree. The main course consists of a dhal and chicken dishes over boiled rice. Delicious!

It is an emotional time, sharing our 'last supper' with Ingo, Bernd and Heidi. We've experienced a lot together since meeting up in Iran. Ingo heads back home to Germany now, and Bernd and Heidi continue their journey at a much slower pace than Brian and me. We plan to meet them in Australia next year.

We always seem to be saying goodbye to too many good people. While we wait for our taxi, Pujan presents us with traditional Tibetan farewell scarves. There are more tears and more promises to return to Nepal.

Brian: There is an email from our friends Nikos and Judy in Athens. Nikos tells us they had an accident on their scooter. Judy is recovering from her injuries and Nikos has a new

Piaggio 500 scooter. Nikos has a great line: 'Life without a motorbike is worth nothing.'

Shirley: Flying out of Nepal, we pass the Himalayas. They are nothing short of spectacular. The mountains are breathtaking in their rugged beauty, and awesome in their danger. We leave Nepal with fond memories.

ving in Nepal

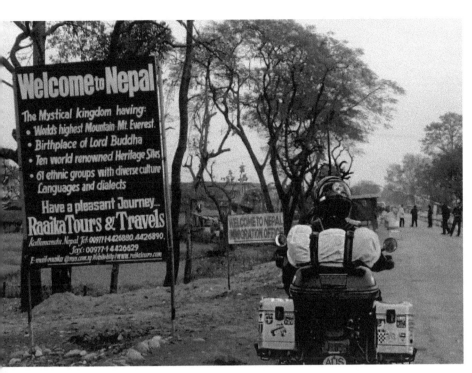

I got Shirl to walk across first — to make sure the water wasn't too deep!

Bath time at Chitwan

Snake charmers, Pokh

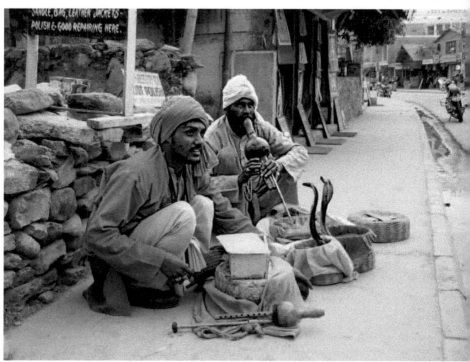

FOURTEEN

THAILAND

16 February – 23 March 2004

Shirley: Our hotel provides a shuttle service to the airport and the driver is happy to drop us off at the international cargo section. Before we can get out of the car, a man jumps into the front seat, says he's from customs, takes our bill of lading for the bike and directs us to follow him. He leads us into a building teeming with people and tells us to wait. He comes back with the news that it will cost 10,000 baht to get the bike out of customs. That's more than $300!

Brian: I immediately smell a rat. It is now clear he is a customs agent and not a customs official. I tell him 10,000 is too much so he drops the price immediately to 7000, without any argument. I still don't agree and tell him I want to see the paperwork with costings. He then tells me I have to pay 3000 up front and the rest when we come back at 2 p.m. after his lunch break! He doesn't want to give us a receipt so there is no way he is getting any money up front.

One of his minions ferries me to the Thai airlines freight centre, where an official tells me everything is in order: 'Come back after 2 p.m.'

While we wait for all the airport workers to have their lunch, we check out what others have paid for the same process. The going rate seems to be 2000 baht. I resolve to pay this guy for his services and do the rest myself, or bargain a reasonable rate. Looking at the mayhem at the freight centre, Shirl is very keen on the second option and I tend to agree with her, but I'm not going to let this shyster rip us off.

At one o'clock, we head back to the airport early, and find Mr Smooth has all the customs paperwork lined up. I walk straight past him into the customs hall and then go back to him. I don't actually talk to anyone in the customs hall, but he doesn't know that. I start by telling him I know he is trying to rip us off and that I will not put up with it. I am prepared to pay him a reasonable fee but no more. If that is not good enough, I'll take all my paperwork and do it myself. I tell him that I will be generous and pay him 3000 baht. We eventually settle for 3200, which is still a bit over the odds, but not much. He does not look happy, but bad luck – he knows he has been caught out.

The Bangkok cargo hall is frantic, with people running in all directions and crates of all sizes being carted around on forklifts. When we finally get to talk to a real customs official, he tells us they don't need to sign the carnet to prove we will export the bike. We just have to fill in a form promising not to sell the bike.

Our crate appears on the forklift and we are horrified to see that there is a hole punched through the side and the left side handlebar is sticking out. I gingerly break away some plywood and am relieved to find no real damage, and the bike is still standing upright. A worker produces a claw hammer and proceeds to break open the crate. A crowd gathers on the other side of a fence. There's nothing like an audience in the hustle and bustle of a freight terminal to ensure you lose vital screws or drop things in your haste.

There is very little air in the tyres and we wobble the bike through the exit gate to a petrol station just outside. We fuel up and ask for air, but we are told the nearest air pump is about 2 km away. We wobble off again and I put the hazard lights on as cars and trucks whiz past us. We pull into the next station and a nice man pumps up the now-very-hot tyres to the right pressures.

With a couple of illegal U-turns and scraping the right-hand pannier against a concrete barrier we make our way to the hotel. There is no real damage and it takes an hour or so to get the bike back in the condition it should be.

Shirley: Without Brian's sense of direction, I wonder how far we would have got. Even when I have the map, he has a better idea of where we should be heading. With a couple of wrong turns and a major U-turn on a freeway, we finally get to Kanchanaburi and the River Kwai. The roads here are modern, well-maintained and the drivers tend to obey the road rules. It's a huge difference from the ones we've travelled in recent months.

River Kwai is infamous for the Death Railway bridge, part of the Burma Railway built by the Japanese during World War II using prisoners of war, many of them Australian. What spans the river today wasn't built by the POWs, but has been reconstructed using the original curved sections of the bridge, retrieved after the war ended. It is a narrow railway bridge, with small aisles along the edge. Its looks belie its brutal beginnings.

There are more Japanese here than tourists of any other nationality. This doesn't surprise us, but we wonder what they know about the atrocities that occurred here during the war. I am sure they are here to commemorate the soldiers killed in the allied bombings, but their understanding of the rest of the history of the railway would be very different from ours.

We walk over the bridge. I'm not comfortable with heights, and the fact that I can see the river below through the railway sleepers makes this a very unnerving experience. Despite a fairly bad case of the jitters, I manage to get all the way across the river and marvel at what a feat of engineering this was, constructed by men starving to death and fighting disease. It is believed 16,000 allied POWs died building the Thai–Burma railway between 1942 and 1943, and as many as 150,000 locals were forced to work on it. It is a sobering thought. In the Kanchanaburi War Cemetery lie the thousands who died during the construction. The graves of 3000 Dutch soldiers, about 1500 Australians, 1500 Brits, unknown soldiers, a woman and the ashes of 300 men who died from disease at the one time are laid out in neat rows in manicured lawns. Like other war cemeteries we have visited, it is a moving sight. There are more Japanese tourists here and we wonder just what they think happened here during the war. Do they know of the treatment of the POWs and forced labourers?

For the Australian POWs Hellfire Pass, through which the railway was constructed, was hell on earth. The prisoners had to cut through a rock face using only pickaxes and sledgehammers. To walk Hellfire Pass is an emotional experience. The cutting runs through rock about 15 m thick. Men cutting this using only hand tools and the odd piece of explosive is a staggering thought, especially considering they were half-starved, fighting illnesses, and had no proper medical treatment or adequate food.

This was where they had to work 24 hours a day to finish the railway line on time. It was the twinkling lights that gave it the name Hellfire Pass. At the head of the pass are Australian flags stuck into the rock and a sign saying this was where the ashes of Weary Dunlop, 'The Surgeon of the

Railway', were scattered. It is an important place in our nation's history and we are humbled by being here. We walk along the old railway line over the original sleepers. We feel the sharp rocks beneath our boots and imagine what it must have felt like for the men in their handmade sandals and worn-out boots. Lest we forget.

Back in the town, there is a museum displaying life-sized statues of emaciated POWs working on the railway line. A collapsed prisoner is being helped by his mates. It is a moving depiction of what happened every day on the railway. A group of young Japanese tourists clamber into the display and pose for their holiday snaps. They seem annoyed that we won't move out of the background of the photos. What they don't realise is that we are deeply offended by their actions. This is not a place of fun. We wonder what kind of reception we would receive if we did something so disrespectful at Peace Park in Hiroshima. Or perhaps we are too sensitive.

I am dreading riding back into Bangkok. I can only imagine how lost we will get. We cross over a bridge on the edge of the city and I can find the bridge on the map. We see the Democracy Monument, which even looks like the drawing on the map! Wonders will never cease. We work out (or should I say *I* work out) that if we keep going straight and then cross the smaller river and turn right, the hotel should be on our left-hand side. This seems far too simple, but we try it. Within 15 minutes we find the hotel and ride straight into the parking area. This has been the easiest entry into a major capital city to date! Brian is delighted and I am staggered by my own ability. Maybe my map reading is improving at last! (Or it could have been a fluke.)

We've come to Bangkok to take part in the Bike Fest. Getting around the city is amazingly easy. We have no trouble finding the start point opposite the Royal Grand Palace, and see golden rooftops and spires towering over the walls. Inside is the Emerald Buddha, but that will have to wait for another day.

Only 500 bikes are permitted in the ride the locals call a 'caravan', and, despite the fact that registrations have closed, we are presented with an official registration in exchange for a donation of 1200 baht. For this we get a T-shirt, patch, two stickers, membership pass and instructions. We throw on the T-shirts and become part of the crowd – everyone is wearing their official T-shirt.

We meet bikers from Bangkok and across the world. Many expats have made their homes in Thailand. There is a real sense of camaraderie among the biker community. We are given business cards for everything from tyres to resort hotels, and contacts in the north of the country, Malaysia and Singapore. We meet a bloke who knows someone who knows someone who might be able to help us with shipping the bike to Australia.

The ride itself goes over the city's elevated roadways, usually off limits to motorbikes. The views are incredible and we really get an idea of the vastness of this city of 19 million people, if you believe the authorities, or up to 30 million, if you believe the cynics.

The marshals keep the whole thing moving smoothly. When we stop for lunch, we are given cold water and cold towels. At the end of a queue is the most delectable Thai meal of chicken curry and rice – all included in the registration fee.

Brian: Chiang Mai and northern Thailand are said to be biker heaven. At a service station on our way there, we meet an Englishman who gives us the name of a bar in the city where expat bikers meet.

Even the road to Chiang Mai is good. Long sweepers and a few hills get the lean angles happening. I maintain 120 km/h and overtake the throttle jockeys in their souped-up utilities and cars that can only go fast in a straight line. It is good fun. Despite the weight, the bike is performing flawlessly today and the better fuel – 95 Ron – is having a positive effect.

Shirley: About 70 km out of Chiang Mai is the Elephant Conservation Centre. Here elephants are bred, old elephants are cared for in comfort, and young ones are trained. Each day they put on a show of work and tricks combined. While some might think the elephants have been turned into performing animals, they seem very happy with their lot and without shows like this at the conservation centre they would be dying off, their natural habitat eroded by human habitation. The elephants bow, run up the flag, drag wood, roll wood with their trunks, pick up wood with their trunks and tusks, play musical instruments and paint. You can buy a painting for 500 baht. We decline.

The temples in Chiang Mai feature golden Buddhas in all shapes and sizes. Here they have a Buddha for each day of the week. The day you are born is your special Buddha. Brian is convinced the reclining Buddha will be mine because of the amount of time I like to sleep, given the chance. He is surprised to learn that we are both 'Thursday children' – reclining Buddhas!

At many of the temples, visitors are encouraged to speak to the monks and learn more about Buddhism. Judging by the length of the queues, it is a very popular offer and we can understand why; we have nothing but praise for the Buddhists we have met.

Chiang Mai's Sax Music Pub is where expats hang out and there's a group of them there when Brian and I arrive.

This place serves cold beer and is packed with friendly people. They all offer good advice on the roads we should take and the places we should stay at. Dave, an Australian who has lived here for years, even produces a map of the Mae Hong Son Loop, a must for all bikers due to its twisting roads and striking scenery.

The road to Mae Hong Son takes us through forested national parks high in the hills on very twisty roads. The road surface is extremely rough in places, but nowhere near as bad as those we travelled on in India and Pakistan. We stop in the town of Pai for an early lunch. This is a backpackers' town, with cheap food, cheap shopping and dreadlocks and tie-dyed clothes everywhere you look.

In Mae Hong Son, we find the guesthouse recommended by the guys at the Sax Music Pub. It's right on the lake and next door to a most magnificent wat. Add to this a pub and restaurant within walking distance, and we've got it made.

We unload, change into jeans and head back to Nai Soi, a 'long-neck' village inhabited by the Karin people from Burma. For centuries the men have placed golden rings around the women's necks to make them unattractive to marauding tribesmen. The tribe had to flee Burma because they were mistreated by the Myanmar people and still refers to Burma as its home. These people are refugees in their new homeland and are virtually made prisoners in their houses by the Thai army.

The road passes small villages with blue signs depicting a woman with rings around her neck tacked on posts and trees. The soldier on duty at the military base just raises the barrier and waves us through. We get to a river crossing and we remember the advice we received at the Sax Pub: 'There is a water crossing that's so deep I had to leave the bike and get a lift with some locals in a truck,' said Marcus.

'You should have turned left,' said Mark. 'The water is only a few inches deep there.'

Poor Marcus looked very embarrassed.

Sure enough, the water looks pretty deep and there is a lot of algae on the bottom. We remember Mark's words and turn left to the spillway. It has only a couple of centimetres or so of water on it and we have no problems at all getting across.

The soldiers man the checkpoint outside the village. We have to sign in the visitors' book before we are permitted to enter the village. Just inside there is a ticket booth – we pay 250 baht and hope that all the money goes to the villagers and not the soldiers.

As we walk through the narrow dirt streets, we look at everyone, wondering when we will see the women and their long necks. When we turn a bend in the road we see many stalls selling handwoven cloth, jewellery and other trinkets. Each one is looked after by a woman with a long neck. We feel very uncomfortable looking at them. It is as though they are exhibits rather than people and we are voyeurs. But we realise that without visitors to the village, they would probably have no income at all. This is their industry.

We get talking to Ma-Nang, a 48-year-old long-neck woman, who looks much older (or am I kidding myself, as I am a year older than her?). She speaks pretty good English and tells us she has four children and is the only one working, selling her fabric and jewellery to visitors like us.

Ma-Nang tells us the rings around her neck weigh six kilos and she wears three kilos of rings on each of her legs. They are never taken off. She also lets us into a secret: the long neck is actually an illusion. The rings force their shoulders down, not stretch their necks. Ma-Nang tells us about her father forcing the rings down onto her shoulders when she was small. It seems brutal.

Life can't be easy here, where the locals live under 24-hour army guard. The tourists come and go but the big tour groups don't visit. They go to see tribes further north. Knowing that eking out a living must be difficult, we are happy to buy some of their trinkets.

Brian: As the map suggests, the road south is straighter and the corners are more open than the tight mountain roads yesterday. This feels good. The bike is going very well, the camber of the corners just right. It's not long before I start scraping my toes on the tarmac. When we turn east, we immediately start a steep climb back into the mountains. Slow trucks and cars are merely a nuisance to us as the bike grunts up the hills. Following a ridge in the mountains the road is mainly good, but we have to beware: sometimes there are landslides that have left very loose dirt right across the road. Hitting one of these on the lean could be disastrous.

Shirley: Homesickness is a problem, so we are like excited kids when we wait at the airport for Frank and Phil to arrive from Melbourne. We met them a few years ago on a bike ride and have become firm friends. Brian says we should hide, but I can't. As soon as they are close I run to the barrier and wave my arms like a mad thing. We exchange hugs, kisses and tears.

We booked an apartment at Pattaya for a week before we realised the beachside town is famous for its sleazy sex industry. Walking Street is where all the tourists go. It is a sea of neon lights and certainly different from Thailand's temples. The seafood is great and the cocktails affordable, but it is people watching that makes it interesting.

Pattaya has between 30,000 and 50,000 prostitutes, depending on the time of the season. There are young female and male prostitutes and endless bars. We come across 'Boys

A Go Go', 'Amazon Girls A Go Go', 'Lucky Girls' – the list goes on and on. Outside many of the bars, groups of girls are sitting and waiting. There are dancers trying to entice men into the bars and touts trying to haul men off the street. Add to this kick-boxing bouts between local fighters and tourists – just like the old 'tent shows' in Australia in the 50s and 60s – in several of the bars and you have the picture. It is an amazing sight.

The saddest part, however, is the number of older men with very young Thai women. They may not be prostitutes in the strict sense of the word, but they are clearly after all they can get from these men. We get the distinct impression that the men think the women love or like them, rather than perceiving them as cash cows. It is depressing and somewhat sordid. And there are young men who seem to come here just for the sex trade. Little wonder HIV-AIDS is a major problem in this area – it's sad, but it is the way of the world.

The temperature is in the high thirties every day and humidity is high. We manage to fit in a fair amount of shopping in Pattaya between making the big decisions of the day, such as do we go to the beach or spend the day by the pool? Over drinks we must work out which restaurant to eat in. As they say in Thailand: 'Same, same.'

The only thing that breaks the routine is a huge storm that blows up on our last day. We feel guilty about sitting around and doing no sightseeing, so we head to the local wat and the golden Buddha we can see from the apartment windows. It is guarded by golden dragons, and worth skipping the beach for, but we still find time for a swim before the skies open in a typical tropical downpour.

We make up for our laziness when we get back to Bangkok with a huge list of sights to see. The guidebooks warn of the tuk-tuk drivers' ruse: 'Jim Thompson's House is closed.' They claim this colonial mansion is closed to tourists and then get you to go shopping with them rather than sightseeing. So we are prepared for what happens this morning. We have arranged to meet Frank and Phil at the main entrance to the Grand Palace and Temple of the Emerald Buddha at 10 a.m. There is no sign of them when we get there, then Frank arrives in a tuk-tuk. He tells us the temple is closed until one o'clock and his tuk-tuk driver will take us on a tour until then. Brian and I are very suspicious. There have been people going into the temple and palace the whole time we've been there. It certainly doesn't look closed. Frank is adamant.

The tuk-tuk driver proves to be as shonky as all other tuk-tuk drivers in this town. He is happy to do the tour for three hours until the temple 'opens' for just 20 baht for one tuk-tuk and 40 if we take two and as long as we agree to visit two shops of his choosing. The shops are always tourist traps that pay off the drivers to bring unsuspecting tourists through their doors.

We convince Frank and Phil to ignore the tuk-tuk driver and walk to the main entrance. Sure enough, there are plenty of people going into the palace. Frank isn't convinced. He still thinks the temple is closed but we convince him to trust us and pay his money.

We are gobsmacked by the grandeur and beauty of the buildings inside the palace and temple complex. They are bejewelled with semiprecious stones and guarded by demon guards, sculptures that stand about 6 m tall and have faces so demonic they warn away evil spirits and ne'er-do-wells. They are magnificent and reminiscent of the Siam we all know so well through the movies. There are golden chedis, or stupas, covered with tiny golden tiles and supported by golden monkeys and demons. Everywhere we look, something takes our breath away.

We move on to the Temple of the Emerald Buddha and –

guess what? – it is open! At last Frank and Phil have to admit they have been had by the tuk-tuk drivers. And we're glad we convinced them to visit the temple. The Emerald Buddha is exquisite. It is tiny and perched high on an elaborate dais. The Buddha shimmers in the dim light and the ceiling is rich red and gold. The walls are decorated with paintings depicting the life of Buddha and the lords of Siam (Thailand). The Emerald Buddha was originally just covered in stucco until it was damaged during a lightning strike and a monk noticed the white was peeling off. The stucco was removed and inside was the Emerald Buddha, made from jasper. Today it is the most revered Buddha image in Thailand and the temple is a very sacred place for Thais.

The taxi and tuk-tuk drivers in Bangkok continue to be a real pain in the arse. They all want to organise a 'program' for you or take you to shops. It is virtually impossible just to get into a cab and go where you want to go. Even when you offer to pay more for the privilege of not going shopping, they want to argue the point. Or they take you where you are going but try to con you into shopping on the way back.

The canals of Bangkok give visitors a completely different impression of the city. The rich live in their waterfront mansions and the poor live in tumbledown shacks that seem ready to fall into the water. Children frolic in the water while their mothers cook and wash on the verandas. A woman in a small boat comes up to sell us cold drinks and encourages us to buy a beer for the driver. As we leave, she hands over the drink to him plus a couple of 20 baht notes – his payment for bringing us to her.

Life on the canal and river today is in stark contrast to the past. The Royal Barges National Museum gives us a hint of what life on the river must have been like. The sleek, long barges are decorated with semiprecious stones and wonderful carvings. The gilt mastheads depict demon guards and dragons, charged with keeping away the evil spirits. The main royal barge at the museum has a crew of 50 oarsmen. It must be quite a sight when it is out on the river for special occasions.

Patpong Road – the site of the night markets, girlie bars, and a haven for transvestites – is high on the tourist agenda. Here you can buy a fake Rolex or fake designer bags for a few dollars and see some of the more unusual club acts on offer in Bangkok.

The touts offer the boys free drinks or 100-baht drinks to come and look; there's no cover charge. A woman even offers Phil and me a drink and free look at the 'Ping-Pong' show. I can't imagine seeing anything more depressing than women degrading themselves by throwing Ping-Pong balls out of their fannies. I've seen enough sad Thai women in Pattaya.

The Reclining Buddha at Wat Pho is worth the fight with the local traffic and the taxi driver wanting to take us shopping. The reclining Buddha that we saw in Chiang Mai was probably 2–3 m long. This one, in gold, is a massive 46 m long! It is really hard to get a photo that shows the Buddha in all its glory. And it is virtually impossible to get a shot without someone's head poking in. The Buddha's feet are inlaid with mother-of-pearl in elaborate patterns and depicting elephants, horses and other animals.

It is time to say goodbye to Frank and Phil. I thought spending time with them would cure my homesickness, but seeing them has made me realise even more how much I miss my family and friends. It leaves me with mixed emotions. I want to go home, yet I don't want the adventure to end.

That night we'd been in bed about 10 minutes when Frank rings to say, 'We miss you guys already'. It sums it all up!

We've spent far too much time off the bike lately. It is time to get back into our bike holiday with a side trip to Cambodia and the Angkor temples. At the border there are scores of trucks queued up. We go to the top of the queue, where hundreds of Cambodians cross on foot, pushing handcarts loaded with produce. They are wearing conical hats, loose-fitting pants and rubber thongs. It is an amazing sight.

Getting the bike's paperwork authorised is time-consuming and frustrating. Then we queue up in the sun for more than an hour to get our passports stamped. Cambodia better be worth it.

We only have to ride 152 km to Siem Reap and the Angkor temples. We expect the road to be bad – and it doesn't disappoint us. The first 50 km are rough, as though the road has been bombed and not repaired. On its side are signs warning of landmines. Then the road turns to red dirt that sticks to everything. The track is potholed and slows us down to about 50 km/h. It's dangerous, but it is the bridges that are potentially lethal. Some have holes in them big enough to swallow the bike and drop it into the water. One bridge is down altogether, so we have to ride off the road and around a small lake (at least we don't have to cross a river) and then back onto the road.

About 25 km from Siem Reap the road improves and we are able to increase our speed. We do hit one huge bump coming off a bridge and we hear that now-familiar cracking sound – sure enough, the bloody frame is broken again, but just on one side.

Brian: Before we can go sightseeing, we have to get the bike fixed. We cross over the canal and the main street and get to the industrial part of Siem Reap. There are mechanic shops and welding shops to spare. I pull into one that looks busy and the boys all down tools to come and stare at us and the bike. No-one speaks English and, of course, we don't know Khmer. They nod knowingly as I try to impress on them that I need a specialist aluminium welder to repair it. They all nod, so I set to work pulling the bike apart. One gets two red plastic chairs and sits them down by the roadside. Shirl sits down in the already blazing sun. When I get the sub-frame out, it is whisked away into the open workshop. Before I know it, the boys have fashioned two additional steel bracings and think that this will do. I know they won't last long and insist on the aluminium being repaired. I finally get the message through and find out they can't do it! So it's three up on a step-through scooter – rider, underling carrying the frame and me on the back (we get a lot of laughs) – weaving its way through the heavy traffic to what looks like a garage. A young man is there squatting on the ground in front of his work – welding aluminium. In no time he melts and re-welds the frame.

Shirley: The lost city of Angkor wasn't found until the 1860s. The Khmer ruled this area until the thirteenth century, and it was a city of palaces, temples and houses. When they abandoned the city, after it was looted by the Thais, the jungle took it back, protecting it from the elements over the ensuing years. Today it is remarkably well preserved.

Our first stop is Angkor Thom, a fortified city built in the early stages of the twelfth century. The massive stone gates are 'protected' by a long line of stone warriors holding a huge stone serpent. On the high tower above the centre of the gate are carved faces looking down on the visitors.

Inside the city we visit the Bayon in the exact centre of Angkor Thom. From a distance it seems like a huge series of columns, but when we get close we realise each 'column' is covered in intricate carvings. There are 54 towers; each one features massive carved faces. The crumbling walls show quite clearly the bas-reliefs depicting ancient Cambodian life. They say there are 11,000 figures around these walls. It is breathtaking.

The Terrace of the Elephants was used by the king as a reviewing stand. It is a large flat area elevated for good views of the passing parades. Its walls are decorated with elephants and garuda, the mythical human birds.

It is incredibly hot. We are dripping with sweat and I have turned a very interesting shade of puce, but we still enjoy the sights of Angkor. The steps on some of the temples are so steep they literally take your breath away and clambering up and down is a slow process, particularly in this heat.

Our last stop of the day is Angkor Wat, a massive temple that is so closely associated with Cambodia it is depicted on the country's flag. A massive moat protects the temple. When you walk through the gateway in the stone outer wall, you see the wat with its three soaring towers and connecting sections. The towers are intricately carved and dominate all else. You can spend hours walking around the corridors and galleries of this wat. The outer gallery is carved with intricate bas-reliefs telling of the battles between good and evil and warring gods, but our favourite is the Churning of the Ocean of Milk where the demons and the gods churn up the sea to extract the elixir of immortality. Of course, good overcomes evil and the gods win the battle and become immortal. The carving is incredible, with fish and crocodiles being turned upside down in the churning water while good and evil fight above them.

Many of the temples are undergoing archaeological restoration by teams of international scientists and craftsmen.

They are working to preserve what time and war hasn't destroyed. Each temple is a wonder to behold but just when we think we have seen all they have to offer, we come to Neak Poan, a rectangular pool surrounded by smaller pools on each side. In the middle of the centre pool is a tower, similar to the towers at all the temples. It is guarded by two serpents that wind their way around the tower's base. There is a group of musicians playing traditional Khmer music near the entrance. They are amputees or blind – victims of war.

Ta Prohm is probably the most famous of the temples and has been featured in some Hollywood movies. It has been left pretty much as it was found in the mid-nineteenth century by the French. The jungle is king here. It is eerie – massive trees have grown through the temple, tearing apart stone vestibules and smaller inner temples. They soar 15 m above the ground, with massive roots searching for moisture and nutrients. They have overtaken in many places, wrapping the stone walls with their huge root systems. The trees seem to be crushing the life out of Ta Prohm.

Outside we meet an unusual seller – a national policeman in full uniform.

'Would you like to buy my badge? It is a real Cambodian police badge,' he says.

'Won't you get into trouble?' Brian replies.

'No. I will say I lost it. Do you want to buy it?'

'No. I have one of my own.' Brian shows the policeman his police ID and he is very impressed.

'Do you want to swap?'

'No.'

I guess this is one way of getting some extra cash. What surprises us is how blatant he is. There was no hiding the fact he is a policeman – the full uniform is part of his sales pitch!

Angkor is truly a field of stones in the forest. But a field of stones that never ceases to take your breath away. Just when you think you have seen everything, you come across another fascinating carving or another soaring tower, or just a steep staircase, and you are gobsmacked all over again.

The more recent history of Cambodia is apparent in this part of the country. The government worked hard to remove the landmines from the area around the temple, but they can't remove the scar of the Pol Pot years: the killing fields.

On the outskirts of Siem Reap is a memorial to those who died during Pol Pot's five-year reign of terror from 1974 to 1979. A glassed-in temple is filled with smashed skulls and broken bones. Our guide informs us his father was murdered, because he was deemed to be an intellectual. The sign nearby tells us that the people of Siem Reap can't afford to build a proper memorial to the thousands killed here and asks for donations. Being one of the countries that stood by and let this atrocity happen, we feel compelled to donate some money toward the memorial fund. It is still hard to believe Australia and the rest of the world would rather have seen Pol Pot's systematic killing of every intellectual and anyone who opposed him than the Vietnamese-backed communist regime that would overthrow him in the 1980s.

We hit the road for Thailand early in the morning, but the temperature is soaring and hot wind is hitting us head-on. It is Saturday, market day, and we share the road with little bikes carrying all sorts of produce. Bags of corn are the norm, along with baskets of green vegetables. Some of the bikes have baskets filled with litters of squealing piglets strapped to the back seat. We even see one with a huge pig strapped into a bracket. The rider tells us, with a big grin, that the pig is 'died'.

Back in Bangkok we have one last tourist sight to visit, the Golden Buddha. It is impressive to say the least – a solid gold seated Buddha, five tonnes, 3.5 m tall and 4.5 m wide at the base! It was only discovered when a stucco-clad Buddha was dropped while it was being moved. It had been covered, like the Emerald Buddha, to protect it from the marauding Laotians.

We need a holiday, so we decide to head to Phuket to catch up with Giovanni, a biker we met at the Bangkok Bike Fest. It should be a pleasant two-day ride to the beach.

Brian: We plan to break the journey at Rayon, a pretty town on the west coast where there are thermal springs. The bike is humming along nicely until we go over some bumps. These aren't a problem, but the little rise allows me to see the warning lights at the bottom of the instrument panel, over the now-packed tank bag. To my horror, the alternator light is on, indicating that we are running on battery power alone. I don't know how long this has been going on, but we are in the middle of nowhere and I know we can't continue for too much longer.

We pull into Prachuap Khiri Khan and find a Honda motorcycle dealership. It's just after 1.30 and the mechanic is not back from lunch, so I pull off the alternator cover and find the belt drive has disintegrated. Bits are stuck in the alternator and I prise them loose, hoping like hell that there is no serious damage done. The mechanic takes one look at it and then jumps on his scooter and scours all the motorcycle and car dealerships, looking for something to replace the belt. He has no luck, so we ring BMW in Bangkok. They will send the part by train, as long as we get to the bank and deposit the money into their account. The Honda dealer, Jiradet

Pongtawaradet, kindly gives me a brand-new step-through scooter to ride around town and gets one of his men to escort us to the bank to transfer the money. He then organises for his driver to take our entire luggage in their work ute down to the only hotel in town. How do you ever repay such hospitality? Such is life on the road.

The hotel is a bit of a surprise. Unfortunately, it's booked out due to a sky-diving convention and the only room they have is in the basement. There are no windows or fresh air and the smell from the drain is overpowering, but a bit of incense covers that. It is cheap, is right on the beach and has a good pool. After a swim and a beer, things don't look too bad. So what if we are stuck here for a couple of days? It could be a lot worse.

Shirley: We check with the bike shop and they let us know the part will arrive on the train at 7 p.m. We should come back at 8 p.m. to pick up the bike. We cross the railway line on our way back to the bike shop and hear the train's whistle. We hope the part is on it. Jiradet is at the station and when he comes back he holds the parcel high in the air triumphantly! His two mechanics have come back to work after their dinner to fit the part. Despite the fact they don't have the right tools, they fit it in 10 minutes. And the total price for all of this: nothing!

'Welcome to Thailand,' is all Jiradet says.

The bike is running like a charm and we make it to Patong Beach, Phuket, in a day. There are two Aussies here who make us feel a little homesick. Paul Anderson is the managing director of the hotel and Anne, from Sydney, likes the place so much she bought an apartment in the hotel block and lives here.

This is holiday time. There is plenty of swimming to be done, food to be eaten, wine to be drunk and books to be read. We don't just veg out. We do venture to Phi Phi Island for some snorkelling and take a trip out to James Bond Island. Fans of the 007 movies will recognise the pillar of rock balanced on a narrow tip standing in a picturesque bay. We visit Monkey Beach, which is clear of all monkeys, and a monkey temple in a huge cave where monkeys climb all over you to get to the bananas they know you have for them.

Giovanni, or Gianni to his friends, shows us around the area on his bike. Phuket is a picturesque area and we can understand why people come and stay here. The only problem for bikers is the slippery road surface. Gianni makes some interesting manoeuvres on the tight corners, where his back wheel takes on a life of its own.

He takes us to Nicky's Handlebar (get it?) managed by a Malaysian biker who came to Phuket and stayed. Nicky runs Harley Davison tours for visitors and his bar is great and filled with biker memorabilia. Like all the other bikers, Nicky and Gianni go out of their way to show us a good time.

Brian: We've spent five good days here in Phuket, but now it's time to move on. Mind you, Shirl is quite keen to spend another day here. I want to start moving south.

Heading out of Phuket, everything is lush through the verdant foothills leading into the mountains. The further south we go, the blacker the skies become. The road takes us up into the mountains and we work out why everything is so green. We experience our first tropical downpour; it's like turning a shower on and off. It's not cold, but the road becomes slippery, and several cars race past us right on the verge of aquaplaning.

We stay overnight at Hat Yai, 30 km from the Malaysian border. Tomorrow we will cross into Malaysia – another step closer to home.

Mae Hong Son, Thailand

The locals love Brian's be

Prohm, Cambodia

You have to have your wits about you on the road in Cambodia

FIFTEEN

MALAYSIA AND SINGAPORE

23 March – 4 April 2004

Shirley: The number-one highway in Malaysia is a perfect road and it's beautiful. There are manicured lawns along the edge of the roadway. Gardens are planted at every exit and there are palm-tree plantations as far as the eye can see. You can tell they get plenty of rain, as everything is green, lush and clean. On every overpass, signs showing a bike and umbrella point to areas where motorcyclists can pull off the road and shelter from the torrential downpour.

We come to the bridge that connects the mainland and Penang Island. It's believed this is the longest bridge in South-East Asia, and our odometer shows it's 9 km! We are tracked across the bridge by a family – Mum, Dad and son – three-up on a motorcycle. What is unusual about this sight is that they are all wearing helmets. That doesn't prevent us from seeing their huge smiles.

Georgetown is a city of one-way streets and that makes getting to our hotel a trick. We can see it, but we always seem to end up one street away from it. Just when the footpath seems the best option, Brian lucks onto a street that runs right past the front door. The one-way system is probably great if you know where you are going. Not so for us.

Brian: The first job here is to try to sort out some little niggles with the music system. It's been very scratchy and intermittent lately. Checking the wiring, I'm sure some inquisitive fingers have been pulling at the wires leading into the top box and loosened the connections. I use the soldering iron and after two hours I finally get some semblance of sound out of it. Shirl (God bless her) comes down and offers to sit with me and listen to me swear at it for two hours. She soothes me by suggesting a beer at the Irish bar over the road. What a woman.

After a couple of beers and watching the barman practise his Tom Cruise impersonation with the cocktail shaker – not bad, either – we head into Chinatown for dinner. We find a nice little place with a few foreigners sitting outside and order Penang-style noodles and soup.

When we check our emails before heading back to the hotel, our motorcycle contact in Singapore tells us the freight company wants more than $500 Singaporean dollars just to build a crate! Considering that Nepal charged $55 and Melbourne nothing, I'm not happy. We will have to sort out with Qantas what they require – and quickly!

Shirley: Georgetown is an interesting mix of British Colonial architecture, modern glass and steel, and a strong Chinese influence. The Cheong Fatt Tze Mansion, Georgetown's perfect example of a feng shui house, is striking, particularly in contrast with its surroundings. Its walls are a brilliant blue and the traditional Chinese architecture is so much more visually appealing than the bland box-like constructions of today. The house was built by Cheong Fatt Tze in the 1880s. His is a real rags-to-riches story: he left China to seek his fortune in Indonesia; working for a wealthy merchant as a 'water carrier', he did the sensible thing and married the boss's daughter. This head start allowed him to build his own wealth and accumulate eight wives and countless offspring. His Georgetown home was built to the exacting requirements of feng shui, to bring good fortune to all who lived there.

After his death in 1914, at the age of 76, his will stipulated that none of his vast fortune, by this time including gold, tin and copper mines, rubber plantations and properties, could be broken up until the death of his youngest son, who was just two years old when his father died.

Over the years, running the house got more and more expensive and all available space was rented out to families. They lived and cooked in the corridors. How the house survived at all is a miracle. A consortium of businessmen bought the wreck and oversaw its award-winning restoration.

The house is fitted out with magnificent pearl-inlaid furniture of the period and much of the gold leaf on the carved panels has been uncovered or restored. It was protected by the layers of dirt that built up over the years of neglect. There is a lot to be said for poor housekeeping – the dirt also protected the imported English floor tiles. There was no expense spared in the construction of the house – hand-carved wooden blinds keep the sunlight out and fresh air inside. Channels carry water through the internal courtyard, which keeps the house cool and is good feng shui.

The air in the streets of Chinatown is permeated by the aroma of incense. It's easy to understand, when you see the size of the joss sticks burning outside the temples – they are more than a metre tall and as thick as small tree trunks. And the Chinese brought their snakes with them, too. The Snake

Temple makes my skin creep, with death adders draped across the trees inside it. This is obviously a popular spot for some, if the signs are anything to go by: 'Mediums are forbidden to fall into a trance in the Snake Temple or its precincts to avoid causing inconvenience to worshippers and visitors.' And another: 'All snakes are live snakes, but visitors are requested not to prod or harm the snakes in the temple as they may be injured.' We can't work out if they are concerned for the welfare of the snakes or the visitors.

After all those creepy snakes we need a good dose of serenity, so we head to the Ten Thousand Buddhas Pagoda, a Buddhist temple which is the largest in Malaysia on a hilltop above the city. The Goddess of Mercy is here towering above the temple, with an incredible collection of Buddha images guarded by massive, ferocious gilded warriors. And there is the soothing smell of incense coming from normal-sized joss sticks.

We wake in the middle of the night to the sounds bikers dread: thunder and pouring rain. The lightning illuminates our room even though the drapes are drawn. We hope it rains itself out overnight. At 7.30 a.m. it's done just that – the rain has stopped and the clouds have cleared.

On the highway to Malacca, there are more palm plantations and gardens of lush, flowering shrubs. And instead of trucks belching out putrid black smoke, we are riding alongside Mercedes Benzs and other luxury cars.

We skirt Kuala Lumpur on the highway – it doesn't intrigue us; it's just another huge city – and get a glimpse of the twin towers. At 88 stories with a spire, they are the world's highest buildings. Now we've seen the city's main tourist attraction.

The hotel we choose in Malacca is a converted Chinese

mansion built by a businessman in 1822. It is like a smaller version of the feng shui mansion in Georgetown, with mother-of-pearl inlaid furniture in an open courtyard, marble floors and English floor tiles. It is luxurious. In a small room off the reception area, tiny swallows nest on the walls. The owner of the hotel uses the nests in traditional Chinese medicine. Unfazed by the constant disappearance of their nests, the swallows build new ones. There must be about 50 of the small birds snuggled down for the night.

What a difference 600 km makes. We are that much closer to the equator than we were yesterday and it is hotter and more humid. The locals have worked out some ingenious ways to make the heat and humidity bearable. Our hotel restaurant has a waterfall and all the tables are set under huge frangipani trees, which creates a cooler haven, but it is still hot and steamy. It's the cafes in town that have the best idea. Above the doorways and outdoor tables, small watering systems have been installed, that spray water in fine streams from an overhead sprinkler. Sitting under the fine mist, we feel cool and don't want to leave in a hurry. That has got to be good for business. The only minor problem I have is that it fogs up my glasses when I try to read the menus. Still, that is a small price to pay for the comfort and respite from the heat.

To get a different view of Malacca, one day we opt to take a rickshaw. Our rickshaw driver is late and arrives very puffed and hot – he's had a flat tyre. He's expecting a trouncing, but we sympathise with him. Flat tyres are something we understand.

In Chinatown, he takes us to the cobbler who makes shoes for women with bound feet. This ancient art is just about lost now as there are no longer women with the absurdly small feet that resulted from binding. This company was the last to continue the art of tiny-shoe making. The miniature silk shoes look as if they are made for a doll, not a woman. It was such a cruel fashion. The women's feet were actually broken and their flesh rotted under the metres of cloth used to bind them. Strangely, some men, it is said, found the rotting flesh quite exciting!

From here we go to the oldest Chinese temple in Malacca, Cheng Hoon Teng. It is a few doors down from the Kampung Kling Mosque and just a couple of doors away from the Sri Poyatha Venayagar Moorthi Temple. Across the Sungai Melaka river is the Christian British Church. This was once known as Harmony Street, a true sign of the melting pot that is Malacca. It's a pity these religions and nationalities can't live in harmony in the world today.

After yet another dinner under a cooling mist, we take a walk through Chinatown. The community halls are being used for various activities. At the first there is a group of people of all ages line dancing to such great classics as 'Hands Up (Give Me Your Love)'. I am very surprised that Brian has never heard the song. What a sheltered life he must lead . . . At the second hall there is an orchestra and choir performing more classical fare.

There is just one piece of advice we have for anyone who wants to take a motorcycle or car into Singapore: *don't.* Our carnet has been enough paperwork to get the bike into every country we have entered and some countries haven't even bothered with it. That is not the case for Singapore and we don't discover it until we actually get to the border.

It's Sunday and the border is quiet. We get our passports stamped and no-one bothers about the bike, so we ride over the bridge to the Singapore border. Our entry visas are issued and stamped into our passports and a young woman comes out of an office and takes the carnet. She takes us into another office, where we have to pay a permit fee to bring the bike into the country. Then we are asked about our 'International Circulation Permit' and we don't have one. We didn't know we needed this, as we've never even heard of it.

We are happy to buy one. They don't sell them at the border. We have to go to the Automobile Association in Singapore for this. It's Sunday and the Automobile Association is closed. And we can't take the bike there anyway, because we don't have an International Circulation Permit.

For the next two hours, we sit and discuss the need for this permit, the fact that we don't have one, and that no-one, especially on a Sunday, is going to help. It is a nightmare. No-one knows why we need the permit. No-one knows why they don't sell them at the border and no-one cares. They can actually let us into Singapore, but they won't let us leave the bike at the border. The only advice they give us is to go to the Woodland Border Crossing, because we can leave the bike there, and get a bus into Singapore – tomorrow. Oh great!

We ride to Johor Bahru and discover the town is right on the border or the border is right in the town. The people at the hotel are far more helpful than the officials we dealt with earlier. We can get a taxi to the centre of Singapore for 50 ringgit (AUD$20), and that includes crossing the border. From there we can get a local taxi to the Automobile Association and then back to the bus station in the centre of Singapore, from where we can get a Malaysian taxi back to the border. And there is no problem leaving the bike and our luggage at the hotel. This is the first good thing to happen to us for hours!

The next morning, after breakfast, Brian rings the Automobile Association and reaches a woman named Alice Fan. She says there is no problem, we can just come over. The cabbie taking us to Singapore has immigration forms for us to fill in, checks our passports and makes sure they are in order – far more efficiently than many border guards we have dealt with. He deals with the stamping of passports and we are in Singapore. He drops us at the Ban San Street bus and taxi station and we jump into a local taxi to the Automobile Association.

The staff are very friendly and two women named Rosie and Alice look after us. All is going swimmingly until they want proof that we are taking the bike out of Singapore. We, of course, don't have anything in writing, so they ring Qantas to speak to the person we've been emailing there. Now it gets expensive. The International Circulation Permit is free; we just have to pay $10.50 Singapore dollars for the administration fee. And insurance is $105 for a week. On top of this there is the autopass, which gives us permission to ride on the roads. This costs $4 per day. And there are toll roads in Singapore and we are told we must have a reader for the toll roads at a hire fee of about $100. They have got to be kidding. The upshot is that if we avoid the toll roads we don't need the reader, but if we get caught on one without a reader the fine is $70.

Alice gets notification from Qantas and wants something in writing from our freight agent. Now, here's a problem: we don't have a freight agent. Finally, after many smiles and a minor threat of tears, Alice says she will issue the permit as long as we get back to her as soon as we have a freight agent, so she can issue the permit for us to take the bike out of the country. This really is a load of bullshit.

Alice has some final advice for us as we leave: 'You know, if I was doing what you are doing I'd ship the motorbike from Kuala Lumpur and just come to Singapore as a tourist by bus, to enjoy the sights.'

Thanks, Alice. We'll remember that next time.

En route to the bus station, the cab driver gives us directions to get from the border to our hotel and our hotel to the airport without using a toll road. I mark the roads on our map of Singapore. There is no way I can let us get lost here.

The cab driver taking us back to Malaysia has more immigration forms for us to fill in and checks our passports to make sure they are in order. These cabbies are very efficient. At last we can load up the bike and head back across the border, filling in even more forms and getting another set of exit and entry permits stamped into our passports.

In Singapore we get our passports stamped again and head into the customs area. The people behind the counter don't seem to know what to do with us. Finally, a customs official tells Brian we should have come through the articulated vehicle entrance – these people expect visitors to absorb everything by osmosis! Brian heads off to get the carnet processed. While he's away I put on my best smiley face and deal with paying for the autopass. We have to pay 6 Singapore dollars for the card and then $4 toll per day. I offer to pay the $30 now, but they don't want that. It would be too easy. Instead, I pay $10 and then we can add another $20 to the card at any 7-Eleven convenience store. And then, when we have proof we are actually leaving the country, we have to go to the Land Transport Authority office to cancel the card and pay any monies owing. This country really is a red tape horror.

Finally with the carnet signed off and autopass in Brian's wallet, we head out of the border control and end up in a long line of little bikes going through the 'nothing to declare' line. The customs officials are getting everyone to open their top boxes. We expect a thorough search, but don't get one – just a big smile and a wave. About bloody time!

At the hotel Brian hits the phone running to get the bike organised. This is going to be hell. Rajendran at Qantas Freight is Brian's first call. We've been emailing him for weeks. He gives us a contact who can get us the Dangerous Goods Certificate we need to put the bike on the plane. Through this contact, Brian gets the name of a shipping agent who can help us. Qantas also suggests we contact their handling agent.

We have all bases covered now and while too many people are duplicating the process, at least everything is getting done. The only problem is that all these people want payment and our costs are mounting.

In Turkey, we met Max Ng, a biker heading west. We meet up with him again through contacts in Singapore from the Chiang Mai bikers. He's back home. He introduces us to Phuah, and a few more bikers who wine and dine us in Singapore. The only thing we don't do is ride the bike! All our time is taken up with making phone calls about it. The more calls we make, the more confusing things become. Finally, we get everyone helping with the freight to agree to meet us at the airport on Friday afternoon so we can lodge the bike and finalise the paperwork.

Singapore is pristine. There isn't a piece of rubbish on the street. Chewing gum is banned, but they have recently relaxed that ruling if you are in need of nicotine chewing gum to help you stop smoking. When heading back to the hotel after a trip to the shops we jaywalk and immediately become paranoid we will be booked!

Tonight I do my last interview with Red from foreign soil. He tells me he is getting masses of emails from listeners who don't want us to come home; they are enjoying our chats so much! What began as an 'occasional' chat has become a regular weekly interview with me ringing in every Thursday morning. We've talked about everything from politics to local food and the highs and lows of our journey. Going live to air means getting up in the middle of the night, but it's been fun.

With the bike as sorted as it can be, we finally get to do some sightseeing. Our first preference, of course, is a cruise on the Singapore River past the flash office blocks, steel-and-glass monstrosities towering over the water. Some old warehouses on the river's edge show the city as it once was and their charm is a real break in the sterility of modern Singapore. But not everyone agrees – like the two American tourists sitting in front of us: 'I wonder why they have left those old warehouses there,' one says.

The shops seem to be offering everything we can get at home, and for about the same price. After the shopping in Nepal and Thailand, it is all too expensive and boring. A haven from this rat race is the Singapore Botanic Gardens. They are beautiful and clean (of course) and offer a wonderful respite from the steel and concrete of the city. The highlight is the National Orchid Garden, which is exquisite. Brilliantly coloured orchids with delicate petals are shown in their natural habitat, including a greenhouse that is also a great relief from the heat and humidity. Waterfalls and fountains add to the display.

But what would a visit to Singapore be without a Singapore Sling at Raffles Hotel? While it has been renovated, the hotel is still charming and very old-world. We can't walk through the lobby – men must wear long pants and shoes (no thongs or sandals). We are directed around the corner and into the courtyard. Here we pay $40 – that's right,

$40 – for two drinks! But it is lovely sitting in the cool gardens and overall very classy.

It is 'B' day and stress levels are high. We are both extremely anxious about getting the bike to Qantas. With all the confusing phone calls over the past three days, we are sure there will be problems.

We have to make one last journey to the Singapore Automobile Association to get our exit permit. Rose and Alice are dealing with a German biker who is having trouble getting his head around the need for the International Circulation Permit. He has left his wife at the border with their bike and is far from happy. We understand his frustration and he is dealing with it all in his second language. We help out as best we can.

Armed with the cab driver's directions we make our way to the airport. My map-reading skills come into their own when we head towards a gantry over the toll road and a $70 fine for not having the reader. It is only a small mistake, but it will be expensive. Brian grabs the map and works out where we should be. He doesn't need to say anything. I know he's not happy.

When we are on the freeway to the airport he reads me the riot act: 'Today is not the day to get lost. We've got very little petrol and I don't want to have to refuel before we load the bike.'

I understand what he's saying. We've deliberately run the fuel down so we don't have to tip too much out when the bike goes into the plane. Fuel is not permitted in the bike. It's okay, though; I'm not lost. I know exactly where we are going. The problem is that we are heading in the opposite direction to the airport.

Brian is now seething. We pull off the freeway and I ask

a girl about how to get back onto it in the opposite direction. In a matter of minutes we are heading to the airport. Brian's mood isn't improving, because the airport seems to be a long way out of town and the petrol gauge is dropping. Then, just to make sure this is a day we never forget, it starts to rain. And it doesn't just rain, it pours. Because of the heat, we are wearing jeans and T-shirts. Our riding gear and wet-weather gear is all packed – back at the hotel. It is bucketing down and we are saturated in minutes.

When we finally get to the cargo terminal we have to get a pass, and that means filling in forms and producing our passports. As another fine example of Singaporean red tape, we are meant to leave our passports to prove we will return their pass. It takes some time to explain to the petty bureaucrat that we will need our passports to lodge the bike. Begrudgingly, he accepts our Australian driving licences as security.

Soaked to the skin and with no sense of humour left, we ride to the freight agent. They laugh uproariously at our wet clothes. I am glad they find it so funny. The more they laugh the shittier I get. Brian is over it too. Things go from bad to worse when we learn that because too many people were involved in our shipping plans, our booking on the plane has been cancelled by one organisation which thought someone else was looking after that aspect. Luckily, there is space on the plane for the bike!

Then, out of the blue, things start to go right. Mustaffa arrives to process the Dangerous Goods Certificate. He takes us to the Qantas freight terminal, and the men there take over. The bike is weighed and comes in at 294 kg! Pretty heavy when you're paying by the kilo.

Rajendran, the Qantas rep, comes down from his office to say hello on his way home. He takes our paperwork to the customs officials, who say we don't need an exit permit because we have a carnet! We told them that, but no-one listens to us. Now the freight agent realises he has nothing to do because we don't need the permit. He was going to charge us an arm and a leg to process the permit, so he says he won't charge us anything now. He just hangs around to see how we go.

It is all falling into place. Once we hand over the money, our last job is to get the carnet signed at customs. While the customs agents take their time, they eventually sign on the dotted line and we are free to load the bike. Before we can load the bike, though, Brian has to empty any remaining fuel out of the tank. I have bottles and funnels ready for the task. He takes off the tank and tips it upside down . . . and nothing comes out. Not a drop. Not even half a drop. We've ridden into the freight yard on vapours alone – now, how's that for planning? Secretly, I count my lucky stars. If we had remained lost for a minute longer we would have run out of petrol in the rain. It doesn't bear thinking about.

The bike is rolled into a metal container and everyone becomes an expert in how best to tie it down. Eventually, after considering laying the bike on its side, they defer to Brian and his expertise. They even break the 'no photography' rule so we can get a pic of our baby in the Qantas box.

In a perfect end to our foreign adventure, Max and Phuah take us to a Buddhist vegetarian restaurant on Orchard Road. I'm not sure how they do it, but we are served vegetarian shark-fin soup and it is excellent.

Tonight we head home, but it wouldn't be possible to get out of Singapore without one more encounter with bureaucracy, and that comes when we have to cancel our autopass. We get a number at the Land Transport Authority office, and wait and wait. A little street theatre keeps us amused, as a man trying to help his brother get a licence ends up abusing an official for making everything so difficult. We silently cheer in support.

Of course, when we get called up to the counter the man behind it doesn't have the vaguest idea of what needs to be done, and even asks if we are in a hurry. Eventually, he tells us we need to pay another fee. At this point our smiley faces disappear and our grumpy 'don't mess with us' faces appear. In a split second he says that he will waive that fee. Just as well. Finally, we have all the paperwork signed. Getting our bike in and out of Singapore has been hell, and, again, our advice to anyone wanting to try such a foolhardy thing is *don't*.

Malacca, Malaysia

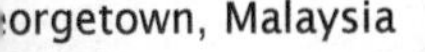

orgetown, Malaysia

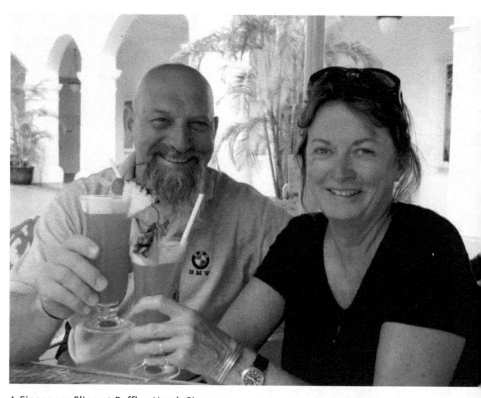

A Singapore Sling at Raffles Hotel, Singapore

The bike is packed and ready to fly home to Australia from Singapo

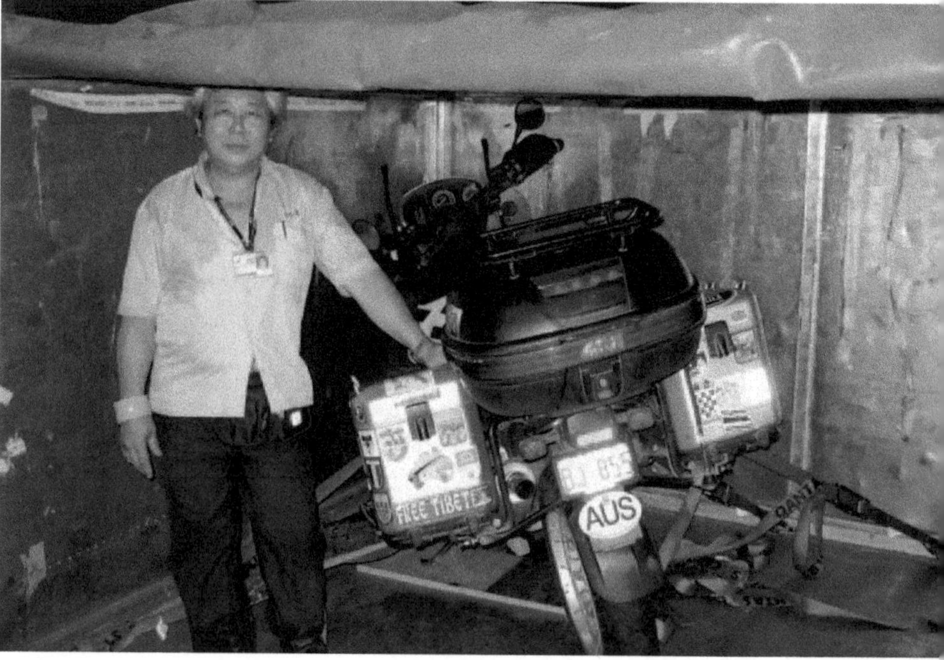

SIXTEEN

HOME

5–24 April 2004

Shirley: Brian feels every bump on the flight from Singapore to Darwin, knowing the bike is strapped into a container in the cargo hold. Luckily, it's a reasonably calm flight.

We count our blessings. Jane, an old friend from Melbourne – now living in Darwin – whom we haven't seen in years, is at the airport to meet us even though it is 4 a.m. And three friends, Ian, Mike and Ros, have ridden all the way from Melbourne to share the final stage of our journey.

We wait until 5 a.m. for Ian to turn up at the airport but he doesn't show so we head home to Jane's and hit the sack for a couple of hours' sleep. When we catch up with Ian, he tells us he did get to the airport but went straight to the cargo section. He saw the bike and it is in one piece, so that is good news.

When we all get together at Jane's we just sit and talk and talk. It is magnificent to be home with friends – no more talking to strangers and no more talking in broken English.

We hardly draw breath before heading out to lunch at the Museum and Art Gallery of the Northern Territory, right on the water.

Ian has been in Darwin for a few days and has become quite the expert on things to see and do in the city. After lunch, he gives us a personal tour of the museum, including the Cyclone Tracy exhibition. In a darkened room we hear a recording of the cyclone. It is terrifying and people who have lived through the storm are advised that it may upset them. I can imagine it would.

Sunsets in Darwin are legendary and Jane has a treat for us on our first night in town – pizzas and wine on the East Point overlooking the sea while the sun sets. We watch the changing colours of the sun as it makes amazing images on the light clouds along the horizon. God, it's good to be home! Our lives are filled with many wonderful, and some not so wonderful, memories of our adventure, but there is no place like home – even though we are not really there yet.

Brian: It's Monday and time to get the bike after the mandatory customs and quarantine checks. The customs paperwork is a breeze. They just need to see the carnet and will clear the bike – once it is cleared by quarantine.

The quarantine inspector meets us as the airport, where the bike has been taken out of the cargo crate and put onto a pallet. This is going to become a real bugbear. The inspector checks the bike with his fingertip, seeking out any foreign soil hidden in crevices. He gives our helmets a thorough going-over and even wants to destroy the air filter until I assure him it is a reusable one and has been thoroughly cleaned. He is sceptical, but lets it pass – thank goodness.

Now the inspector wants to destroy the wooden pallet. I've got no problem with this, but Qantas might. And no matter how many times I tell him, the inspector won't believe it is an Australian pallet and not a Singaporean one. I can't work out why it is my problem. He just doesn't seem to get it, so we leave him to argue the point with the Qantas officials.

The bike is delivered to us by forklift. If you ignore the broken frame, on this adventure the bike has suffered its most serious damage somewhere between being tied into the crate in Singapore and coming out of the cargo shed in Australia. The screen is broken and the supports for it are bent. It looks as though it's been rammed into something while on the forklift. I am a bit pissed off but decide to let it pass. I'm just glad to have the bike home. Now all we need are new tyres and we'll be on the road, heading south.

Shirley: For the next couple of days, in Darwin, we just eat, drink and talk, enjoying the companionship of friends, good Australian food and the magnificent Darwin sunsets.

Having been away for so long, we don't realise Easter is coming up, school kids are on holidays in Australia, and accommodation prices are at a premium. Ian is going to cut and run to get home in a couple of days, while the rest of us take our time. Mike and I hit the phone to organise somewhere to stay. Uluru will cost us just over $100 per person per night. Crikey – we know we are in Australia and not Asia.

We make one last trip to the post office to get rid of the few items we bought in Singapore and re-pack the bike. Looking at our luggage, we realise we have just about changed our wardrobes entirely, and things we didn't think we could live without at the start of the journey have been jettisoned. This includes my hairdryer and hair dye! Peter Baird once asked us what item proved indispensable while we were on the road. I have no doubt it was my pegless clothesline, a farewell gift from our old friends John and Nancye Cain (the former Victorian premier and his wife). It came in so handy when we needed to get our smalls dry in hotel rooms. Brian thinks he couldn't have lived without the CamelBak, the freshwater bag he wore on his back.

It is a scorcher as we begin our journey south. Brian and I have never visited the Northern Territory and we thought that, as we've seen so much of the world, we should see this part of Australia, too. Our first stop is Adelaide River to visit the War Cemetery. Here are buried all the servicemen and one woman killed during the bombing raids on Darwin and in operations in the Timor Sea. The men were so young – one was only 16, a naval cadet in the Merchant Navy – it is very sobering. At the back of the cemetery are the graves of civilians who were killed in the bombing raids. This includes nine killed in a direct hit on the post office. Among the civilians were many Aborigines, some only known by the single name given them by the station owners. Without seeing something like this, it is so easy to forget that war did come to our shores and more than 200 died in bombing raids.

Another wartime memory is revived when we stop at Mataranka for a swim in the thermal pool. Dad served in Mataranka during World War II and we have many photos of him and his buddies swimming naked in the pools. Ian and Brian want to recreate this image, but there are far too many people about. We change into our bathers on the side of the pool, having worked at perfecting the art in Greece. No-one cares. The pool is a pleasant break away from the heat of the road. The water is warm and crystal-clear and is surrounded by massive palm trees that shade the entire area.

We stay overnight at Daly Waters, a town with a population of 16 people and 20 dogs. The pub is the hub of the town. No, that's not quite right – the pub *is* the town. Inside, it's Australiana at its worst. Bras and knickers donated by previous visitors are pinned over the bar! And we really know we are at home when a snake slithers through the bar and we find a frog in the shower. Dinner, however, is a T-bone steak as big as a plate – yum!

We take the bikes for a ride down the Daly Waters airstrip, Australia's first international aerodrome. It is incredible to think that flights from London to Sydney stopped here in the 1930s because the Darwin airport was too small. Now it is time for Ian to head back home and it's yet another sad farewell. At least we'll see Ian when we arrive at Melbourne in a few days' time.

At Tennant Creek, we meet up with Brian's cousins, Craig, Pauline and Caitlin, who are heading to Darwin for a sea change. It is the perfect opportunity for a good old-fashioned Australian barbie, but having a drink will be a bit difficult. Today is 'Thirsty Thursday' and there is no takeaway alcohol for sale in the town. Alcohol abuse is obviously a problem here, so one day a week the pubs close their bottle shops. If you want to drink, you have to go to a pub, where the over-consumption of alcohol is barred. One of the locals tells us that the drinkers in town don't like the ban, but for those who have a drinker in the family, it is a pleasure to have that family member sober for one night a week.

One of the service stations on the highway is trying to curb the alcohol-abuse problem by having a strict limit on the amount of money you can withdraw from the ATM. This stops drinkers from spending their entire pension in one day. It's a difficult problem and people are obviously trying their best to combat it.

The natural beauty of Australia is at its greatest in the out-back. The red dirt and the scrub are beautiful to us. And the Devil's Marbles are breathtaking. The deep ochre boulders, perched precariously on top of each other, are a sight to behold. They look like they will topple over, but defy gravity with boulders the size of rooms atop much smaller ones.

We stop at the Tropic of Capricorn for a photo. Ian rings to let us know he made it to Uluru en route to Melbourne, has climbed the rock and walked into The Olgas. He estimates he will do 15,000 km on his trip from Melbourne to Perth, Darwin and home again. So far, Brian and I have travelled 51,000 km to get from the UK to Australia. It just shows how big this country is.

Ayers Rock Resort is very expensive, but when you want to stay at Easter and you book only three days beforehand, you have to expect that. Sunset is at 6.40 p.m. so we head to the pub, on the other side of the resort, to get some sparkling wine to drink while we watch the sunset. At the pub we discover they, too, have a problem with alcohol abuse. Guests can only buy one bottle of wine or a six-pack of beer per person. Spirits are not sold in the bottle shop at all; the resort is in very close proximity to an Aboriginal community. It is unbelievable that guests would buy alcohol to sell to the Aborigines, but that is what the bar staff claim.

Our aluminium panniers make very good Eskies, and we fill one with ice and the sparkling wine. The nibbles go in the other and then we head to the rock. Like the Taj Mahal, we know what the rock looks like. We've seen it a thousand times on television and in the movies, yet nothing prepares you for its awesome beauty. It is enormous. The sunset viewing area is getting crowded, but we find two parking spots and wait for the sun to go down. Even though there is massive cloud cover tonight the rock does change colour a bit as the light fades, but probably not as much as it would on clear nights.

When the sun goes down we head back to the apartment and I get to work in a kitchen for about the fourth time in 10 months! It's amazing I haven't forgotten how to cook pasta.

We get up early and ride out to the rock before dawn. When the sun rises the cloud cover is gone and the rock's colour display is wonderful. Every time you look it is a different shade of red. We munch our way through some hot cross buns while the sun rises on this symbol of ancient Australia.

The traditional owners ask visitors not to climb the rock, but it is a temptation too great to resist for many people and this includes Brian. I have to admit that I am in no way fit enough to climb the rock anyway. Sitting on your backside on a bike for 11 months takes it out of you! Brian straps on the CamelBak and starts his climb. We watch as he goes higher and higher. Every now and then he stops and sits, catching his breath. I have to admit I am anxious about him doing the climb, but then, I am a worrier. We watch through binoculars and Mike's video camera as Brian disappears over the top of the rock. I presume this is the top and wait for him to reappear. When 45 minutes have passed I have to admit I am getting very worried. Even Mike has misgivings and goes to ask some people coming down if they saw Brian. They tell him no-one is in trouble at the top.

Then he finally appears. I can't believe how long he has been out of sight. We watch as he comes down, making one small stumble. When he gets to the bottom I go to meet him. I am furious – and relieved. I tell him how worried I was and how much I love him. Brian admits it was one of the hardest things he has done and that he won't do it again. It was a once-in-a-lifetime experience.

There is one thing we have noticed since arriving here – the bloody flies. Ridiculous-looking nets over the face are all the rage here, but I think they look so silly I don't bother buying one. Then we get to The Olgas and the flies are big enough to carry a small child away and so sticky the usual 'Aussie Salute' doesn't shift them. Brian has one of these stupid face nets and offers it to me – and I take it.

We thought the flies were bad at the Rock. At Coober Pedy they are even worse. The flies are big enough to carry a *large* child away and nothing shifts them. This opal-mining town is outback Australia personified. Most people live underground, to get away from the heat – even the churches are underground. The town is hot, dry and dusty.

However, the skies are clear and we have the most incredible night stargazing with a local amateur astronomer. For a bit over an hour, we stand in the dark watching the stars and planets both with the naked eye and binoculars. We see Venus change from a white light to bright red as it dips below the horizon. Those with steadier hands can see the rings of Saturn and three of Jupiter's moons. We see Orion (the saucepan), the Southern Cross and the Coober Pedy duck. You won't find the duck written about in any books, even though once it is pointed out to you it is the most obvious one. Our guide can't believe the Ancient Greeks didn't see the duck.

You have to be a bit careful walking through Coober Pedy. Mineshafts are everywhere, and some are a 30 m drop. The signs warn you not to walk backwards – that last step to get the right photo angle could be a real doozy! Everywhere are piles of white sand that have been removed from the mines, and the mine machinery lies dormant on this Easter Monday.

We brave the flies and the heat to see the dog fence, an ingenious construction that runs for 5300 km through New

South Wales and South Australia, to keep the dingoes out of cattle country. Brian even thinks a maintenance job on the fence would be good – out in the middle of nowhere away from the city rat race. He's been away too long!

At Broken Hill in New South Wales, our friends Al and Trish have come up from Melbourne to meet us and by the time we get here the temperature is soaring. We while away the afternoon in the pool and then adjourn to the shade of the trees to have a few cold drinks and catch up.

We've travelled halfway across the world without having anything stolen and here we are, a couple of days' ride from Melbourne, and we get robbed! It's a frustrating robbery: kids have broken in to our cabin through the bathroom window and stolen my Swiss army knife and a couple of cans of alcohol from the fridge. They were obviously looking for money and must have been disappointed when the only thing they found was Cambodian money worth nothing there and even less here.

The annoyance of this petty theft is forgotten when we get to Pro Hart's Broken Hill art gallery. We delight in his view of Australia. And there is a real thrill in store at Jack Absalom's gallery. Jack himself is there and is happy to pose for a photo and discuss travel around Australia. He is a wonderful man – still vibrant and still painting.

Brian's mum and dad were founders of the 'keep Brian and Shirley in Australia' committee before we left Melbourne and are keen to have us home. When we ride into their orchard just outside of Mildura, everybody bursts into tears. There is room for everyone to stay and a round of parties has been planned to welcome us home. Even Brian's number-one son,

Stephen, travels from his home in central Victoria to see his old man.

After three days, Brian and I better get off this party merry-go-round and get to Melbourne soon. But while the parties are still in full swing, Brian savours some very old Scotch with his old mates Jeff and Grant. Jeff had been given the bottle on his twenty-first birthday and he's now nearly 50. He promised himself he'd open it when we got home – and the boys aren't disappointed. It must be all right, because they polish off three-quarters of it!

On our way home there is one more stop to make: Apollo Bay, along Victoria's Great Ocean Road, where Paul Carr is buried. He has prime position, if there is such a thing, in the cemetery: high on the hill overlooking the ocean. There is a bench seat next to the grave, so we sit with Possum for a while.

Brian: I have been carrying Tibetan prayer flags since McLeod Ganj, just for Paul. I take my time adding them to the strings of flags already flying around his grave. I always promised myself and Poss that I would come here to say goodbye. To bring him luck I light some Buddhist incense we bought in Nepal and then I say a silent farewell to my mate.

Poss's grave tells of him passing away while attempting to achieve a dream. We achieved ours. I always believed Poss's spirit would ride with us, and maybe it did. We have travelled 56,671 km over 350 days with virtually no trouble. Perhaps Paul and Fran, Shirley's sister, rode with us. Our guardian angels.

ck on Australian soil — Darwin

Uluru

Termite hills in the Northern Territory

On the road hom

SOMETHING FOR THE TRIVIA BUFFS

Days on the road – 350
Kilometres travelled – 56,671 (17,437 on the clock when we put the bike in the crate in Melbourne and 74,107 when we ride into our garage at the end of our journey)
Litres of petrol – 2550
Flat tyres – four
Mechanical breakdowns – one broken alternator belt
Bike damage – rack supporting top box snaps four times
Come offs – four, at very slow speed (no damage, no injuries)
Countries visited – England
Isle of Man
Northern Ireland
Republic of Ireland
Scotland
France
Belgium
Germany

Austria
Czech Republic
Spain
Switzerland
Italy
Slovenia
Croatia
Bosnia
Montenegro
Kosovo
Macedonia
Greece
Turkey
Iran
Pakistan
India
Nepal
Thailand
Cambodia
Malaysia
Singapore

Beds slept in – 166
Best bed – the five-star Taj Mahal Hotel in Mumbai
Worst bed – the minus-star dump-a-rama in Dalbandin in Pakistan

BIKE LOGISTICS

Planning an overseas holiday isn't that complicated. Once you have your tickets, visas and a credit card, you're away. Extend that trip to a year and throw in a 290 kg-plus motorcycle and it isn't quite so simple. Here's some information we thought might be helpful to anyone planning something similar – but please keep in mind that while these prices and other details were correct at the time we did our trip, they might since have changed.

Vaccinations

You don't venture off the beaten track without making sure you've got all the right shots. We visited a doctor who specialised in travel medicine. Just to keep ourselves safe we had vaccinations against hepatitis A and B, typhoid, rabies, tetanus, meningococcal meningitis and polio. We couldn't get cholera, because the vaccine wasn't available and the doctor advised that it wasn't really that good anyway!

Visas

Because of the time we'd be on the road, many of our visas would expire before we got to the relevant countries, so we applied for some along the way. We contacted the embassies in Australia to find out where we could organise the visas or if they were available at the border.

Carnet de Passage

The bike needs its own 'visa', known as a Carnet de Passage. This document allows you to import and export the bike into and out of countries without paying any duties. We organised ours through the local RACV but it is issued by the Automobile Association of Australia. The carnet isn't cheap and this is where it gets tricky. There's a one-off, non-refundable fee of $350 and a refundable deposit of $250. Then there is the charge to ensure you don't sell the bike overseas and avoid the sales tax and duties payable here and there. This is worked out on the value of the bike and the countries you are visiting. Our journey would take us through Iran, so the insurance premium was 470 per cent of the value of the bike! You can leave this money with the Automobile Association in cash, as a bank guarantee or take out an insurance policy, which is by far the most cost-effective way of dealing with it – unless you have a spare $70,000 lying around.

The Australian Customs Service needs to see the carnet before you take the bike out of the country.

Packing and shipping the bike

The costs of taking the bike by air were high, so we opted for sending the bike by sea – 40 days door to door (or so they promised). We contacted BMW Southbank in Melbourne, where we purchased the bike. They gave us a crate, and one of the apprentice mechanics helped pack the bike into it. The shipping agent then collected the crate and took it to the docks. The next time we saw it was in the UK. What we didn't know was the bike was off-loaded in Singapore and took 60 days to get to England.

Packing

There is a real art to packing for a motorcycle trip – minimalist is the key word. We thought we had it organised, but all along the way we sent home clothing we didn't need. Following is the ideal list of clothing and items:

For her –
Seven pairs of jocks and socks, three bras
Two short-sleeved T-shirts
Two long-sleeved T-shirts
Two collared shirts (for when T-shirts are not acceptable)
One skirt
Two lightweight (e.g., cheesecloth) shirts (one sleeveless and one long-sleeved)
Good pants
Jeans
Cargo pants that cut off into shorts
One pair of shorts
Two pairs of track pants
Long-sleeved good jumper
Cardigan
Thermal underwear
Swimming costume and sarong
Travel towel
Polar-fleece jumper
Runners, thongs, black sandals and black slip-on shoes
Winter- and summer-weight gloves
Cap, beanie and sun hat

For him –
Seven pairs of jocks
Four pairs of 'normal' socks
Three pairs of thermal socks
Five T-shirts
Four collared short-sleeved tops
One short-sleeved 'going out' shirt
One long-sleeved shirt
One long-sleeved polo shirt
One pair black 'Draggin' brand jeans
Cargo pants that cut off to shorts
One pair casual trousers
One polar-fleece jumper
Two belts
One pair board shorts
Two pairs Lycra pants (good for exercising and 'extra padding' under riding pants)
Speedos
Travel towel
Runners, thongs, boaties and boots
Winter- and summer-weight gloves
Cap, beanie and sun hat

Extras – First-aid kit
CamelBak water carrier

Spare parts

Even a relatively new bike needs maintenance, so on the advice of our mechanic and good friend, Phil Marshall, we packed:

A torque set
Selected sockets to fit most parts, such as brakes, front forks, etc.
Selected ring spanners

Pointed nose pliers
Flat screwdriver
Star screwdriver
12-volt soldering iron (to run off the accessory plug from the bike)
Feeler gauges for exhaust and inlet valve settings
Special tool to remove oil filter
Spare fuel filter
Two spare spark plugs
Length of high-pressure EFI fuel hose
Extra puncture repair kit
Purpose-built tyre-changing kit for tubeless motorcycle tyres
Most importantly, black electrical tape and black gaffer tape – the modern day version of eight-gauge wire – capable of fixing anything.

ACKNOWLEDGMENTS

You can't undertake a journey like ours without the help of many people. For their help and support, we would like to thank: Alix Beane for her web page expertise; Benno Rentick for the technical support of our web page and email; Phil Marshall for his assistance in getting the motorbike up to scratch for our departure (sorry about its condition on our return, Phil); Diane Flett from Travelscene St Kilda for help with visas and sound travel advice; Elissa McCallum, Jenny Fitzpatrick and Dee Stewart for keeping Hardy-Rix Media Services afloat in our absence; Peppina Sorbaro from the Australian Automobile Association for advice and assistance with our carnet; Bettina and Tim Harrison for looking after us so well in London on more than one occasion; Alan Hardy for dealing with our sometimes complicated finances (and not selling the house); Bruce McKenzie who took on the mammoth task of looking after our very spoilt pets and the house; all our family and friends for being so understanding, and all the magnificent people we met along the way who gave us advice, assistance or just shared the experiences that made our odyssey so memorable.

And thanks to Alex Craig, Sarina Rowell and Annie Coulthard at Pan Macmillan.

Printed in Australia
AUHW011454191118
305416AU00003B/3

9 780646 91851